One Small Village: Kearneysville 1842-1942

by Elsie Hamstead
2000

One Small Village: Kearneysville 1842-1942

Copyright © 2000, 2024 Elsie Hamstead

All rights reserved. No part of this book may be used or reproduced in any manner whatsoever without written permission of the author. Published 2024.

Printed in the United States of America.

ISBN: 978-1-63385-547-2
Library of Congress Control Number: 2024925645

Published by
Word Association Publishers
205 Fifth Avenue
Tarentum, Pennsylvania 15084

www.wordassociation.com
1.800.827.7903

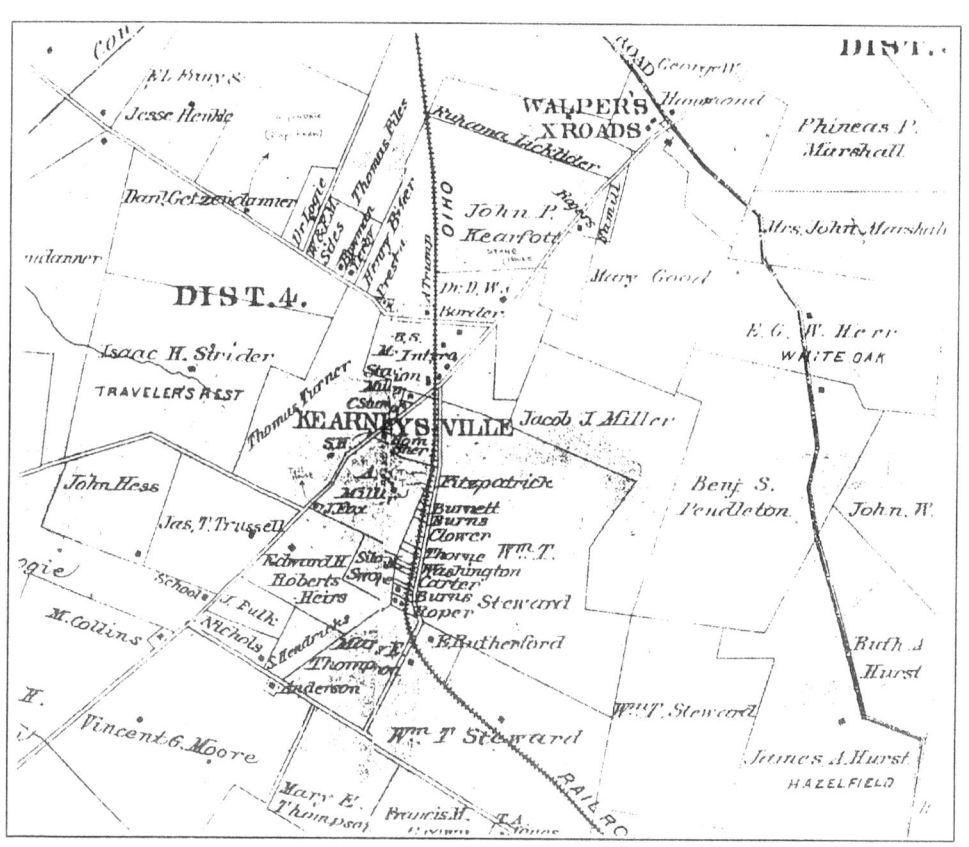

S. Howell Brown Map, 1883

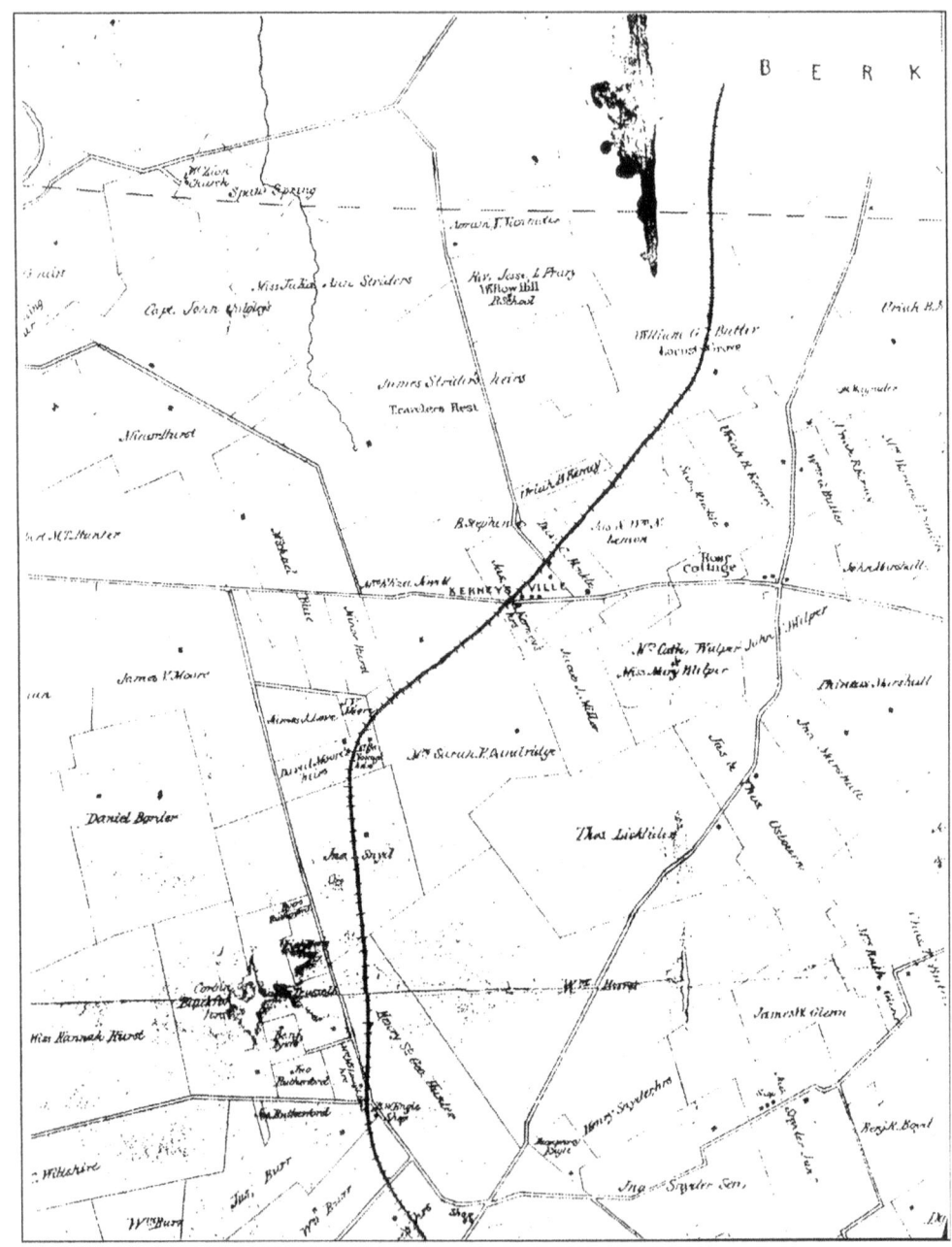

S. Howell Brown Map, 1862

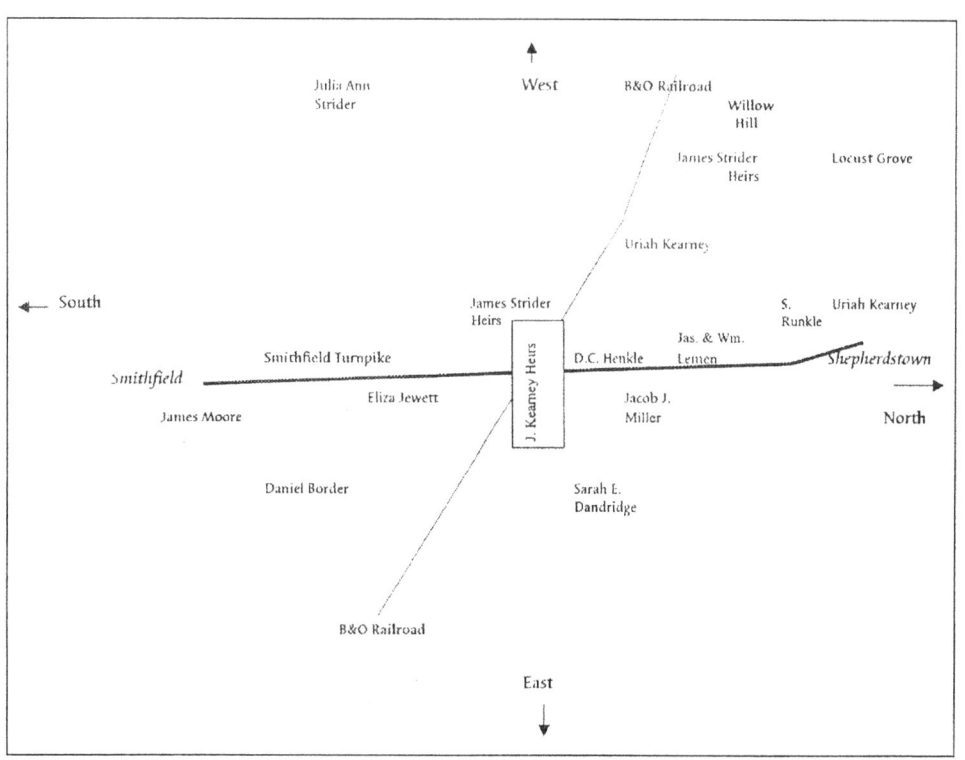

From S. Howell Brown Map, 1852

Contents

Author's Note	ix
Introduction	3
People	1
Horatio Gates	4
Nicholas Lemen III	6
The Kearneys	9
Thomas Turner	11
Ann Elizabeth Stilwell and	
* James M. Rutherford (Roderford)*	13
Samuel D. Rutherford	15
Charles E. Rutherford	16
William Fulk	17
Dr. James Logie	19
J.J. Miller	21
Daniel Webster Border	24
Theodore Homsher and Lewis Wilt Families	32
John and Blanche Miller Stanley	36
John H. Fox	39
Public Services	47
Transportation	49
Roadways	49
Baltimore & Ohio Railroad	58
Post Office	66
Hartstown and Beyond	71
Economics	85
Baker Limestone Quarry	87
Agriculture	97
Milking Enterprise	98
Orchards	100
Merchants	101
Housing and Construction	110
Taxi Services	114
Education	115
Private Schools	117
Beginning of the Public (Free) Schools	118
Free School for Black Children	132

vii

Social Activities 135
  Sports 139
  Informal Sports 142
  Trips 142
  Toys for Adults 143
  Clubs 144
  Politics 148
  Churches 150
    Presbyterian Church 150
    St. Paul Baptist Church 154
    Grace Reformed Church 154
    Methodist Episcopal Church 159
    Old School Baptist Church 159

War Years 161
  Civil War 163
  World War I 166
  World War II 169

Conclusion 171

Appendix A — Cemeteries 175
  Existing Tombstones at Presbyterian Cemetery 177
  Elmwood Cemetery, Shepherdstown 178
  St. Paul Baptist (Kearneysville) 183
  Stewart Chapel Methodist Cemetery 185
  Hart Graveyard 187

Appendix B — Selected Names from Federal Census 189
  Selected from Federal Census
    of Jefferson County 1850 191
  Selected from Federal Census
    of Jefferson County 1870 195
  Selected from Federal Census
    of Jefferson County 1880 199
  Selected from Federal Census of
    Middleway Magisterial District 1900 204
  Selected from Federal Census of
    Middleway District 1910 217
  Selected from Federal Census of
    Middleway District 1920 232

Author's Note

Writing this history has been an interesting journey across the past ten years. As I worked, I noticed that the villagers grew in stature in my mind as research revealed their accommodation to their surroundings.

There are many who have offered information and suggestions in the writing of this Kearneysville history. I would like to mention a few: Margie Johnston and Bertha Fox Jones, for the stories and memorabilia; Lige and Jane Miller for conversation and encouragement; Kelly Rudolph for belief in the project; the late Mary Border Snyder, who had a positive vision of Kearneysville before the turn of the century; Katie Payne for her computer skills; Emily M. Gassler, the graphic designer; my children, for their support during the project; and most of all for my daughter, Margaret, who has been steadfast through all the editing and rewriting.

N.B. *The first edition of this book was printed in 2000. The edition you are holding now was published in 2024, meaning that it has been assigned an ISBN and Library of Congress number and is now Mother's legacy. However, none of the text has been changed. It is exactly as it was in the first edition.*

— **Margaret Hamstead**
November 2024

People

A great variety of events preserved in newspapers and in memory give the author power of selecting as well as adorning the facts he relates.
— ***Hume, D. History of England***

Introduction

Local historians tell and retell stories of the Shepherds and others who settled Shepherdstown; those versed in Charles Town history beguile one with stories of the Washingtons. Harpers Ferry has a unique place in history: The federal arsenal there became the target of John Brown, whose attempt to capture that installation set in motion a chain of events that are woven into the Civil War and have been included in U.S. history texts ever since.

Often when newcomers move into this area, Kearneysville is referred to only as the location of Traveler's Rest, home of General Horatio Gates. Gates was one of three Revolutionary War generals who built a home in the eastern panhandle of West Virginia, which actually was Berkeley County, Virginia in 1786 when he settled here.

However, there are many other stories and actors woven into the history of Kearneysville. What the reader will find in these pages are glimpses of men and women who found a fertile area with opportunity to make a livelihood for their children and themselves. They created an environment conducive to attaining a measure of security. They participated in government and in providing schools and churches for the growing population. They were creative in solving problems and voiced, sometimes quite loudly, approval or opposition to some measures being forced on them from outside sources. They rejoiced together in success and shared their burdens of sorrow. In short, they built a community. These are the people who stood out in my research as significant in their contributions. Surely there were others not mentioned who also contributed in important ways, but for whom I could not find information. Their story is left for other authors.

The following pages reflect one person's respect and appreciation for those who developed Kearneysville during its first years, to about 1942. Stories in this account were pieced together from newspaper archives, census data, courthouse records, and recollections of community residents. The first section of this brief history highlights some of the families that settled here. The remainder weaves together their stories of commerce and play with those of others who have shared the journey but about whom less is known.

People

HORATIO GATES

In the telling of a history, one must begin somewhere. And although Horatio Gates, a retired general, had no direct influence in building this community, his name appears much larger than that of the Kearneys for whom the town is named. Nevertheless, Horatio Gates must be included here since the home he established, "Traveler's Rest," is the oldest existing house in the area of Kearneysville. By one account, he bought 659 acres from Joseph Grable; by another, the property was a Fairfax land grant, which would explain how he came to the area in the first place. In either case, the stately farm he established provided a livelihood for several families long after Gates had left the area.

The British would have called Horatio a turncoat. At age 22, he was sent from Great Britain to command King George III's Independent Company in Halifax, Nova Scotia. For whatever reason, Horatio left his position with the British army and built the western section of Traveler's Rest in 1773 on a hill over-looking Spa Springs. Shortly after, to fulfil an obligation to his community, he accepted an appointment as a justice by Lord Dunmore, the Governor of Virginia. He was also listed among those who collected tithages or head taxes in his district, which included Warm Springs Road and the road that is currently Route 480 to Shepherdstown.

Eventually Gates's sympathy was swayed to the colonial cause for separation from Great Britain. In 1776, his name was

Plate 1. Recent photograph of Horatio Gates's Spring House.

Plate 2. Recent photograph of pastureland and stream on Gates's Farm.

included in a new commission in which all references to "our Sovereign Lord" were conspicuously absent. Gates was given the rank of adjutant general when the conflict began between the American colonies and Great Britain. After the defeat of the British at Saratoga, he was given the status of general. In 1782, his command was defeated at Camden, N.C., and shortly thereafter Gates retired to Traveler's Rest, but he did not remain long in the area. His home was sold to John Mark in 1790.

John Mark then sold Traveler's Rest to Bowley, who sold it to Isaac Strider II. From about 1852 until 1965, the James Strider heirs owned the acreage on which the mansion was built. Currently "Traveler's Rest" includes a tenant house, a large barn and a free flowing spring. The present owner, Martha McIntosh, acquired the property of more than 200 acres from John F. and Nancy Campbell Ambrose in 1965.

In the 1990s brass bells on old leather with the initials W.E.B. were found about a quarter mile east of the residence, on property that was part of the original tract of Gates, then owned by Donald Heinz and his wife. This artifact was possibly used as a harness for horses. Also found were Spanish coins dated 17[ ], 1804 and 1808 that have since become part of a personal collection.

NICHOLAS LEMEN III

On September 5, 1756 — before Horatio Gates was even aware of this fertile area, Nicholas Lemen III received a grant of 570 acres from Lord Fairfax. The parcel was north of what is now the B&O Railroad and Grace Reformed Church, along the Shepherdstown road. Land grants required that a home of specific dimensions be built on the property, and that a survey be presented to Lord Fairfax's office so that it could be recorded in the Frederick County, Virginia courthouse. It also required that the land be used for agriculture, and that annual taxes be paid.

Lemen immediately built a heavy log structure near a spring as a home for his family. The Lemen family was the earliest of record to make their home in the area that became known as Kearneysville. Their second child, Robert, became somewhat of a hero in the area, although this is an example of conflicting historical records. Reporting on a ceremony sponsored by The State Chapter of the United States Daughters of the War of 1812, *The*

Plate 3. Robert Lemen Marker

Shepherdstown Independent of October 28, 1938 notes that:

> ...Robert, born Nov. 7, 1760, who married Esther Bowers on March 31, 1792. This Robert was a soldier in the Revolution and was with Washington at Yorktown when Cornwallis and his British Army surrendered. He was in the War of 1812. He contracted a fatal illness from which he died February 27, 1815. This is he whom we are dedicating this marker.

The following year, Pack Horse Ford Chapter, DAR, dedicated a marker to Robert Lemen. The story in *The Independent* of Oct. 25, 1939 reported:

> ...Robert Lemen, ...second child of Nicholas Lemen and Christian Lemen, his wife was born at the homestead of his parents in Frederick county, now Jefferson county, West Virginia, on November 6, 1751. His wife was Miss Esther Banes. They were married in Virginia on March 19, 1779...

It seems that he received good religious training, later becoming a deacon of the Shepherdstown Baptist Church. Although acquiring only a "common" school education, his interests led him to extensive reading and gathering of information. No fault could be found in his character, and he was highly regarded by all who knew him.

Being of large build and great strength, he could not resist the temptation to stand for his rights. In 1775, Robert was in eastern Virginia (possibly Williamsburg), where he publicly denounced King George III for his heartless oppression in America. A British Officer over-heard and could not accept such criticism of the king.

Being fully armed, he assaulted Robert. It was said that the blow from Mr. Lemen's right arm to the mouth of the officer felled the latter to the ground. To the delight of the crowd Robert then removed the officer's sword.

The articles differ as to when Robert was born, married, who he married and when he died. Nevertheless, he is buried in the graveyard on the original Lemen estate. Another probable descendant, a Robert Lemen born in 1791, wrote the following to the editor of *The Shepherdstown Register*, April 2, 1876.

> Mr. Robert Lucas: Sir, I see in the *Shepherdstown Register* that there is a call for publication, for all old soldiers of the War of 1812, yet surviving, as well as their ages. I will be 79 years old on May 23, 1870. I was born near Kearneysville, Jefferson County, Va., I served in Capt. Cockrill's company under Col. Griffin Taylor. I served as First Lieutenant in above named company.
>   Signed, Robert Lemen, Missouri

The Lemen property passed through family descendants for well over 100 years, the latest being J.P. Kearfott, a great grandson. Mr. Kearfott added a large brick home in 1880, and the log house

Plate 4. Kearfott's Rock Dale, built 1880. Picture taken 1997.

was removed at that time. By 1900, James and William N. Lemen's land was reduced to 98 acres after lots were sold to Samuel Ruckles, J.J. Miller, and the B&O Railroad. The property was known as Rock Dale until Mr. and Mrs. W.H.S. White renamed it White Rocks sometime in the mid-1900s.

THE KEARNEYS

Two brothers, Uriah and James Kearney, Sr., seem to be the source of the name of the Kearneysville community. There are two spellings of the family name, however, both of which appear in various contexts. For example, gravestones and news articles show "Kerney", whereas the Brown 1852 map shows "Kearney."

By the time the Baltimore and Ohio Railroad passed through the area in 1842, the large land holdings had been reduced in size. Uriah and James Kearney, Sr. had acquired modest-sized farms through which the railroad passed. Legend tells us that a Kearney ran a boarding or rooming house for the B&O workers. The house, altered beyond recognition, still stands at Trump's crossing, at the intersection of the railroad track and Kearneysville Lane.

In the 1850 federal census, Uriah Kearney is listed as being a farmer worth $19,000. (See Appendix B for a listing of his holdings). An 1852 S. Howell Brown map shows two plats owned by Uriah: The smaller lies along the old Martinsburg Pike; the second, a larger farm, lies between the Samuel Runkle and William Butler properties. Uriah's residence was a stone house built in 1820 that lies just south of Grace Reformed Church along the old Smithfield-Shepherdstown Turnpike, currently Route 480. (This house came to be known as Calico Cottage). Uriah married Elizabeth Woods on November 17, 1836. Speculation is that the unmarked grave site on the property is one of the Kearneys.

James Kearney Sr.'s holding was bisected by both the B&O Railroad and the Smithfield-Shepherdstown Turnpike. He was married to Ara Edna Gibbons, who was descended from pioneers. A daughter, Eliza J., was born in 1813. She was to marry Daniel G. Henkle in 1845. His parents were John and Barbara (Troxell) Henkle, who had originally settled in Frederick county, Maryland, although Daniel was born in Harpers Ferry, Virginia in 1815.

Eliza and Daniel also owned property on the Shepherdstown-Smithfield Turnpike, between holdings of the James Kearney heirs and James and William N. Lemen. The couple had two children: Bettie Hall Henkle, born September 6, 1848, and Mary Jessie Henkle, born in 1853. In the 1850 census, Daniel is listed as a manufacturer.

Little is known of the children. Apparently Jessie attended the Captain W.H. Morrow Female School in Shepherdstown, since she was chosen queen at the May Party in 1867 and was photographed with her court by a Mr. Darnele. At the Morrow school, she could have studied English, mathematics, and classical literature, offered by Captain Morrow. There was also a music department where she might have learned to play a musical instrument or taken voice lessons. To get to the school, Jessie may have used a conveyance provided by James A. Adams of Shepherdstown. His advertisement in the *Shepherdstown Register* claimed that tickets could be obtained at the Kearneysville Depot or any store. Daily times were scheduled for trips between Kearneysville and Shepherdstown.

Jessie never married and was living at home with her parents in 1880. Two black servants and two children were listed at the home also: Ann Smith, 29, Lewis Smith, 8, Vinson Smith, 2, and Erby Smith, 62. Then, in the 1910 census, Jessie is listed in the household of her brother-in-law and sister, John Calvin and Bettie Henkle Bitner. A daughter of this couple, Agnes Bitner, married Bailey McIntyre and had five children. One of them, Effie Moore

Plate 5. Kearney home in 1966. View facing B&O Railroad.

McIntyre survived her siblings and acquired the property formerly held by James Kearney, Sr.. An interesting point is that she willed this property to Tabb Janney, a previous fiancee of one of her sisters — provided that he did not marry a cousin. He didn't. The house still stands today next to the Kearneysville underpass, although it is in disrepair.

Plate 6. Kearney home prior to 1920 when the underpass was built. View facing R. 480.

My research did not ascertain if one or both Uriah and James, Sr., should be given credit for naming the village. Notwithstanding the name, a greater contribution might be found in the list of descendants of James who made their homes in Kearneysville. Among these are the Bitners and McIntyres. These families will appear later in this story.

Thomas Turner

Thomas Turner was born January 22, 1818 in Washington County, Maryland. In October 1849, he married Sarah A. Thompson, who was born August 27, 1833 in Huntington,

Pennsylvania. They were parents of twelve children according to information recorded in Personal History of Jefferson County Residents.
- Robert, born on July 25, 1850, married Nannie McKinney and moved to Kansas.
- Winfield, born October 24, 1852;
- Mary S. born October 12, 1855 married Abram Miller;
- Jemima E. born December 31, 1857;
- Martha, born March 1859 married George McClincy;
- Rhoda born 1861; Sarah Annie, born 1863;
- David born July 21, 1867.

Three additional children were born after the family moved to Kearneysville:
- Joseph, born October 13, 1869;
- James born July 4, 1872, and
- Edward born May 23, 1876.

In 1867 Thomas purchased the 141 acre estate of Eliza Jewett. Little is known of Eliza, except for a brief mention in the census of 1850. At sixty-four years of age in 1850, she had moved from somewhere in Pennsylvania and was worth $9,525. A son, John M., who was an attorney, and Anna McElroy, 65, lived with her. It seemed, according to the census, that she boarded at least part of the year at the Entler Hotel, Shepherdstown. In any case, the property that Thomas Turner purchased from Eliza was part of the original land owned by Horatio Gates. The farm of 141 acres was bisected by the Smithfield-Shepherdstown Turnpike and was located about a quarter mile south of the B&O Turnpike intersection. A home was situated on the eastern extremity. (See Brown Map, 1852).

In the census of 1870 Mr. Turner claimed $4,000 in real estate and $1,500 in personal property. By profession he was a farmer; perhaps he raised wheat, since this was an especially important cash crop at the time. In 1878, he became purchasing agent for T. Homsher who was shipping local farmers' wheat via the B&O Railroad. One account shows that Mr. Turner went to Hampshire County on one occasion as agent, where he purchased 150 head of sheep. In addition to farming, he was active in turnpike upkeep and road-building decisions.

In 1876 Mr. Turner built a comfortable brick home just west of the Pike. His eldest daughter, Mary Susan, who had married Abram Miller, had two children according to the 1880 census:

Alice, 5, and Gilbert, 2. Perhaps they were living in the original home place that stood on the east side of the Pike. This home burned about 1888 and a large colonial style house, still standing, was built close to the Pike.

Thomas Turner died in May 1894. The following was reported in the local paper:

> Thomas Turner died at his residence last Friday morning at the age of 76. He was a veteran of the Mexican War, a private in the Battery 4th Regiment U.S. Artillery on the Ship Empire when it wrecked at Fort Key. He went to California when the gold rush was at its height. He is survived by his wife and 10 children and will be buried in Elmwood Cemetery.

Thomas's widow, Sarah A Turner, was granted a Mexican War widow's pension shortly after his death.

ANN ELIZABETH STILWELL AND JAMES M. RUTHERFORD (RODERFORD)

Some early residents worked on various land holdings, often living in a tenant house. Such was the case of James and Ann Elizabeth Rutherford. James was the third son of Thomas H. and Elizabeth Pultz Rutherford of Berkeley County. From records, the couple, with a new son and two older boys, were living on the Woodbury property near Leetown in 1848. The 1850 census lists James 38, Elizabeth 32, and their children W. Thomas, 10; Sarah E., 9; John A., 7; Samuel D., 2; and Margaret Butt, 13.

In 1852 James purchased a small farm of 10 acres near the B&O Railroad in Kearneysville and moved his family there. Unfortunately, he died of pleurisy in 1855, leaving his widow with three young sons. Sarah E., their daughter, had died previously. In 1855 Widow Betty, so called to avoid conflict with the name of her mother-in-law, purchased the remainder of the property for $90, making the total cost of the 15 acres and house just $120.00.

Two of her sons fought in the Civil War. In 1861 W. Thomas, then 21 and a laborer, and John A., 18 and a carpenter, enlisted in the Confederate Army. W. Thomas was wounded at the Second

Manassas conflict and was on sick leave until December 1863. Then in February 1864, he was AWOL with no further record of activities until the close of the war, when he returned to Kearneysville and resumed his occupation as day laborer. He married Jane Randolph, and the couple became parents of three daughters.

John A. was wounded at the same battle and was taken prisoner. After recuperation, he was released on condition that he no longer engage in conflict on the Confederate side. He happily agreed it seems, as he began employment at a general store in Staunton, Virginia.

There is no record of how Widow Betty supported herself when her two adult sons were absent. It can safely be conjectured, however, that she took as boarders men who were expanding the B&O tracks in the area. During these years, she also brought a nephew, Charles E., born in 1863, into her home. In 1870, Widow Betty adopted this child.

The census of that year shows that she owned personal property valued at $300, which may have included real estate. Her family included W. Thomas, Samuel, Charles, and three grand-daughters: Annie, 7, Mary J., 3, and Emma C., 1. Sometime during this year, though, Samuel, now 22 years old, became dissatisfied with living under the roof of a domineering mother and migrated to Virginia. There he plied his trade as an itinerant carpenter.

In 1875 Elizabeth Pultz Rutherford, Widow Betty's mother-in-law and grandmother of Thomas, John, and Samuel, died at her home in Mill Creek. Her husband had died 20 years earlier. The bulk of her estate was to be divided among her three living sons, Uriah, William and Joseph. She also bequeathed the children of deceased daughter, Catherine, and deceased son, James, $1.00 jointly. Her signature, an X, was properly notarized. We can only imagine how her grandchildren used this windfall.

Records show that across time the Rutherfords, Thomas H., his son James M., and W. Thomas, son of James, had Presbyterian leanings as evidenced by the following: Rev. John Matthew performed the marriage ceremony for Thomas H.; James M. and his bride were married by Rev. James Watts; and W. Thomas is listed as a member of the Kearneysville Presbyterian Church.

By the census of 1900, Annie, Mary J. and Emma C. were no longer in the home with Widow Betty; Charley, at age 30, is considered head of the household, and Samuel, at 45, has returned home. Further research is needed to determine what happened to Annie; Mary J. married an American-Indian and migrated to Oklahoma, and Emma C. married John C. Heinz. John built a home on land deeded from Widow Betty. By 1900, he and Emma had two children, Samuel C., 5, and Laura E. 3.

Although advanced in years, Betty appeared to be much in charge. Having of necessity lived a frugal life, it was said that she wasted nothing. At the dining table, she kept the loaf of bread close by and cut each slice on request. An extremely small woman in size, she knew how to command attention. She made neighborly visits to Jim and Mary Head, who had purchased and now occupied the house built by John C. Heinz. There was a winding path up a hill and a gate to pass through at the top. By the turn of the century, at age 84, Widow Betty was still able to make the climb and visit her neighbors with the use of her cane. Instead of a friendly knock on the door, she banged on the door with her cane, announcing her arrival as few people would have dared.

Betty Rutherford died in 1905, age 89. Three of her five children survived her. When her will was probated, Samuel was to receive some real estate and personal property, but the house and nine acres were to go to Charles E. The house is currently owned by Tommy Bowers and stands at the Rutherford Crossing. Bequests of $25.00 were willed to John A., her son; Emma C., and Mary J. Day, her grandchildren; and to the five heirs of Anna Engle. The will was witnessed by Joseph E. Engles and Charles C. Lucas, M.D.

SAMUEL D. RUTHERFORD

Samuel, the third son of James E. and Elizabeth Stillwell Rutherford, appears to have been a restless individual. Born in 1848, he was too young to join the Confederate Army in 1861, as did his brothers W. Thomas and John A. When the public school opened in 1872, he was already 24, too old to attend as did Charles, his adopted brother, and Emma C., his niece.

He followed a profession of many self-taught men of that time and became a carpenter. He may have found use for his talents in the nearby growing village of Hartstown. Sources say that he also migrated to Virginia where his older brother, John A., had settled when he left the Confederate Army. As an older man, he made several trips to Oklahoma to visit a niece but always returned feeling that he belonged in Kearneysville. His adopted brother, Charles E., owned a 1925 Ford Roadster, which he drove the many miles to bring Samuel home.

Samuel married a girl named Susan. The only remembrance I have of her is a china doll that she gave to my sister, Anna (a great niece); the doll was stuffed with sawdust and had arms, legs, and head made of china. When Samuel's mother died in 1905, she left him a small inheritance. His principle residence from then until his death in 1936 was his mother's home, with his brother, Charles.
Two events that seem to be related stand out in the life and death of Samuel. As a youth, he had climbed out the window on the second floor to gain a position on the roof from which he could see the smoke from a skirmish between Confederate and Union forces in 1864 at Duffield's Station. In 1936, at age 88, in attempting to climb out a second story window, Samuel D. Rutherford fell to his death.

CHARLES E. RUTHERFORD

Charles E. Rutherford was the adopted son of the widow Betty Rutherford and became her primary heir. He attended the Kearneysville Free School, and at some point afterward became a well-driller, or so he is listed in the 1900 census. He was to continue this work well into the 1930s, keeping his own records and collecting money for his work. He could be seen frequently driving throughout Jefferson County, but not on Sundays. Then he would be seen at the Methodist Church (Bethany) at Bardane. His civic commitment was evidenced by the great pride he took in having received a 50 year membership pin from the Elk Branch Lodge of A.F. and A.M. at Shenandoah Junction. As a hobby, he and his brother, Samuel, worked at bee keeping, selling the honey for which there was a great demand.

Charles never married. While he was known as an honest, friendly individual, there is no anecdote of a fling with a member of the opposite sex. Even his great niece refused to kiss him until he shaved off his mustache. Alas, his mustache was sacrificed without the promised reward.

Before 1900, the family had used a horse and buggy or wagon (as needed) for transportation. Later, Charley drove a Ford

Roadster. But before he died in 1948 at age 85, he was again walking — as he had done when he attended the Kearneysville Free School, but this time it was the mile to the neighborhood grocery to "gab" with friend, Charlie Widmeyer. After a century of being in the family, the house at Rutherford's Crossing was sold out of the family.

Plate 7. Rutherford house, 2000.

WILLIAM FULK

"Sunnyside," a beautiful farm that borders the Smithfield-Shepherdstown Turnpike, has been a profitable farm for more than a hundred years. Mr. Robert S. Helms, Esquire, had owned the farm in 1874, but when he moved from the area to Rockingham, Virginia, he sold the farm in two parcels. Twenty acres were bought by Dr. James Logie, whose property bordered Bower Road; another 200 were sold to Dr. Charles Stephens for $32.50 an acres. In 1891 at age 26, William Andrew Fulk purchased those 200 acres and later bought back the 20 acres from Dr. Logie, which brought the farm back to its original size of 220 acres. Sunnyside has been held by his descendants since then.

Mr. "Bill", as he came to be known, was born in 1865 and

raised in the area, residing with his parents and siblings (see 1880 census) on the Border Farm, which lay along Border Road. At the time Mr. Bill brought his growing family to Sunnyside, only a small dwelling was available on the farm. By 1910, his household included his wife, Mary Entler; two sons, Henry (Harry) and Charlie, and a daughter, Nellie, in addition to Mary's sister, Sallie Entler and a servant, Sallie McCoy. Worthy of note was that Sallie McCoy, although listed in the 1880 census as a servant at the age of 40, was in truth considered to be an integral part of the Fulk family. Neighbors jokingly commented when Mr. Bill built the dairy barn, that he first should have enlarged the home. Quickly he countered, "It is the barn that earns the money." In fact, though, by 1911 he had built a stately brick home facing the Pike. It incorporated the original house at the rear, and still stands.

During Mr. Bill's tenure, Sunnyside was considered a model farm, as was the nearby Border Farm. Kearneysville lay in a slightly rolling plain of lush fields and woods, and Mr. Bill was not the first to note the advantage of dairy farming. Other farmers were raising dairy cows, also, which is one of the reasons why Mr. Bill was active in organizing the Kearneysville Creamery business as described later in this history.

Due to the location of Sunnyside, Mr. And Mrs. Fulk's children, Nellie, Charles, and Harry attended the Woodbury School and continued their education at Shepherd Normal School. Through the years Mr. Bill stayed involved in the education of his children. He became a member of the Jefferson County Board of Education and regularly visited the Kearneysville and Woodbury Schools to evaluate the quality of teaching and identify problems. He also served his community as a shareholder in Jefferson Security Bank, Old National Bank and Bank of Charles Town.

We can imagine the earlier lifestyle from the charming story about Miss Nellie's method of getting to the Woodbury School beginning about 1910. To begin with, Miss Nellie had a special partnership with her horse named Maude. Maude was respectful of automobiles wanting to keep her distance. But Miss Nellie had to be taken to school and she respected Miss Nellie more, far more.

Before school Maude would be hitched to the buggy and Miss Nellie handed in. At Woodbury Miss Nellie would alight, fasten the reins to the buggy and Maude would trot home. In the afternoon, Maude would be hitched to the buggy again and the reins fastened securely. Maude knew what her mission was. She quickly trotted to the school to convey her mistress safely home.

Mr. "Bill" died at Sunnyside in 1942 at the home he and his wife created. He is remembered as a community builder through his contributions as a farmer, dairyman, and an entrepreneur. Sadly, Harry was killed as a young man during a farming operation. When driving a pair of mules pulling a disc, the mules bolted, dragging him beneath the disc. The younger brother, Charles, inherited a farm outside the Kearneysville area. The beautiful Sunnyside farm eventually went to Bill and Mary's daughter, Nellie, who was married to Hugh Hill. In June, 1986 according to the will of her mother, Mrs. Hugh Hill, the farm went to Mrs. Elizabeth Hill Moores. At that point in time, it included four houses. Elizabeth's son, Chuck, and his family reside in the brick home built under the direction of Elizabeth's grandfather, Mr. Bill Fulk.

Plate 8. Miss Nellie and Maude, circa 1910.

DR. JAMES LOGIE

To local residents in later years, Dr. Logie is only known by reference to a dusty, pot-holed road off Route 9 known as "Logie Lane." But to his peers in the last half of the 19th century, he was well regarded for his activities and many aspects of his character.

In 1856 Minor Hurst conveyed to Dr. James Logie what was referred to as Lot S, with more than 44 acres including the Smithfield-Shepherdstown Turnpike (now Route 480). In the federal census of 1870, it was noted that his real estate was appraised at $24,000 with personal property of $2,000. Also, by this time, Dr. Logie had built a stately home, was already 47 years of age, and had a wife and three small sons. Three other individuals lived in his home, one of whom at 13 years of age was listed as a domestic servant. Many references to his community activities appeared in local newspapers, some of which will be reported here.

During the November term of court, he was named a magistrate for his district. At that time, Braxton Davenport was the presiding justice and other magistrates included John Grantham and Edmund Chambers. Ten years later Dr. Logie had become President of the Supervisors Court (later called the County Court) in which H.C. Entler was clerk. One of the duties of the Court was to hear complaints of those who thought their real estate was overappraised and needed remedy.

In 1869 Dr. Logie was listed by the Virginia Free Press as an officer of the newly-organized Valley Mutual Fire Insurance Company of West Virginia. In the next years, he served with Dr. O.G. Mix as a physician for the Poor Farm for which he received $1.00 per year. He also assisted J.J. Miller and John G. Ruckle as road viewers for a fee of $2.00. And as a trustee for Robert Lemen, he was charged with the sale of personal property at the Lemen farm.

Plate 9. Dr. Logie's home, Bower Road, built before 1870. Picture taken 1998.

Dr. Logie should be remembered for his many civic contributions, foremost of which was his idea that all should have a right to an education. Dr. Logie was a significant promoter and provider of schools for the children of the community, both black and white. In 1872 he collaborated with one Mr. Motrin Collins in constructing and opening a log, one-room school for black children. This was located on Dr. Logie's farm, opposite the Jacob Fulk farm and on the west side of the Smithfield-Shepherdstown Pike. (See S. Howell Brown map, 1883). Also, Dr. Logie was a member of the Temperance and Masonic organizations that collaborated to construct a two-story building on property owned by Homsher, opposite the Presbyterian Church. The first floor of this building was used as a public school for white children. Of his own family, his daughter, Jessie, graduated from Mt. Vernon Institute in Baltimore; his son, John, became a minister; and Frank, his other son, was granted permission to appear before the judge of the courts in Jefferson County to apply for a license to practice law. This was much later, though, in 1891.

In 1884, about one year after being thrown by his horse, Dr. Logie gave up medical practice. However, we note in the same year he was administrator of A.H. Kearney's estate, deceased and was paid Civil War claims amounting to $252.

Dr. Logie moved several times in the next ten years — from Kearneysville to Baltimore, from Baltimore to the Miller Farm in Halltown in 1890, then to a home he built in Charles Town in 1894. In 1897, while living in that town, he suffered a fatal stroke. He was buried in Elmwood Cemetery. In 1921, Harry Wagely bought the Logie Farm of 172 acres at a price of $125 per acre.

J.J. MILLER

From newspaper articles and other sources, Jacob J. Miller appears to have been a loving husband, a devoted father, and prosperous farmer. In addition, he gave liberally of his time to civic organizations and contributed to the general well-being of the community.

His farm, valued at $4,000 in the 1850 census, lay near the Smithfield-Shepherdstown Pike just north of the B&O railroad. Neighboring farms include that of Mrs. Catherine and Miss Mary Walper, James and William N. Lemen, David Henkle, the James Kearney heirs, Eliza Jewett and Mrs. Sarah Dandridge.

J.J.'s astute farming abilities were put to good use, because his family was large. By age 33, he and his first wife, Catherine Susan Snyder, were the parents of six children. Three more were added in the subsequent 10 years. Also, a seamstress, Elizabeth Joy, age 75, had been added to the household. Catherine died in 1860, and Jacob married Catherine Ronemus, age 45, on November 25, 1862. No children were born of this marriage.

There seems to be no record of J.J.'s formal education, but evidence of his active involvement in and knowledge of local government is recorded in weekly publications of the time. He served as Assistant Marshall for the Federal Census in 1850. In 1867 J.J. was named a road surveyor of Chapline Township (south of Shepherdstown), for which he was paid sometimes $2 or $3. The road was the Smithfield-Shepherdstown Turnpike (Route 480) and was continually in need of repair. J.J. also served as Supervisor of Roads for his township and was authorized to expend $500 to open the road from George Seibert's on the Berkeley County line that would intersect the Pike at Kearneysville[1]. The panel to view and open the road included: J.J. Miller, chairman; William Lemen, Thomas Licklider, M. Helm, and G.D. Wiltshire.

J.J. — as his great-grandson, Lige Miller refers to him — at 52 years of age, was obviously a frugal man. In addition to his many other income-producing activities, records show that he was also paid $3.00 for fox scalps. In 1867 his real estate was valued at $11,000 and personal property at $4,000. Consistent with his belief in accountability, he appealed for a reduction in this appraisal, thereby reducing the tax from $58 to $50. In 1876, shortly after this compensation review was completed, J.J. expanded his farming operation by adding 150 acres of land adjoining Walpers Crossroads at $35 per acre from Phineas Marshall.

J.J. was a consistent proponent of religious training. When H.C. Bitner deeded one acre of land for a Presbyterian Church and cemetery in 1868, J.J., along with B.S. McIntyre and James V. Moore were named trustees. His second wife, Catherine, and children Sarah, Abraham, and Solomon became members of this church in 1869. J.J.'s name also appears as chaplain of the Patriotic Order Sons of America in 1877. Some of his descendants are still living in Kearneysville, including Lige Miller.

One other significant civic duty stands out in J.J.'s life, and this occurred when he was about 40 years old. Although research has not shown that J.J. Miller ever owned slaves, he was called to serve on the jury that found John Brown guilty of treason against

---

1 On the census records, Kearneysville at various times is considered part of Averill, Chapline, and Duffields Depot before it is consistently designated in the Middleway District.

the State of Virginia and criminal conspiracy to incite insurrection. The trial lasted from October 25 to October 31, 1859 in Charles Town, Virginia, then the county seat of Jefferson County. One may think his jury duty to be a dire omen, because there is no factual evidence to explain why J.J. Miller should have hanged himself in his barn on November 12, 1886. He had always shown concern for his family, participated in religious life, and been involved in the community. Still, legend holds that John Brown predicted all jury members would die a violent death.

> **DIED.**
>
> At his home near Kearneysville, in this county, November 12, 1886, Mr. JACOB J. MILLER, aged about 70 years. His remains were interred in Elmwood Cemetery on Sunday, Rev. Mr. Ghiselin officiating. The deceased was a man of the highest Christian character, respected and esteemed by all who knew him. In his death his family lose a kind and affectionate protector, his church a liberal and consistent member, and the community a valued and exemplary citizen.

Plate 10. J.J. Miller's obituary, Shepherdstown Register.

J.J.'s son, Abraham, established a farm in Kearneysville before 1905. Charles H. Miller, his grandson, recalls his father (Paul E. Miller, Sr.) telling of Abraham's hitching a horse to the wagon and peddling pears, quinces, apples, and vegetables throughout the village. Abraham also sold vegetable plants grown from seed on another of his plots of land. He established an orchard in 1905, which Paul, Sr. inherited. In 1933, C.S. Musselman, who operated an apple processing plant in Inwood, asked local growers to raise cherries as part of their fruit-growing, so that he could keep the canning plant running throughout the summer months. So it was that Paul Miller, Sr., planted the first cherry orchard in the area.

Today, the Miller Orchard is widely known, but perhaps not so well known is the fact that it is the oldest family owned and operated orchard in the area. When his father died in 1957, Charles operated Miller Orchard for his mother and became sole owner in 1983. Charles told me that his grandfather's expertise and thrift enabled all seven of his children to earn a college education.

DANIEL WEBSTER BORDER

Born in 1850, Daniel W. Border and a sister, Sara, were orphaned in 1866. Their parents owned two large properties, one in Shepherdstown and another in Kearneysville. An article in the *Shepherdstown Register* reports that Abraham Snyder, an uncle, had been named guardian of the children, heirs of Daniel Border, deceased. As guardian, Mr. Snyder offered a property for sale opposite the Entler Hotel in Shepherdstown that contained a two story brick house, brick kitchen with cistern and pump. There were five rooms on the first floor and four or five on the second. The other property in Kearneysville, consisting of extensive acreage and a dwelling, is shown on an 1852 map. It seems that these two properties were part of the inheritance left to Daniel W. and Sara, which means that the children were probably wealthy at an early age.

Having completed a medical degree at Johns Hopkins University Hospital in Baltimore, Dr. Daniel W. Border took up residence in Kearneysville sometime prior to 1872, at about the same time that he was voted president of the Friends of Temperance. He purchased the small stone cottage, sometimes referred to as Calico Cottage, in 1876. This property is significant in Kearneysville history, having been owned previously by Uriah

Plate 11. Recent photo of Calico Cottage, built circa 1820.

Kearney. Simon Shunk was somehow involved with its construction between 1815 and 1820. The property extended to the railroad on the west with a stone barn on the south side. Later the Grace Reformed Church was built on the north side. A daughter of James and Ariadne Kearney, Jr., who married Daniel Henkle, had lived there. In 1880 Dr. Border placed the deed to this newly-acquired property in the name of his second wife, Clara Getzendanner Border. This is the first evidence we see of his tender nature toward his wife. On the deed was written: "In consideration of one dollar and love and affection." The couple's first daughter, Margaret, died at the age of seven. The first son, Daniel Worth, born in 1881, lived less than five months. Ralph Winebrenner Border was born in Calico Cottage in 1882, followed by Marguerite in 1894.

Part of Dr. Border's medical interests can be found in the *Register* of April 16, 1884. He had read an article "The Corset Curse" written by Alice B. Stockman, M.D., which began, "If women had *common sense* instead of *fashion sense*, the corset would not exist." She further writes, "I am a temperance woman. No one can realize more than I the devastation and ruin alcohol in its many tempting forms has brought to the human family. Still I solemnly believe that in weakness and deterioration of health and moral principle, the corset has more to answer for than intoxicating drinks." He sent the article to the editors and urged them to print it, which they did. His introductory comments can be seen above.

COMMUNICATED.

KEARNEYSVILLE, W. VA., April 14th, 1884.

Editors Register.—During a period of eight years as a physician at this place, I have always condemned the wearing of the accursed corset by the opposite sex, believing them to be the cause of most of the diseases of women, so well known to our profession. And not long since I saw an article on this subject, written by a female physician, which is so pertinent to the question that I send you a copy of the same, requesting you to publish it for the benefit of parents who have daughters growing up, and who consequently hold in their hands the destiny of our future wives and mothers.

Respectfully,

D. W. BORDER, M. D.

Plate 12. Dr. Border's corset correspondence to the Shepherdstown Register.

Between 1883-1885, Dr. Border purchased the property across from Calico Cottage and caused to be built a magnificent home, known as Mendenhall Hall. The land had an interesting history dating back to 1756 when Lord Thomas Fairfax gave a grant of 570 acres to Nicholas Lemen. James Kearney, Sr. bought 50 acres of this land. The property had also been owned by Amos M. Kearney, Daniel G. Henkle, husband of Eliza J. Kearney, and Robert L. Roberts, from whom Dr. Border bought the land. Through the years, the property has been substantially reduced in size, however.

It has been reported that the bricks of Mendenhall Hall were fired on the property. The two story structure was crowned with a cupola. Servants' quarters were included in the plan. Carrie McDowell became the first house keeper and her husband, Will, served as outside man. Dr. Border used a small frame building near the corner of the stone cottage for his office, where, it has been said, he kept medicine for dispensing to his patients in a barrel. Mendenhall Hall still stands — across from Calico Cottage on Route 480. The office is now owned by George and Annabelle Ferguson.

During his residence in Kearneysville, Dr. Border was active in community affairs. He gave the land for the Reformed Church in 1884. In 1889, he fascinated his audience at the M.E. Church in Leetown with a talk on "Identification of the Lost Tribes of Israel." He maintained an active role in Friends of Temperance, filling several positions at various times. In addition, he was an active member of Elk Branch Lodge A.F. and A.M. at Shenandoah Junction.

Perhaps the most important contribution of Dr. Border's was his interest in orchards and promotion of the apple industry. Annie E. Border, his daughter-in-law, noted in a presentation before the Jefferson County Historical Society in October 1927:

> Sometime prior to 1876, Dr. Daniel Webster Border visited W.S. Miller in Berkeley County to view his orchards on Apple Pie Ridge. Following this visit, Dr. Border decided to plant forty acres in commercial apple trees at his residence in Kearneysville, Jefferson County, and this is considered the first commercial orchard of any size in this end of the county, being planted in the year 1876.

In his later life, Dr. Border became far more interested in apple production than in the practice of medicine. His vision for this area became a focal point for commercial orchards, and led him to start an apple tree nursery, named Mendenhall Nurseries. In an ad in the *Register* on September 6, 1889, he offered 50,000 first class apple trees ready for fall and spring planting at a cost of ten cents each. He later added cherry and pear trees as well as a vineyard. The nursery idea was later abandoned as he concentrated on commercial orchards. In 1913, Dr. Border was continuing to oversee his farming operations. He had contracted William Boxwell to build a stable and large barracks at his Elkwood Farm, which is near Sunnyside on what is now Border Lane, for a cost of $1,000. Dr. Daniel W. Border's grave marker shows that he died in 1914, and that his wife died twenty years later in 1934.

Ralph, the oldest surviving son, had spent most of his life in Kearneysville. He began his education at the public school but was transferred to a private school at Willow Hill, the home of H.A. Bitner and family. Much of his story here comes from a biography that his daughter, Mary Border Synder, shared.

Ralph was known for pranks. One of these was joining "Duck" Rinehart, a friend, in planting all the potato sprouts in one hole so that the task would be completed quickly. Another occurred at the Shepherd Normal School, where he joined several youths in removing a skeleton from the Physiology Department, seating it in a carriage, and placing the arrangement on top of a professor's desk.

By 1909 Ralph had completed several levels of education and graduated from the West Virginia School of Law in Morgantown. Before settling into a career, Ralph joined a steam shovel crew that was building the Panama Canal. Eventually he became the boss of the crew. No date is given for this journey into adulthood.

Following this adventure he accepted an invitation from General Lee Gurney, an Irishman, to take a three-month trip through the Panamanian jungle. Mary Border Snyder noted that at this point he drank river water before discovering a dead alligator in the pool. Another time during this adventure, he was frightened by a large tropical snake in the crevice of a log.

Journalist: It's a queer saying that the truth lies at the bottom of the well.

Lawyer: You wouldn't think that way if you ever knew the amount of pumping we lawyers have to do to get at it.

No information is available as to his reason for beginning a law practice in Texas, but it was noted in a 1911 issue of the *Register* that he was one of El Paso's leading attorneys. A legal case that first brought acclaim to Attorney Border was known as the Hotel Dieu Case. A Mexican woman, working at the Catholic Hospital, sued the hospital after her arm was caught and crushed in a mangle iron. Mr. Border represented the woman and won the case, making legal history. He was paid $3,000 for his efforts.

He boarded at the home of Mrs. A.L. Etheridge. Her daughter, Annie Laura, was a Spanish translator for Judge Fall and other prominent lawyers. Annie and Ralph fell in love and exchanged wedding vows on August 8, 1912.

Two years after their wedding to the day, on August 8, 1914, the first of their two daughters, Clara Alice, was born. Mary Virginia was born July 8, 1916. Ralph's father, Dr. Daniel Border, had died in 1915; the following year, Ralph brought his family to Kearneysville. At first, they lived in the "Old Thompson" house on property owned by Margaret May Border. This house, although much altered, still stands on the south side of Border Road.

The lives of Ralph and his family were drastically changed with the move back to the area. Ralph became a farmer, plowing the land, raising pigs, cows and horses; Annie became a country wife. In 1920, the family moved to Mendenhall Hall, Ralph's childhood home. The house was set between apple orchards with a bank barn in the back sheltering the carriage and sleigh of Dr. Border. Ralph, however, drove an open Ford.

The Border women engaged in many of the activities at Morgan Grove Fair each summer. Although Ralph transported them to and from the fair, he never attended himself. He was known as a strong minded and somewhat opinionated man. He was also quite protective of his family. For instance, Mary was permitted to attend 4-H camp for only two summers. After that, her father decided the woods and underbrush were fire traps.

Matters of the spirit and soul were important to Ralph. Believing in the teaching of the Philosophical Society of America, he read and faithfully studied this literature. He briefly joined the Society and also attended the Episcopal Church in Martinsburg. Annie was a Christian Scientist, subscribing to the literature and reading extensively.

Across the years it became evident that, although Mr. Border was an exceptional lawyer, he had little business acumen, at least when it came to managing the orchards he inherited. Banks customarily lent an owner of a large orchard money as necessary until the crops were harvested and sold. During the 1930s, the Bank of Charles Town was a beneficial holder of items against the Border estate. The bank called in its money, in spite of the fact that an uncle of Ralph's was a stockholder at the bank. Ralph's property

Plate 13. Mendenhall Hall, built circa 1882 by Daniel Border.

was put up for sale at $12,000. Fortunately, it was saved by Mr. Gatrell of the Rothwell-Gatrell Orchard Company of Martinsburg, who took over the orchard with an agreement to pay off the debt.

At age 50 Ralph again turned to the practice of law and purchased an expensive set of law books. He handled very few cases although he served as Justice of the Peace for a short time.

Throughout these years, his two daughters attended the four room school in Kearneysville. Clara graduated with the highest grade average in the county in 1928 or 1929, and then attended Martinsburg High School. Seeking a career in nursing, she graduated from Johns Hopkins School of nursing in Baltimore. Ralph sold two horses for $700.00 each to pay for Clara's education. Mary attended the newly built high school in Shepherdstown. After graduating from Shepherd College in 1937, she joined the ranks of teachers in the local area.

Mrs. Annie E. Border was loved by many and respected by all

who knew her. She was very active in the local area and through her many contacts was successful in having a caution light installed at the intersection of what is now Route 9 and Route 480. Many of the Border family are interred at the Elmwood Cemetery in Shepherdstown.

A story of Ralph Border and Samuel Heinz stands out in my memory. Sam, who was clever at making "home brew" and hard cider as well, would often entertain his friend Ralph Border. A word of explanation concerning the production of these two drinks — they did not come under prohibition. To make home brew, Sam could easily purchase malt and yeast, the two principal ingredients. Water was added and the concoction "set" in a ten gallon crock and placed in a cool dark cellar. After a number of days, when Samuel had assured himself that the brew was finished working, he strained it, capped it in dark brown bottles, and stored it in a dark cool cupboard. Few bottles ever exploded, so careful was Sam in his craft.

Hard cider was produced with less trouble. Apples, often those that had fallen to the ground, were taken to a cider press. One of these presses was located in a building owned at that time by Mr. F.O. Trump, which stood next to Trump's residence on Creamery Road. The cider needed only be kept until just before it turned to vinegar. Hence, the name hard cider. Without knowing what the alcoholic content might be, those who imbibed simply recognized a good flavor and the heady sensation that hard cider produced.

When Sam entertained his friend Ralph on summer evenings, either home brew or hard cider were part of the routine. As the sun set, the two rocked on the front porch, enjoying the potent refreshment and reciting poetry. Some of Sam's young children listened attentively as the poetical stories unfolded.

The poetry of Robert Service was a favorite, especially the tales of the Klondike Gold Rush. A few that stand out in my memory are *Dangerous Dan McGrew*, *My Friends*, and *The Cremation of Sam McGee*. Some well-remembered lines from the latter poem are:

> There are strange things done in the midnight sun
>   By the men who moil for gold.
> The Arctic trails have their secret tales
>   That would make your blood run cold;
> The Northern Lights have seen queer sights,
>   But the queerest they ever did see
> Was the night on the marge of Lake Lebarge

I cremated Sam McGee.

On this particular night, we children listened with rapt attention as the story unfolded of the death of Sam McGee and the author's promise to cremate his body. On and on through the Yukon, the frozen body fastened to a sled, the author describes his search for wood to fulfill his promise. Abruptly, as the story intensified with hardship and momentum — Ralph stood up and parted with these words: "That's all for tonight, Sam. I must get home. Mrs. Border will be waiting for me."

Although we knew the remainder of the story, the finding of a derelict boat and the author's final verses, we were disappointed not to hear Mr. Border's melodious voice concluding the saga, which I remember well.

> Some planks I tore from the cabin floor,
>   And I lit the boiler fire;
> Some coal I found that was lying around,
>   And I heaped the fuel higher;
> The flames just soared, and the furnace roared–
>   Such a blaze you seldom see,
> And I burrowed a hole in the glowing coal,
>   And I stuffed in Sam McGee.
>
> Then I made a hike, for I didn't like
>   to hear him sizzle so;
> And the heavens scowled, and the huskies howled,
>   And the wind began to blow.
> It was icy cold, but the hot sweat rolled
>   down my cheeks, and I don't know why;
> And the greasy smoke in an inky cloak
>   went streaking down the sky.

Memory is the old
paradise from which we
cannot be driven.

THEODORE HOMSHER AND LEWIS WILT FAMILIES

The enterprising Theodore Homsher added to the growth of the village when he opened a general store in the 1860s. I found no record of when he came to Kearneysville, but sometime prior to 1870, as included in the federal census of that year, Mr. Homsher and his wife Letitia, had moved from Middle Octorara, Pennsylvania. A servant, Eliza Camanra, accompanied them. The Homshers were parents of four children: Mary, Arabella, Frank, and when Virginia was born in 1879, a 9 year old local girl, Margaret Ford, came to the household to care for her.

By 1870, Theodore reported his personal property valued at $6,000. Compared to other businessmen in the area, he was modestly wealthy. About 1868 he took Alex Drawbaugh as a partner in his business. His store ads appeared during the next twenty years in the *Shepherdstown Register*. On occasion, Mr. Homsher would make buying trips to eastern cities, purchasing staple as well as fashionable garments that would adorn the local belles and their families.

In about 1879 Alex Draubaugh left the partnership. Although he did not establish a business in Kearneysville, there was other competition for Homsher. Augustus Trump and his family had moved into the area and, in the 1880 census, Mr. Trump was listed as a merchant, operating his store a short distance from the center of town. Other competition came from Major Hamill, who advertised "fresh fish."

NEW GOODS
AND
TREMENDOUS EXCITEMENT
AT
KERNEYSVILLE
AT THE
CHEAP CASH STORE
OF
T. HOMSHER !

I take great pleasure in informing the Public that I have received a Splendid Stock of new FALL AND WINTER GOODS, of every description, for Ladies, Misses, Children, and Men and Boys, which I will sell VERY LOW strictly for CASH or BARTER, without any deviation whatever. My stock is complete. BOOTS AND SHOES, HATS and CAPS, READY MADE CLOTHING, GROCERIES, choice and at lowest figures. Please give me a call, I warrant satisfaction. Terms strictly Cash or Country Produce.
T HOMSHER
Kerneysville, Oct. 25, 1879.

Plate 14. Homsher General Store advertisement published in the local newspaper.

Keeping an eye on business opportunities, Mr. Homsher hired Thomas Turner as a purchasing agent. Mr. Turner transacted business with farmers as far away as Hampshire County. His purchases — wheat and other farm products — were shipped on the B&O. On one occasion 150 head of sheep brought him a tidy profit.

Two events of note occurred in 1879 for Mr. Homsher. First, he purchased an additional seven acres of land from Thomas Turner. Second, he took his son, Frank, into the business. It wasn't until 1884 that his new home was completed on a lot opposite the Presbyterian Church, a property now used by the Kearneysville Branch of the Bank of Charles Town.

As a Democrat, Mr. Homsher and his son, Frank, worked for the party on the local level. This work enabled Theodore to become postmaster in 1885, a position that he maintained during President Cleveland's first term, the term of Harrison and the second term of Grover Cleveland.

Perhaps the event of 1888 was the wedding of Theodore and Letitia's oldest daughter, Mary, and James V. Moore, owner of "Western View," a magnificent antebellum home located opposite Sunnyside. Juanita Stuckey Anderson, whose parents lived at Western View for many years in the 20th century, describes the house in great detail. Aspects that stands out in her memory are the slave quarters at the rear of the mansion and a large barn and tenants' house that stood to the right. Another memory is of the awe-inspiring entry way with its chandelier high above one's head and the winding staircase that ascends to the third floor. It was here in the entry way that the young couple exchanged vows in the presence of both family and intimate friends.

Boom times were reported in the last decade of the twentieth century, when growers were paid $1.00 per bushel for wheat and 80 cents per bushel for potatoes. However, Mr. Homsher had already sold his general store to Samuel Lickleider, who continued the operation from what was known as the "Depot Store." Having lost the position of postmaster to Augustus Trump in 1897, it appears that Theodore Homsher retired from public life. His wife died in July 1903. His death followed less than a year later at age 76.

Of the four Homsher progeny, two remained single. Little has been noted of Frank other than that he became a business associate of his father. Mention was made in an April, 1927 edition of the *Shepherdstown Register* that he was buried with military honors upon his death at age 66. Belle, who never married, lived with her parents until their deaths. Mary continued living at Western View. At this point, the Wilt and Homsher families were joined.

The Wilt and Homsher families first became acquainted and found much in common in Kearneysville. A member of each family was to serve as postmaster during a Democrat administration. Both Mr. Wilt and Mr. Homsher were owners of general stores. And finally, the only son of Lewis Wilt married the youngest daughter of Theodore Homsher.

Mr. Lewis Wilt and his wife, Georgiana Texas (Fleming), moved from Virginia to West Virginia sometime prior to 1874, the year their son, Walter, was born. Three daughters were to follow: Irene, born in 1879, and the twins, Margie L. and Mabel C., born in April 1880. Mr. Wilt operated a grocery store in Kearneysville and added "salesman" to his occupation on the 1900 census. As far as can be determined this store occupied a room in Mr. Wilt's home on the northeast side of the B&O.

The 1920 census lists Lewis as merchant. Lewis Wilt's death preceded that of his wife, Georgina, who died October 4, 1923. The twin daughters moved from the village upon marriage and returned only for brief visits. Irene married J.P. Brown. After the death of her husband, Mrs. Brown raised her four children, Max, Tracy, Lucille, and Tyler while living in her parents home. None of the Brown children remained in the community.

The only son of Lewis Wilt, Walter, married Virginia, the youngest daughter of Theodore Homsher and the couple moved in with her parents. After Lewis and Georgina died, Belle continued living with her sister and brother-in-law in the home place that the two sisters had inherited from their parents. Belle was to live 22 more years, dying at the age of 72.

This must have been a difficult threesome. Belle, born in 1857, was twenty years older than her sister, Virginia. Since she never married, and from reports of her personality by those who knew her in later years, one wonders if Belle felt unloved. At any rate, Virginia seems to have become the target of her bitterness and domineering attitude.

Belle spent much of her last fifteen years in her upstairs bedroom. It was incumbent on Virginia to carry meals when Belle could not or would not descend to the dining room. Also, a fire had to be kept in the upstairs bedroom during the cold months. Henry Stanley recalls vividly the day Belle started the fire in her room. While Belle was attempting to burn some papers, the stove became over-heated and flames burst between the inside and outside walls and into the roof. Belle was quickly escorted to the parlor as Virginia attempted to sooth her sister's jagged nerves.

The Shepherdstown Fire Department roared to the scene with klaxon signaling by-standers to make way. Those loafing in the area quickly gathered also, unintentionally getting in the way and intentionally giving advice. But it was the hook and ladder crew that saved the home. Firemen ascended the ladder and forced water between the walls to extinguish the fire. And neighbors had another example of how difficult it was to accommodate Belle's behavior.

Walter Wilt was a rather reserved man. He was also known for taking advantage of every opportunity within his reach. Physically he was short of stature, clipped his mustache to cover his mouth and endured walking with a misshapen foot. However, what he lacked in appearance and personality was compensated for in determination. He became active in local affairs and was selected as a delegate to the West Virginia Democrat nominating committee in June 1912. Those accompanying him to Grafton were C.E. Jones, Thomas Campbell, and J.P. Kearfott. In 1925, he held the office of Vice President of the State Camp of Patriotic Order Sons of America (P.O.S. of A). The local organization was known as Washington Camp No. 3. In the same year he was called for jury duty.

He served as postmaster from 1915 to 1922. In 1917, he became a business partner with Carl Fleming and bought M.M. Jenkins's general store, known as the Depot Store mentioned previously. By this time, it housed the express office, station waiting room, post office and general store on the first floor. On the second floor a social room was available for community activities referred to as Trump Hall.

In 1919, while Walter was standing in front of the store stove to warm himself, he was badly burned. An accumulation of coal gas caused the stove door and pipe to puff out. His mustache and eyebrows were singed such that they became non-existent. His hands were painfully burned as well.

Two occurrences caused the change in his store operations during the early 1920's. First, his father died, leaving a vacancy at the Wilt's Store; second, Carl Fleming, his partner, returned to farming. Thus he sold the Depot Store and took over the business run by his father. His sister, Irene Brown and her family occupied the living quarters of the same property. Across time, Mr. Wilt's deformed foot didn't stop his walking from his home across from the Presbyterian Church to his place of business, just northeast of the B&O Railroad. This daily activity continued six days each week, until his last illness and death prevailed in 1943.

During the following years, his widow, "Miss Virginia," continued to tend her flower gardens with the help of "Uncle" Will Dixon. As a close friend of Mrs. John Stanley, she used her sewing talents to create pretty aprons to sell at the Reformed Church Bazaars. She was also a steadfast participant in the annual Stanley ritual of apple butter boiling.

Having no children, Virginia was removed from the community by her nephew, Tyler Brown, following a small stroke. She died in May 1962, although her death date was never added to the family grave marker in Elmwood Cemetery.

To learn the value of money, try to borrow it.

JOHN AND BLANCHE MILLER STANLEY

As with writing of the contributions of many to the development of this village, it is impossible to give a complete picture of Mr. and Mrs. John Stanley. From personal knowledge and historical accounts they both nurtured the community and willingly helped those in need.

Both had spent their youths on farms among many siblings, and were accustomed to the rigors of country living. In 1909 we find them living in Kearneysville with their two children, David Henry and Margie. Mr. Stanley had built an eight room frame house on land purchased from F.O. Trump for $150. The house still stands on Stanley Lane. Federal census records of 1910 indicate the value of this real estate was $800.00.

Mr. Stanley kept meticulous records of his work as a construction contractor. His books which have been retained give much insight into new construction, repairs and various costs, including labor during the first half of the twentieth century. For example, his records indicate that he was paid $1.50 per day in 1906, and that a day's work was 10 hours with a break for lunch. In the next few years, Mr. Stanley repaired the roof on the Presbyterian Church for

Plate 15. Stanley home, circa 1940. Homsher Barn on right.

$1.00. Also, population trends can be inferred from his records of construction activity in the community. Across his lifetime, he did carpenter work for the people listed below.

D.W. Border	Annie McDonald
Mayberry McKee	Sniederhan (for State Farm)
George Bradford	D.L. Magruder
John Tucker	Ruah Trump
F.O. Trump	A.J. Umps
T.O. Everhart	Walter Wilt
Will McDowell	J.P. Kearfott
Jane Myers	Mrs. Will Fowler
H.C. Miller	Mrs. C.C. Border
Hodges and Lemen (elevators)	Vernon Stuckey & Company
Mrs. Clower	Bertha Horn
Francis Miller (store)	Lee Creamer
Fred Winston	Israel Hunter (house)

By 1911, the record shows that the family was selling farm products — four pigs at $2.00 each, one pound of butter for 18 cents. Mr. Stanley was also hauling apples to the cider mill. At some point in his career, assisted by his wife, he delivered milk for the Clarksburg Dairy Company, which preceded the Kearneysville Creamery.

There is a gap in the records from 1917-1924. Perhaps it was during these years that John Stanley worked for the Creamery in maintenance. On advice from his doctor that this work was harmful to his health, he began working in construction in Washington, D.C. He was earning a salary of between $122 and $125 per month. The family at home was adding to the Stanley coffers, also. Henry, the only son, received $12.00 per month as janitor for the school which stood just behind the family home. This was hard work: Henry did not enjoy carrying coal from the basement and tending the stoves! Mrs. Stanley provided board and room for one or two paying guests who needed extended accommodations; there were few or no other options for transitioning to the village.

About 1917-1918 an influenza epidemic spread through the village. Mrs. Stanley gave of her time and resources to serve the community, and tirelessly provided care at any home to which she was called without concern for her well-being. Before the epidemic had ended, though, she became ill. Miraculously she recovered. Mrs. Stanley cared for the sick in the community at other times as well. She served as mid-wife if a doctor was not available, and helped prepare bodies for burial if undertaking services were inaccessible, such as during snowstorms.

Both Mr. and Mrs. Stanley were stalwart members of Grace Reformed Church and contributed to the community through their work there. Mr. Stanley held the position of Superintendent for many years and Mrs. Stanley taught a Sunday school class. Many children first attended Sunday school when Mrs. Stanley stopped by their home and shepherded them to the Church.

As the nation drifted into the Depression, construction also declined in Washington, D.C. Mr. Stanley returned to Kearneysville and resumed his work here, building houses for Herb Carter and Frank Powell. After Norval Johnston and Margie (Mr. Stanley's daughter) were married in 1935, the two men worked together constructing a home for the young couple and later a home for Gilbert and Virginia Willingham. His records show that he built barns, silos, and made repairs for community residence, wherever he was called. He continued sharpening carpenter's and crosscut saws long after the age when many men retire. Further, John Stanley provided employment for a number of men as the Kearneysville community continued to feel the effects of the

Depression.

John and Blanche's son, Henry was an educator. He married and moved to Berkeley County. At the end of WWII, the Stanley's daughter, Margie, bought the Esso Station on the corner of Routes 490 and 9. She combined the sale of gasoline and groceries, and provided service to the community for the next 25 years.

Mr. and Mrs. John Stanley added to the spirit of community through their service to and interaction with the people. Mr. Stanley died in 1968 at 91; his wife survived him by three years.

Wife: Hubby dear, may I have $5 to go shopping?

Husband: Of course, would you like a $5 bill or a new one?

Wife: A new one, of course.

Husband: Good. I'm $4 to the better.

- The Pathfinder

JOHN H. FOX

The life of John H. Fox is compelling in the remarkable strength and perseverance of an individual born with the odds against him. He overcame many obstacles to achieve the respect of those whose lives he touched and to leave a rich heritage for his descendants. His son, Dewey Fox, (at age 102) and his niece, Bertha Jones, recently shared some of the family legends with me. Dewey recalled that his father, John, was born in 1845 on the Dandridge Plantation known as The Bower, which is near the Opequon Creek in Berkeley County. Lemuel Dandridge was the plantation owner at the time. John's story begins here when Mrs. Dandrige discovered that her husband had auctioned off a woman slave and left her five children in the slave quarters. She found the little children mewling together, a sound that reminded her of small foxes — hence the family name of Fox, or so the story goes. The children were four boys — Benjamin, Humphrey, Stephen, and John — and Mary, a girl.

The mistress of the plantation brought them to the kitchen and ordered the cook to tend to them. That attention was the same as what the dogs and cats received. That is, the children were fed scraps, skimmed milk and cornmeal placed under the table, and yet they grew well enough, such that in time the Master ordered them to be fed meat to help them grow even stronger. But the cook had other ideas of where the meat would be used and instead smeared their lips with grease in deception. Eventually the situation came to the attention of the Master, who intervened.

From what is known, the children grew and served as family slaves on the plantation. Although they remained slaves until the Civil War, the boys were to become more than field hands. Benjamin learned to read and write and was trained as a butler. Then, in 1863, John seized an opportunity for a different life when President Lincoln signed the Emancipation Proclamation. Although he could have sought his freedom in the North, he placed himself with the Confederate Army. He wasn't allowed to carry a gun, and therefore performed auxiliary tasks to support the troops. No records have been found of his experience in the Civil War, but a few stories survive. One of these is a description of his idea to wrap the wagon wheels for crossing a wooden bridge to reduce the noise, thus enabling the Rebs to gain an advantage. According to Bertha, Mr. Fox spoke of being at Appomattox and apparently was present at the surrender of General Robert E. Lee.

At the end of the war, John returned to Jefferson County, to the Bower, and worked once more for Mr. Dandridge, but this time as a free man. His wages were two dollars per day and one meal. With this small amount of money, he managed to buy an acre of land for five dollars, and then another and another, until he had purchased three acres of land in the Pine Hills. Then he began cutting and selling timber from his land. Bertha says he bought oxen and wagon and was known as "lumber jack."

From this entrepreneurial beginning, he was able to grow and prosper as a large property holder and family man. In 1869 Thomas Turner conveyed to John Fox a property with house known as Toll Gate House, about a half mile south of Kearneysville on the Smithfield-Shepherdstown Pike, for $500. However, it seems that he rented out this property and never occupied it. According to the 1870 census, John Fox at age 24, a male mulatto, had real estate valued at $500 and personal property valued at $100. He was married to Hannah Washington, age 25, female black, with two small children, Emily, age 4 and Lucinda, age 1. At this time he and Hannah were living with her parents, David and Nellie Washington, in what came to be known as Hartstown. Humphrey, a 16-year old youth, lived in this household as well. Now John was working at various jobs, including the flour mill at Leetown.

By 1880 John H. Fox gives his occupation as farmer and is living on the Border Farm. He has married a second wife, Lucy E, sister of Hannah. Emily, his first child, has died but two children have been added. Now the household consists of John and his wife and their children, Lucinda, age 12, Robert E, age 2 and Bertha E. 9 months. Also by 1880 John has added a servant, Emily Coleman, and two farm laborers, Howard and Oliver Denis, maternal cousins. It's interesting to note that John had named one of his sons "Lemmiel D.", possibly in remembrance of his former master. Unfortunately this child died when he was five years old.

John continued to expand his farming operations and his land holdings. He purchased 87.75 acres in 1889 from George McIntyre. This property contained a dwelling. The same year he also purchased 80 acres that were part of the Border inheritance from Dr. Daniel Border. Today this area is known as Fox Glen.

Bertha Jones, his granddaughter and source of much of this story, says that her grandmother died in 1892, when the youngest child was 2. Her grandmother's sister, a school teacher named Mary E., married Mr. Fox to keep the children together — two brothers and five sisters. A son — Dewey — was born to this marriage. They lived on his Wiltshire Road farm near Bardane until he sold it and moved to Johnsontown with the family. The children attended Linwood School at Kearneysville for eight years; later they got their high school education at Eagle School in Charles Town.

John's civic contributions were substantial. He was on the Board of Trustees with George Mason and George Johnson of the Colored Baptist Church of Kearneysville (currently St. Paul). He and Mr. Motrin Collins, a carpenter, were patrons of the Colored School at Woodbury that stood on the Kearneysville-Leetown Road. This building has since been torn down. When the Niagara Movement, an initiative to improve education opportunities of black people, first began in Jefferson County, John loaned money to the organization to build a headquarters. Bertha Jones tells of his last trip to Harpers Ferry to receive repayment of money he had loaned. By this time, he was unable to climb the steps to Storer College, so he remained seated in his conveyance until the sum was delivered to him with grateful thanks.

Unable to read or write except to sign his name, John urged his children and grandchildren to become educated, which they did. Many received advanced degrees. In its entirety, John's story leaves me with a sense of awe, especially related to the mystery of his childhood, the courage and integrity he exhibited throughout his life, and his care in building community.

John Fox died a wealthy man on May 19, 1911 at age 65. Further demonstrating his knowledge of human behavior, he had wisely hired an attorney to write his will, the full text of which is shown below. The will was probated on May 25, 1911.

Last Will and Testament of John H. Fox, Deceased.

In the Name of God, Amen: I, John H. Fox, of Bardane, in the County of Jefferson, State of West Virginia, being of sound mind and memory, do make, publish and declare this to be my last will and testament, hereby revoking any and all former wills by me at any time heretofore made.

1. I desire modest and decent burial, and the payment of all my just debts as promptly after my death as convenient.
2. I give and bequeath to my beloved wife, Mary E., all my household furniture, and one third of all the residue of my personal property (after the payment of debts and expenses of administration therefrom) to be hers absolutely.
3. I give, bequeath and devise to my daughter, Lucinda (wife of Edward Roper) my house and lot of land (about one acre) situated on the Shepherdstown and Smithfield Turnpike, and known as the "Old Toll Gate Property", absolutely and in fee, and do also give my said daughter an annuity of Sixty Dollars per year to be paid her annually (beginning six months after my death) for and during her natural life, equally by my three sons hereinafter named, and the same ($20 each annually) is hereby made a charge and lien upon the real estate herein after devised them respectively.
4. I also give, bequeath and devise to my beloved wife, Mary E., one-third of all the residue (excepting the Toll Gate property) of my real estate for and during her natu-

ral life, and at her death the same to be divided equally among my three sons hereinafter named.
5. I give, bequeath and devise all the residue of my property, real and person, and of every kind, character and description whatsoever, to my three sons, Robert Edward, Charles Washington and Dewey Williams Fox, to be divided among them in equal shares, absolutely and in fee (subject, however, to the charge for the above specified annuity) except that in the event of the death of said Dewey Williams occurring before attaining the age of Twenty one years, and without issue, then his share of all my said real estate shall go to, and be divided equally between his two brothers, said Robert E. and Charles W. Fox, and their heirs, respectively, forever.

This will is not meant to include, or in any way effect the disposal of my tract of land known as the F.M.Brown Farm, which by contract in writing of date April 2nd, 1906, I then sold to my said son, Robert E., except that in the event my death occurs before the money consideration provided for therein is paid by said son, and a deed to him for said farm, as therein provided for, is executed and delivered by me, then, in that event, my said Executor shall, and he is hereby fully authorized, upon the payment to him for my estate of the money then due under the terms of said contract, to execute and deliver to said Robert E. Fox, a proper deed for said farm (not only "for and during his natural life") but absolutely and in fee; but for the residue of said farm which he thus acquires without paying therefor he is to be charged the sum of $2,000.00 then, and that taken into account as that much on his share in the partition of my other real estate provided for hereunder.

I hereby constitute and appoint George M. Beltzhoover, of Shepherdstown, sole executor of this my last Will and Testament.

Given under my hand and seal this 1st day of August, 1908.

                                                  John H. Fox, (Seal)

Codicil

I, John H. Fox, do hereby make and declare this to be a codicil to my will, of date August 1st, 1908, and to be taken as part thereof, to-wit:

1. Instead of an annuity of $60.00 per year to my daughter, Lucinda Roper, as provided for in item 3rd of said will, I hereby so change and modify same as to increase the amount from $60.00 to $100.00 per year, payable as in said item 3rd provided, which in all other respects is to remain unchanged.
2. I also hereby change and modify item 5th of my said will as to provide that the share of my estate therein given my son, Dewey Williams Fox — in the event of his attaining the age of twenty one years — shall not be paid or delivered to him until he attains the age of thirty years, but the same in the meantime to be held in trust for him by my Executor, allowing my said son only the income therefrom during said period, i.e. between his attaining the age of twenty one and thirty years.

Given under my hand and seal this 25th day of January, 1911.

John H. Fox, (Seal)

Witnesses: W.N. Lemen
            Geo. M. Beltzhoover, Jr.

His passing was reported in the May 25th edition of the *Shepherdstown Register*. Clearly he was a man much respected in the community.

> John H. Fox, a well-known colored man, died at his home near Bardane, last Friday night, after a long illness, aged 65 years. He was perhaps the wealthiest colored man in the county, owning a couple of excellent farms, well-improved and very desirable. His estate is worth from $20,000 to $25,000. He was a very highly respected man, and his death will be regretted by many friends, both white and colored. He was a genuine Christian, the soul of integrity and honesty, and his word was as good as his bond.

> Esteemed and highly thought of, he was an example to his race and his life shows how a really good man will be appreciated, no matter what disadvantage he may labor under.

John's remains were buried at the St. Paul Cemetery, where many of his descendants are also buried. He was survived by his third wife Mary E. and three of his sons, Robert, Charles and Dewey, and a daughter, Lucinda. According to his will, Mary E. was to receive all of the household furniture and one-third of all the residue of all his personal property. Lucinda, the wife of Edward Roper, inherited the old Toll Gate property and annuity of $100 per year paid annually during her lifetime. Each of the surviving sons received a farm. However, Dewey could not receive his until he was 30 years old.

Robert and Charles lived on their farms for a number of years. Dewey was forced to sell his shortly after he inherited it in order to pay the remainder owed on it. Had he kept it, he might have been able to acquire a small fortune from it, as it is currently held by the U.S. Department of Agriculture. Across time Dewey has served in local and state government, and continues to play the organ at his home church in Fairmount, West Virginia. For whatever reason, his father's will indicates that if Dewey attains the age of 20 he would receive some property. It's one of Life's ironies that Dewey is now 102 and has outlived all his siblings. I recently heard him speak at an NAACP event held at the Ebenzer Mt. Holiness Church in Mt. Pleasant near Summit Point. He is an extraordinary man and profound speaker. He told us to take responsibility for our lives, and to not go begging for a job but go to the bank for money and start our own businesses. He concluded by saying that he was finished his speech not because he wanted to sit down, but because he wanted to move around.

Living heirs of John Fox in the Kearneysville area are Sarah Roper Walker, Celena Roper Carter, and James Roper, (great grandchildren of John; children of Lucinda Fox and Ed Roper), and Bertha Jones, who lives in the Shiloh Development Route 9 just outside of Kearneysville (granddaughter of John, and daughter of Charles).

Public Services

Public Services

TRANSPORTATION

Roadways

Transportation has always been an important part of building a prospering community. From early times in what was to become the United States, settlers have used the many streams and rivers to move commodities as well as people from one location to another. Kearneysville is in a direct line between Middleway and the Ferry Landing on the Potomac River at Shepherdstown, and between Martinsburg and the Shenandoah and Potomac Rivers at Harpers Ferry. The history of road-building through Kearneysville is tied to this bit of geography. Of course, there were other factors that resulted in two major roads that intersected at Kearneysville, perhaps stimulating growth of the community.

The village of Smithfield, now known as Middleway, was more than 15 miles removed from either the Potomac River or the Shenandoah River. Seeing the need for a dependable route from Smithfield to Shepherdstown, which was a market center as well as a landing stage on the Potomac, the Smithfield-Shepherdstown Turnpike Company was formed in the early years of the 19th century. Thus, the Smithfield-Shepherdstown Turnpike became one of the first major roads that connected the Kearneysville community with its neighbors. This was before West Virginia became a state, and the records were moved from Charles Town to Shepherdstown and then back to Charles Town between 1859 and 1873, possibly resulting in some of the confusion about dates. For example, records show that Mr. Helm, a local farmer at the time, recalled the date that the road opened as being in 1826, although the recollection of others placed the date five or so years later.

However, Brenda Kitzmiller from the Department of Transportation recently gave me much information about the early history of this turnpike. According to her, the larger road, the Shepherdstown to Winchester Turnpike, was chartered in 1816; the smaller section that included Kearneysville was rechartered by Acts of the Legislature of the Commonwealth of Virginia in 1824. Initially, the Turnpike was paved with stone and had three small culverts but no bridges. By 1848 it had deteriorated to a deplorable state. The turnpike company received permission from the Legislature to increase capital stock and also to set up toll booths. The first two were at Shepherdstown and Leetown; gatekeepers were paid an annual salary of $60 and $50.

The General Assembly of the Commonwealth of Virginia, in an extraordinary session on September 4, 1862, ruled that the Turnpike was to pass to the newly created state of West Virginia when it received its charter in 1863, but it had to be purchased. The State failed to pay until they were sued by the General Assembly. West Virginia lost the case and finally paid on June 14, 1915.

The existence of the Turnpike stimulated transportation services. For example, James A. Adams, a Shepherdstown resident, advertised that any person desiring to go to Kearneysville by hack could procure a ticket at the Shepherdstown Depot or at any store — cash only, no credit. In 1894 F.O. Trump established a livery to carry passengers from Kearneysville to Shepherdstown, Middleway, Charles Town and other points. He advertised a one-third reduction in fare for County riders. As will be shown later, Kearneysville residents combined the hack services and the train for transportation.

The system for use of the Pike was fairly ingenious, although similar to other turnpikes in the country at the time. To ensure that funds were available for upkeep, in 1870 the Superior Court ordered "watch boxes" on the Pike. At Shepherdstown, the end of the route, George Bast had charge of the toll gate or watch box; Frederick Fulk was in charge of the midpoint, Kearneysville; and T.M. Kearns gathered tolls at Smithfield. For this service, the "watchers" were to receive 20 percent of the tolls gathered, and the other 80 percent went to the Turnpike Company.

Farmers whose land adjoined the Turnpike played a part in the Pike's upkeep, which often consisted of simply filling in the ruts with rocks. Their maintenance efforts were probably subsidized using fees drawn from the Turnpike Company. For example when James Logie purchased 44 acres of land from Minor Hurst, he also purchased the adjoining length of Turnpike, and thereby had to assume responsibility for its upkeep. When repairs were not made in a timely manner, complaints were taken to the Board of Supervisors, which was later to become the county court. A committee of road viewers, sometimes called road supervisors, was then formed to investigate the complaint. People who performed this service were paid two dollars, an amount that was later changed to three. Also, viewers inspected the roads periodically. J.J. Miller, James V. Moore, and Thomas Licklider all served in this capacity during the early history of the Turnpike.

Although the tolls may seem small today, they were probably considered substantial at the turn of the century, especially because they had to be paid at each watch box. The fee for every horse, mare, mule, jack or jennet (donkey) or gelding that was hitched to a vehicle was three cents; unhitched the toll was one cent. A single horse and carriage, wagon or cart was assessed five cents, and the fee went up from there. Two horses drawing a carriage, wagon or cart cost ten cents; four horses and carriage or wagon, twelve cents; and five horses and carriages, eighteen cents. Travelers paid five cents for every sheep or hog, and ten cents for every twenty cows. Persons going or returning from funerals were exempt.

In 1874, G.T. Licklider erected another tollgate house on the Pike from Kearneysville to Shepherdstown. When the company went public in 1876, admitting stockholders, a determined effort was made to repair the Pike and add even more watch boxes. One of these was located near Shepherdstown and one near Kearneysville. This might have been the former John H. Fox house, now a part of the Miller Orchard. (Of note here is that John Jewitt, a local citizen was Secretary Treasurer of the Turnpike Company at this time). Naturally, the renewed effort to collect tolls drew another outcry from the local citizenry.

Thanks to a correspondent for the *Shepherdstown Register*, known only by her pen name "Mary Beau," some historical events related to roads in Kearneysville were captured for posterity. Ms. Beau lived in Duffields for a time and served as a correspondent for that village for ten or more years. After she moved to Kearneysville, she continued as a correspondent, but for her new neighborhood. She noted the following list of complaints by users of the Pike in her Letter to the Editor, June 10, 1876:

- Tolls were too high for the distance traveled.
- The charges were injurious to inhabitants.
- The Turnpike Company was issuing free passes to county officials, thereby stopping the redress of grievances.

Ms. Beau's letter highlights the plight of the farmer coming to town and traveling just one mile in a two horse vehicle with a few pounds of butter and a dozen eggs to trade for groceries. He pays fifteen cents to get these articles to Shepherdstown. If he is detained and must spend the night in town, he must pay for overnight lodging; finally, he spends another fifteen cents to return home.

In the later years of the 19th century, many travelers were avoiding the Pike to avoid the tolls — even though this added extra miles to their journey — and had humorously renamed what is today Bower Road as the "Shun Pike." At one point the court ordered the option of an advance, yearly toll rate to relieve complaints. This proved to be unsatisfactory, and the locals continued avoiding toll roads whenever possible.

But there was another problem: Local farmers who did not have direct access to the Pike crossed their neighbors' land, leaving aggravating ruts. Actually, Bower Road, across from the Toll Gate House, became a byway in this manner according to Charles H. Miller, present owner of the house. The neighbors, being greatly displeased with this unwanted traffic, appealed to Superior Court for help with it. Mary Beau wrote that the road from Martinsburg to Shepherdstown was better and smoother for ten months of the year than the Smithfield Pike because it had larger boulders buried in the road bed. She advocated for making the Pike a county road that could be covered with clay and made much more passable. In any case, one must marvel at this direct route laid out by such enterprising men.

Other roads were to follow. The history of a part of Route 9 began in 1868. Daniel Getzendanner, who owned Aspen Dale Farm, (later to become the State University Experiment Farm) joined other nearby farmers and petitioned the Superior Court to open a road from the Berkeley County line at George Seibert's, to intersect the Pike at Kearneysville. The road was built, this time crossing the B&O Railroad at Trumps' and entering the Pike at Dr. Border's. Farmers whose land was affected and who were compensated are shown in the table below. The amount appraised by the Court was usually twenty-five percent less than requested by the landowner. The sum total of allowed deductions was $276.88. Another $40 in surveyor fees were paid to J. P. Kearfott, bringing the total to 316.88, which had to come from the County Treasury. Trump's Crossing was later closed, in about 1931.

Name	Compensation Request	Allowed
J.M. VanMetre	$30.00	$22.50
D. and E. Gentzendanner	$145.00	$108.50
Isaac Strider	$45.00	$33.75
Thomas Turner	$56.00	$42.00
Henry Bitner	$39.50	$29.63
H.A. Trump	$24.00	$18.00
J.G. Ruckle	$30.00	$22.50

Table 1. Farmers and fees paid for road-building land, 1868.

Warm Springs Road was also opened in 1868, connecting the Charles Town road to the Shepherdstown road. Encouraged by all the previous, successful openings of new roads, a petition for yet another was presented to the Court in August of 1868. This time, D. and E. Gentzendanner, James M. VanMetre, William Broadwell and Mrs. Hamill proposed a road be opened from Spa Springs to

ROAD MATTERS.

A party of surveyors under instructions of the State Road Commission are making their headquarters in Shepherdstown while they are engaged in surveying a route from Kearneysville to Martinsburg for the proposed State road between Charles Town and Martinsburg. It is said that the present survey is to locate a road that will be south of the Baltimore & Ohio Railroad the length of the whole line. Like the route surveyed through Jefferson county, the proposed route means almost entirely new construction, but little of the established roads being utilized. It is said that a preliminary survey indicated that a practicable route can be secured through that section. The survey, it is said, will follow the line of the Baltimore & Ohio Railroad from Kearneysville to Vanclevesville, thence through the pine hills to Senator Sliver's orchard and on to Martinsburg.

The State Road Commission seems bent on making a road that will be as nearly as possible a straight line between Martinsburg and Charles Town, and every other consideration will be sacrificed to this one idea, apparently. With narrow stupidity the commission ignores the well laid out roads already established, with their solid beds of limestone rock; it takes absolutely no account of the towns and villages that have a right to be considered in making the road; it pays no attention to the centres of population; it utterly ignores the wishes of the county court and the convenience and benefits that ought to be extended to the people; it gives no heed to local desires or advantages of the people who have a right to such advantges.

It takes no genius to build a road on a straight line if there is no regard for expense or any other consideration, and there may be instances where such a road is required. But there is no such necessity in the case of the proposed road between Martinsburg and Charles Town. The direct communication between these two cities is so trifling and unimportant that the commission is utterly unjustified in its attitude of ignoring all other questions involved. It is a sin and a shame that it persists in defying public opinion and public interests and because of political influence wastes the State funds in putting a road where it is not serving the public needs but caters to individual advantage.

We hope that the Legislature at its coming session will take note of the policy of the State Road Commission and head it off either by inducing a change in the personnel or refusing to appropriate money to be deliberately diverted from its proper purposes.

Plate 17. "Road Matters" from Dec. 7, 1922, Register.

the Pike, or what is now the Leetown Road. J.J. Miller, E.H. Roberts, Thomas Licklider, James V. Moore and Thomas Turner were named viewers. For whatever reason, these men returned an unfavorable finding, and the matter was closed.

The struggle over tolls continued for at least a couple of decades. It came as no surprise to some when the State of West Virginia ordered all tolls eliminated in 1911. This act preceded the Department of Highways assuming responsibility for some roads, which came to be known as State roads. All others were the responsibility of the county.

In 1921, the State Legislature passed a measure to construct roads connecting county seats by the most direct route and connecting principle highways with neighboring states. Hearings were held in three locations during that year.

Early in January, 1922, Division Engineer B.E. Grey announced that the new road between Martinsburg and Charles Town would pass by way of the Riley Ford Bridge and VanMetre School through Kearneysville. Although the most direct route from Kearneysville to Charles Town had not been decided, it would lie entirely south of the B&O. It was also announced that a link would be constructed from the proposed road near Kearneysville to Shepherdstown; this link would pass under the B&O tracks. All grade crossings on the main line of the B&O Railroad would be avoided as standard procedure.

It seems that the question of location for the new road slumbered for some months. Finally Division Engineer Grey and his assistant, Mr. Hawkins, came before the Jefferson County Court to ask for immediate approval of the proposed state road from Kearneysville to Charles Town. This approval would be given by authorizing condemnation proceedings so that land could be acquired.

The issue may have appeared to slumber, but this proposal was met with a blustering response, and the Court was ready with reasons to refuse:

- Even if the proposed route were completed from Charles Town to Kearneysville, Berkeley County must have a bond issue passed for additional State funds. Thus Jefferson County Road funds would be tied up in a road of little use.

- The Court opposed damages to land where there were so many roads available. Condemnation costs were estimated at $15,000 to $16,000.
- If an entirely new road were constructed, new side roads would need to be built as connectors, an expense that would continue for years to come.
- Perhaps considered most important by the Court, members felt the Court had not been treated courteously or fairly. While the State Road Commission knew that the Court and a large proportion of the people found the route objectionable, Engineer Grey failed to consult with County officials on this very important matter. Only when approval of the Court was required was that body approached.

In its determination to have a voice in the matter, the Court sent a petition signed by four of the five members to the State Road Commission requesting that the new road be located by way of Shepherdstown.

Hostility toward the new road was fueled when the State Legislature increased real estate taxes to 20 cents per $100. Fifteen thousand dollars of this revenue were allocated for the right-of-way purchases. At this point in time, jobs were becoming scarcer. Residents protested that the local roads were getting worse, that increasing taxes during times of depression was a bad idea, and that no good result could be seen. Some tax payers claimed distance travel by automobile was negligible, since few families owned a car, and most travel was limited to a local town. Besides, they argued, the B&O Railroad was a logical option for journeys of some distance.

Tempers continued to flare as surveyors were seen between Charles Town and Martinsburg. Why insist on a road that was nearly as straight as possible? Why ignore a route that was laid on solid beds of limestone for the most part? Why not pay attention to the voices of villagers in making the final decision? And what was the necessity for direct transportation between Charles Town and Martinsburg, when intercourse between the two towns was practically negligible?

Most often repeated was the question: Why waste State funds to make a road that would not be serving public needs but catering to individual advantage? The questions and criticism seemed to fall on deaf ears.

Articles in the *Shepherdstown Register* from this time note that talk was abroad of political and personal consideration influencing the decision. For example, decisions related to the South Queen Street-Pine Hill route in Berkeley County were said to be influenced by Senator Gray Silver and other notable politicians who had orchards in the area. Mr. Charles Faulkner suggested that Burke Street be followed and continue on through Shepherdstown. President of Shepherd College, W.H.S. White, led the group that insisted such a route would benefit Shepherdstown. Others were insisting that a route from Charles Town to Martinsburg through Duffields had existed for a hundred years.

Apparently three possible routes from Charles Town to Kearneysville were proposed and seriously considered. Shenandoah Junction residents urged that the road pass through their town and thus to Bardane and on to Kearneysville. Another route would leave Charles Town, travel the Leetown Road to Brown's Shop and Bardane, and then to Kearneysville. A third, Cross County Route, seems to have been recommended by Senator Burr.

As contracts were being considered, the *Shepherdstown Register* continued to voice strong protest. *The Advocate Editor,* Charles Town, denounced what was termed the "narrow stupidity" of the State Road Commission and declared it:

> *"..a sin and a shame that it persists in defying public interest and because of political influence wastes the State funds in putting a road where it is not serving the public needs but catering to individual advantage."*

Still hoping to persuade the County Commissioners and other residents to accept the plan, Engineer Grey spoke to their concerns in early March 1923, but few people rescinded their objections. This was especially true of the Shepherdstown populace who continued to insist that an alternate road through Shenandoah Junction to Shepherdstown and on to Martinsburg would connect larger business centers. An additional complaint was that Charles Town already had a full share of improved roads with one to Clarke County, Virginia, and another through Harpers Ferry. No reason was given as to why the Charles Town and Ranson Chambers of Commerce favored the route through Kearneysville. And like "Brer Rabbit," Kearneysville dignitaries "laid low."

The lowest bid for the segment from Charles Town through Kearneysville came from a Warrenton, Virginia company at $139,442.50, or $20,000 per mile. In March 1923, the contract for the first segment was signed. Eighteen parcels of land including a number of houses had been condemned, and county residents were still declaring that the State Road Commission was incompetent to deal with a local situation.

While no homes were removed in Kearneysville, Mrs. Walter Wilt, watching from her side porch, shuddered to see several unmarked graves at the Presbyterian Cemetery fall under the new state road as the intersection with the Pike was formed. On the east end of Kearneysville, the new road cut through the Border property from Oak Tree Road to the eastern entrance of Border Road. Also condemned was a corner from Steward Orchard.

Henry Stanley, then fifteen years old, remembers spending his idle time watching the road crew with shovels and hammers tearing down stone walls bordering the road. Thus the stone walls in front of the Gap View and the Aglionby Farms disappeared, along with others along the route. Miles of stone fences were thus destroyed. Rocks for road building were also brought in from elsewhere. Johnson Everhart recalls a family story of how rocks were quarried from an area of property that was then owned by Thomas Everhart, his grandfather. (This property was owned by the Jewett's and then by Thomas Turner in the early years of Kearneysville). The stones were loaded on wagons drawn by teams of horses. At the construction site, napping hammers were used to break these rocks, which were then put in a trench a foot deep. When the supervisor determined a solid roadbed had been laid, smaller stones and gravel were added.

The men worked a required ten hour day, from 7 a.m. until 5:30 p.m. with a half hour for lunch. In this manner the new state road from Charles Town to Martinsburg was finally completed. A road celebration was held at the Apollo Theater in Martinsburg. Anticipating commercial advantage from this new road, businessmen from Kearneysville attended: T.O. Everhart, W.F. Wilt, A.E. Trussell, J. Trout, Paul E. Miller, Sr., and F.O. Trump.

To be sure, all citizens were not satisfied, partially because of the safety hazards that were built in. Two railroad sidings were crossed. In addition there were two dangerous curves. One passed the Burr farm near Bardane and the other was known as VanMetre's Curve in Berkeley County. The problems with the curves persist to this day, adding annually to the region's death toll, and reminding us how the impact of poor decisions continue to be felt across time.

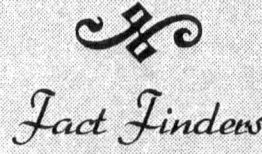
Fact Finders

- An automobile license cost $13 for every car that weighed 2,000 pounds or less.

- If an automobile weighed more than 2,000 pounds, an extra 60 cents was charged for each additional 100 pounds.

- A flat fee of $15 was charged for every automobile that had been converted to another type of vehicle.

- It cost $1 to apply for a Certificate of Title.

- The fine for driving without a license was $25 to $100.

- The gasoline tax was 3.5 cents per gallon.

The Advocate, 1925

Baltimore & Ohio Railroad

Two events of importance came together in 1842. First, the Baltimore and Ohio (B&O) Railroad completed its first run from Baltimore, MD, to Hancock, MD. Three tracks were in use by 1873. The railroad crossed the Smithfield-Shepherdstown Pike as it passed through large farms on its way into Berkeley County and beyond. Two of these farms were owned by James Kearney, Sr., and Uriah Kearney. A legend holds that one of the gentlemen built a boarding house along the tracks to make life more comfortable for itinerant workers who laid the tracks. (See 1852 map). Thus, the second important event was precipitated by the first: Kearneysville received a name and a post office.

A new era was beginning for small communities in Jefferson County that lay along the route. One can imagine the anticipation and perhaps apprehension as residents stood along the tracks to see this new method of transportation. And they could marvel that the locomotive, powered by coal with black smoke and cinders billowing from its stacks, could travel at the speed of ten miles an hour!

It appears that the B&O had become central to the commercial and residential growth of Kearneysville, as it had to other small villages, such as Shenandoah Junction. Local businessmen and residents found the Railroad to be a boon, particularly in the latter part of the 19th and early 20th centuries. On the commercial side, for instance, H.A. Trump was shipping

THE GAZETTE.

ARTINSBURG, VA.

THURSDAY JUNE 2, 1842.

OPENING OF THE RAIL ROAD.

The extension of the Baltimore and Ohio Rail Road west of Harper's Ferry, is now complete to a point opposite Hancock, in Maryland, a distance of about forty-three miles. The first locomotive reached Hancock on Saturday last, with a splendid new car, and a small pleasure party, invited by the officers of the Company. On Monday, the Directors of the Company, the Mayor and City Council of Baltimore, and a number of other gentlemen left Baltimore for an excursion on the new road, and were joined by a number of other invited guests at Harper's Ferry, Martinsburg and other points on the route. The train consisted of three of the new cars, and arrived at Martinsburg about 2 o'clock.

An immense mass, comprising nearly the whole population of the town and a very large number from the country, had assembled to witness the arrival. The passengers, after dining in Martinsburg, proceeded to Hancock and returned here to tea, and on Tuesday morning back to Baltimore.

The road, the locomotives, and the cars are unsurpassed by any in the United States. From Harper's Ferry to Hancock, the location is through a country of great interest. The fertile fields of Jefferson and Berkeley, groaning under the luxuriance of the growing crops, are passed as if at lightning speed, and before the passenger has time to realize the transition, he is whirled along the banks of the majestic Potomac through a mountain region of surpassing grandeur. The deep cuts through the North Mountain, which were first designed to be tunnelled, entirely exclude the Sun's rays and give an idea of approaching night.

Those interested in the road, seemed to regard it as every thing they could desire. It is constructed upon quite an expensive plan, but true economy is in the end promoted, for beside the increased security to life and property, it will require little repair for many years, while all the roads built upon the cheaper and lighter plans require constant tinkering and renewing.

It is the design of the company to push the completion to Cumberland. The graduation and masonry are finished we understand, at every point except perhaps the Doe Gulley Tunnel, and the track is being laid.

Plate 18. The Gazette announcement of opening of the railroad, June 2, 1842.

walnut timber and shingles to Baltimore and Frederick, and to western states as well. Apples, wheat, and milk also found their way to market via the B&O.

Here's the picture. In 1927, the B&O tracks lay parallel to Quarry Road, just as they do today. Beginning on the north side of where the Quarry Road intersected the Smithfield Turnpike were concrete coal bins constructed off a siding such that three different kinds of coal from coal cars could be dumped into the bins and shoveled out by customers desiring to purchase the same for a kitchen or heating stove. Next was a tall grain elevator that housed several services. Both the coal bins and the elevator were operated by Hodges & Lemen and managed by Mr. Arthur Trussell. Next to the grain elevator, the B&O Company had constructed a building for the station agent and a waiting room for passengers. The Company had also constructed an apple shed and "cattle shoot" loading dock just south of the station. After the Depot Station was torn down to make way for the underpass, the Kearneysville station may not have been something to brag about: The Shenandoah Junction village reporter for the *Spirit of Jefferson* mocked that the station was an empty cattle car compared to the modern station and waiting room in Shenandoah Junction.

Individuals were reported to be using train transportation for pleasure as well as business, and women felt quite safe traveling alone to visit relatives and friends in distant cities. Records note that Francis Whittington, the assistant to the agent for the B&O, rode the train alone to spend several days in New York City in 1911 and vacation in Philadelphia in 1912.

Across time, travel by train became even more convenient. By 1910 passenger trains would stop to take on or discharge passengers at Kearneysville. Schedules were published at the station waiting room. An example of such a schedule was published in April 1929 and is shown below.

Westbound	No. 33 Daily	Leave Kearneysville	7:51 a.m.	Arrive Martinsburg	8:07 a.m.
Westbound	No. 31 Daily	Leave Kearneysville	5:04 p.m.	Arrive Martinsburg	5:19 p.m.
Eastbound	No. 32 Daily	Leave Martinsburg	8:50 a.m.	Arrive Kearneysville	9:08 a.m.
Eastbound	No. 34 Daily	Leave Martinsburg	6:25 p.m.	Arrive Kearneysville	6:43 p.m.

Table 2. Passenger train schedule, 1929.

Notice was given that passenger trains would not exceed 55 mph in that year (1929). The average time for No. 33 to make the run between Kearneysville and Martinsburg was 28.0 minutes; average time for No. 31 was 29.4 minutes, for No. 32, 27.7, and for No. 34, 26.6 minutes.

As the years passed and more people purchased automobiles, regular train stops became less frequent. An announcement was published that anyone wishing to travel by train should flag it down. The story goes that Mrs. Nan Myers had an innovative method to get the train to stop: She used a red apron.

The public has ever spoken loud and long when government has neglected their demand for safety. Although residents saw many advantages in being on the railroad line, they were very concerned that there were no safety provisions. So, while concerned citizens were attempting to have a voice in the direction of the new state road, there was much concern with hazards posed by the B&O crossing. When the tracks were laid in the 1840s, the Turnpike was a dirt road. But when it was hard surfaced after the turn of the century, it still crossed the B&O at a point that had become the town center.

In fact, the train did take a toll on human lives through a combination of carelessness and lack of safety protection. In September, 1884, Mr. Tillet's six-year old daughter was killed while crossing the tracks. The train was reported to have been travelling at 60 mph. In May, 1895, George Bradley from Shenandoah, Virginia, fell in front of a train with cars heavily loaded with coal and earth. Dr. C.C. Lucas attended to him and found it necessary to amputate both his legs below the knee.

Then on a balmy evening in July, 1910, Jerry Myers, owner of a small store and eating establishment just east of Stanley Lane, had been reveling in Martinsburg with friends. On the return trip, his car stalled on the tracks. His friends left him in the car, inebriated, while they searched for help at a neighboring house. Meanwhile, a freight train chugged through the crossing. Mr. Myers was instantly killed at the point of impact. He was 40 years old.

In November of the same year, Hiller's Livery team of horses was struck and killed by a helper engine. The wagon was demolished, although the two occupants escaped injury. It should be noted that these "helpers" were not well-lighted. However, when traveling East, they were necessary to assist freight trains on the "grade," an inclined part of the tracks that lay just passed Vanclesville and Rutherford's Crossing. The helper engine then returned to Martinsburg.

In November of 1911, F.W. Balthaser, a representative of Rand-McNally of Fleetwood, Pennsylvania, and the livery driver Robert Moore also happened to be in the path of a helper engine after the main section of the train had passed. Luckily neither was seriously hurt.

Bells were installed at Trump's Crossing in late 1911, but accidents continued to occur. William Lowry sued the B&O Railroad for an injury that occurred while he was alighting from a train. The case was settled in November, 1911, and he was awarded $640.00.

Mr. John Tucker suffered injury in 1913 due to his impatience. He approached the tracks from the north side where a train was standing. Not willing to wait until the train pulled away, he stepped between the cars to get to the other side of the tracks. At that instant, the train began to move, dumping him on the north side with a crushed limb. Dr. Lucas and Mrs. John Stanley, who came to offer medical assistance, could only wait in helpless frustration on the south side until the train passed through, clearing the tracks.

> In 1924 there was talk of adding a fourth track to the B&O Railroad. This gave rise to John Tucker's indignation. His home had been moved when the third track was added. He is reported to have said, "Guess the B&O wants me to steam heat my home. All I need do is raise the window."

In May 1918, Mr. And Mrs. Lynn Grantham miraculously escaped injury when their overland (car) was smashed. Having left their five gallon cans of milk at the Creamery, they found it necessary to cross the railroad to W.F. Wilt's store for commodities when the overland became caught between the rails. Train No. 13, a fast express, sped east with whistle blowing at Trump's Crossing. In less than a minute the train would arrive at the station crossing where the overland was caught. Some men quickly attempted to extricate the car, but the overland became a considerable piece of wreckage while Mr. and Mrs. Grantham watched from a place of safety.

In a late day accident in July 1919, the auto of the two sons of Mr. and Mrs. W.P. Zombro of Millville was smashed when the car stalled on the tracks. William E. Zombro, 23, was dead at the scene according to Magistrate Herbert C. Miller. His brother, Pearl Zombro, was carried to a hospital in Martinsburg by the "helper" engine. Shortly after January, 1920, Mr. Zombro filed suit against the B&O in the death of his son, William.

On the 29th of January, 1920, Magistrate H.C. Miller conducted an inquest into the death of Boyd Ramsburg, who was killed while crossing the tracks at the town center. Boyd had been killed late in the day, again by a helper engine. Running backward, the engine struck the young man and then passed over his body. Reports state that it was likely that four more trains passed before the man was discovered. This time, the investigating jury urged the B&O to equip the helpers with proper lights on the rear as well as on the front.

The *Shepherdstown Register* noted that residents of the village were incensed by the frequent accidents at the crossing and demanded a tunnel under the tracks for highway safety. Finally in July 1930, an agreement between the B&O and the Department of Highways was made. A tunnel would be built, and the B&O promised that local men would do 80% to 90% of the work. The State would share costs. This would become a boon in more ways than one, since many were jobless due to the Great Depression.

Although the B&O suddenly cancelled the agreement in August of that year, by September plans were renewed for the underpass. A contract was given to Empire Construction of Baltimore with Superintendent J.E. Tobins in charge. Total cost of the project was estimated at $250,000. Soon a concrete mixing machine and a steam shovel were unloaded at the site.

About one hundred local men applied for jobs; however, only B&O employees were called to work, which must have been a great disappointment to the community. Housekeepers took advantage of the situation, however, by furnishing room and board — four men per room.

During all of these transportation developments, vast changes were imposed at the town center, which had been expanding for seventy years. On the southwest side, the general store, now owned by C.O. Whittington, and a four room house were moved approximately 50 yards. The old stone building, once used as a milk station and later as a freight warehouse, was demolished. A log house, known

Plates 19 and 20. Construction of underpass, 1930.

Plate 21. Before construction of underpass. Irvie McIntyre training her dog, circa 1920s.

AT KEARNEYSVILLE.

If some of the former residents of Kearneysville should come back to that village they wouldn't know the place, now that the work of constructing the subway has advanced so far. Few persons had any idea of the tremendous amount of work that is required to make the passage of the State road under the tracks of the Baltimore & Ohio Railroad at that place and the estimate of a quarter of a million dollars for the cost of the improvement seems none too great. A number of buildings have been bodily moved to new locations. C. O. Whittington's store was transported several hundred feet to an entirely new site near the filling station and his residence was also moved to a new location. The transfers were made with but little interference to either business or household affairs, and the buildings are said to be better now than they were before they were moved, as weak places were strengthened and the firm that moved them left them in excellent order. On the north side of the railroad the store buildings occupied by Walter Wilt and Francis Miller have also been moved back some distance to new foundations. The old stone building along the tracks was demolished and the log structure known as "the parsonage" has been replaced by a comfortable structure.

The railroad tracks have been moved to the southwest of the old line, and trains are slowed down to fifteen miles an hour over these temporary tracks. Excavation is being made under the old roadbed, and when half of the subway has been completed the tracks will be moved back and the other half constructed. A great amount of rock has been encountered in making the subway, and this has delayed the work to some extent. The big steam shovel, however, is such a powerful machine that it does the work of many men, and eats a hole in the ground in short order.

Of course amateurs know very little about engineering work, but persons with a reasonable amount of common sense believe that the work could have been done for about half the cost if the subway had been constructed a hundred feet or so west of the location chosen by the engineers of the State Road Commission. There would have been but three tracks to burrow under instead of five and a natural hollow would have saved a great amount of expense in excavation. It is whispered that the railroad engineers are also of this opinion, privately expressed.

The contractors have been favored in their work with good weather, and they have been making the best of it. The old road over the crossing has been closed entirely and travelers are detouring by way of Trump's crossing with but little inconvenience.

Plate 22. Clipping from Shepherdstown Register, October 30, 1930.

as "The Parsonage," was replaced by a more comfortable one.

On the north side, store buildings owned by Walter Wilt and Francis Miller were moved. These can be seen in the background of the picture on the preceding page.

Trout's dwelling was barricaded to protect it from bombarding stone. And F.O. Trump constructed a brick post office beside Miller's store. By now there were five tracks; these were moved westward during the construction period and road travelers were detoured to Trump's Crossing. Watchmen were hired to protect the equipment when it was not in use. As work continued, there was ongoing scrutiny by the local people and the news media. Some of the controversy surrounding the project is illustrated in the article on the preceding page from the *Shepherdstown Register*.

Plate 23. Underpass just before completion.

Completion of the underpass progressed quickly. By April, 1931, bids were opened for concrete paving on the subway, as it came to be called. By August, the subway was opened and Trump's crossing was closed.

POST OFFICE

The history of the Kearneysville post office somewhat parallels the development of the railroad. In fact, locating the post office near the railroad was not a coincidence, since trains were a primary method for transporting mail.

The first Kearneysville post office of record was established in 1842 and included a building known as the Depot. This two story building served as a general store, a post office, and a train station with waiting room. The second floor was used for social activities and meetings of civic organizations. The first Postmaster was William Hedges. Several other early postmasters were active in National as well as local affairs. Their contributions will be noted later. When Augustus Trump held the position of postmaster for the first time in 1866, he moved the post office to his home, which was also a general store.

Although this first post office was located on property owned by Bailey S. McIntyre, he did not become postmaster until 1867. Still holding that post in 1878, Mr. Mcntyre had the difficult task of buying up three cent pieces which were recalled by the U.S. Treasury Department in August of that year.

Misfortune fell on Bailey in 1880, when he and his entire family became ill with diphtheria. Others filled in for him. Mr. Powell L. Licklider was named deputy postmaster, followed by Mr. Charles Stump. Both men vied for the position as postmaster when Mr. McIntyre resigned in 1885.

Since the political party in power in Washington, D.C. influenced the office of postmaster, neither man won the position. But Mr. Theodore Homsher, who also owned and operated a general store, won the post when Grover Cleveland became President of the United States in 1885.

Consequently, Mr. Homsher had the onerous and important responsibility of convincing his patrons that a change in the color of the stamps was necessary. The significance of the change was to provide single stamps in the same color as the

Plate 24. Brick post office on Quarry Road

corresponding envelope.

One of the bumps and aggravations in the early history of the Kearneysville post office occurred in March 1889. Much to the vexation of the clerks, the new Postmaster General Wanamaker ordered that all clerks should report to their respective offices at 8:30 a.m. and remain on the job until 6 p.m. Their previous hours had been from 9 a.m. to 3 p.m.

Mr. William L. Wilson, a Jefferson County native, as Postmaster General, established Rural Free Delivery in this county in 1896. Colonel Thomas March, Chief Clerk of the delivery system, noted that in September, a delivery station would be established in Kearneysville. Contracts were to be made with carriers as a trial run until July 1, 1897 in exchange for a $1,000 bond per carrier. However, rural delivery was not begun in the Kearneysville area until 1899. Despite complaints from the patrons at Leetown, the U.S. Postal Department perceived the service as a success. Perhaps it wasn't in Leetown: The Post Office there was closed in 1906.

Sometime prior to 1899, the Depot and post office burned to the ground. Mr. B.S. McIntyre built a large structure on the same location, which again served several purposes. This building with its charming turret came to be known as Trump Hall and was an important gathering place for the community until it was razed in the late 1920's when the underpass was constructed.

This precipitated the need for yet another post office. The son of Augustus, F.O. Trump, had been named postmaster for a second time in 1922. F.O. received the contract to erect the new building on a site east of the old structure. This brick building, which served as the post office from 1931 until 1961, lay on

POSTOFFICE AT KEARNEYSVILLE ROBBED. 10/16/29

The handsome little postoffice building at Kearneysville, a new and attractive structure, was broken into and robbed last Friday night of $36.71 in envelopes and stamps. No cash had been left in the office. The robber got 562 No. 5 stamped envelopes, 1,116 No. 8 large stamped envelopes and 76 cents in stamps.

Entrance to the postoffice was gained by breaking a large window in the front of the building. The safe in the office was unlocked, and small drawers and compartments were broken open and rifled. The entire place was ransacked. State Officer Smith and Detective E. M. Rinker, both of Martinsburg, were called to the scene of the robbery about 7:30 Saturday morning and remained at Kearneysville throughout the day, investigating. The only definite clues found were a number of fingerprints which the thieves left. Garfield King, a colored youth of Kearneysville, was arrested, but his fingerprints did not compare with those left in the postoffice and he was released.

F. O. Trump is the postmaster at Kearneysville and Miss Dorothy Horn is in charge of the office.

Plate 25. Clipping from The Register, *October 10, 1929.*

the east side of Oak Tree Road, more commonly called Quarry Road.

Residents of the community were shocked to learn that on the morning of October 5, 1929, their handsome little post office had been robbed: $36.71 in stamps and envelopes had been taken. Although the safe was found to be unlocked, no cash was kept there. No arrests were made.

The post office was burglarized again in 1934. This time, 25 cents, a few stamps, one C.O.D. and a Fada Radio Loudspeaker were stolen. A local man was arrested and convicted of a Federal offense shortly thereafter.

Mr. Will Dixon figured prominently in the postal service of Kearneysville and is fondly remembered by many. Beginning in 1930, he took over a position held by Francis Whittington. His job was to place the mail bag on the hook that was attached to a pole at a level such that the mail clerk aboard the train could grab the bag as the train passed by. Simultaneously, the mailbag for the Kearneysville Post Office would be thrown from the train. Mr. Dixon used a wheelbarrow to carry out his duties. Morning and evening he met the train, always on time. He continued this task until the mail was delivered by vehicle from the central post office in Martinsburg to the outlying post offices.

During the first 100 years of Postal Service at Kearneysville, clerks' duties were to sort mail and sell postal services. Some of those who served in the position of clerk during the first half of the twentieth century were Alton Thomas, Dorothy Horn, Bill Hammond, James Trump, Margie Stanley, Miss Jessie Johnson, Elizabeth Trump, and Mrs. Walter Wilt.

Kearneysville postmasters for the first 100 years of operation are shown in the table below. Obviously, party politics figured in postmaster appointments.

Postmaster	Tenure	U.S. President/Party
William Hedges	1842	John Tyler/Whig
James Dernnington	1843	John Tyler/Whig
William Roberts	1846	James K. Polk/Democrat
Giles C. Hamill	1851	Millard Fillmore/Whig
Daniel G. Henkle	1860	James Buchanan/Republican
William G. Butler	1862	Abraham Lincoln/Republican
William A. Chapline	1863	Abraham Lincoln/Republican
William G. Butler	1865	Andrew Johnson/Republican
Augustus Trump	1866	Andrew Johnson/Republican
Bailey S. McIntire	1867	Andrew Johnson/Republican
Theodore Homsher	1885	Grover A. Cleveland/Democrat
Augustus Trump	1897	Benjamin H. Harrison/Republican
F.O. Trump	1908	Theodore Roosevelt/Republican
Walter Wilt	1915	Woodrow Wilson/Democrat
F.O. Trump	1922	Warren G. Harding/Republican
W.W. Hammond	1946	Harry S. Truman/Democrat
P.E. Miller, Jr.	1948	Harry S. Truman/Democrat
W.W. Hammond	1950	Harry S. Truman/Democrat

Hartstown and Beyond

Hartstown and Beyond

There is an area of land and homes within what is now known as Kearneysville that is called Hartstown. It is not clear how or when this area came to be known in this way. However, included here are pieces of information that may offer clues.

While Kearneysville was not unique among small communities, one notes with satisfaction the industriousness of its people and the rich mix of cultures and backgrounds. Separate schools for the races were established in 1872. Afro-Americans and Euro-Americans built their own churches as well, and only on special occasions did the two races attend social functions together. But it was in the home setting that association of cultures could be seen as community. Although this was true of much of Kearneysville, it was particularly true of Hartstown, where families of various races lived side by side.

Perhaps the story begins on December 10, 1763, when Thomas Hart received a Fairfax land grant of 49 acres, but then the story stops for almost a hundred years. As can be seen on the 1883 map at the end of this section, Hartstown lies to the East of what is now Kearneysville. In early 1870, John Burns began selling lots from a twenty acre property he had purchased from Serena and Abram Dandridge. Although Mr. Burns built on one of the lots, he intended the remainder to be investment property: It bordered the B&O Railroad and lay southeast of the hub of Kearneysville. Thomas Turner's farm lay on the west and John Thompson's on the south, separated from other Dandridge property by the railroad. Since there was no county road, an access road was laid out between the settlement and the railroad. This enabled residents to cross the B&O at Rutherford's Crossing and travel north to the town center at the intersection of the Smithfield and Shepherdstown Turnpikes. (See S. Howell Brown Map, 1883 at the end of this section).

Toward the turn of the century, the community of Hartstown looked similar to that shown on the sketch below. All of the older houses faced the B&O except that of Mascena Hart, which lay at right angles to the tracks. In its early growth, the development was known in various records as "Benwood," since Ben Carter was a landowner. However in 1885, the Superior Court (County

73

Commission) gave permission for a connector road to be laid from "Hartstown" to Kearneysville, thus giving the settlement a name. This road is now a part of Route 9.

As with other areas of Kearneysville, families in Hartstown wanted to become self-supporting, and to acquire land and homes. They achieved these goals within community spirit and a sense of interdependence. Abbreviated stories of some of these families follow. These are drawn mainly from remembrances of current Kearneysville residents.

Mascena Hart and John H. Fox appear as pioneers for African-Americans in the community. Both were mulattoes; one was born free and the other a slave.

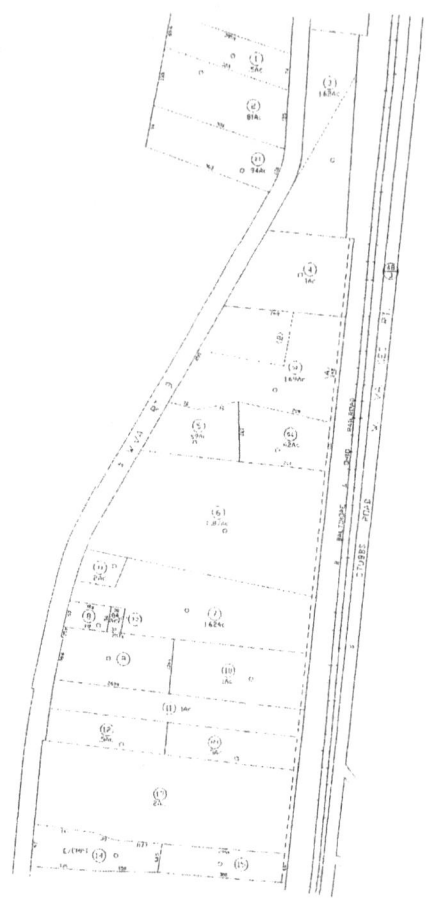

Plate 26. Sketch of John Burns's lots, 1872.

The town was probably named for Mascena. He was born in 1838, one of seven children of Edward Hart. Mascena gives his occupation in 1870 as a stone mason. His home was built in 1883. He received the deed to his 1.2 acres in 1898, after making payments at specified times until the whole was paid. Mascena married Sarah Roper, and their son, Howard, took possession of this home in 1902 by assuming a debt of $200 with interests and costs secured by the property. In the agreement, Mascena reserved an upstairs room, board and care during his lifetime and on his death was to have proper burial with all funeral expenses paid. He died in 1905 at the age of 66, and his remains rest among those in the Hart-Lucas Cemetery, which is located beside the family home.

Plate 27. House built by Mascena Hart in 1883. Picture taken 1995.

John Fox is notable for rising from slavery to high stature as a philanthropist and community leader. When he was mustered out of the Army as a free man, he was given $50. At the end of his life, his real estate was valued at between $20,000 – $25,000. John is first mentioned in the court records when Thomas Turner conveyed a property with a house, known as the Toll Gate House, to him in 1869. More about this notable man is included in the first section of this history.

Another family that came to the area for employment was that of David Washington. The 1870 Federal Census recorded David as a 52 year-old male mulatto who worked as a farm laborer. His wife, Nellie, is listed as a house keeper and his oldest daughter as a domestic servant. Etheline Clinton, a direct descendant, speaks of an ancestor as part Native American. Possibly this ancestor was David's wife, meaning that yet another race would have enriched the make-up of Hartstown and the Kearneysville community.

David and Nellie had seven other children who called home a modest frame one-and-a-half story, four room dwelling with attached kitchen behind. This house faced the B&O Railroad tracks. It's interesting to note that two of the daughters of David and Nellie were married to John Fox, at different times, and that John lived with the family briefly. Sometime later, a second home was built on their two acre lot, facing the connector road to Kearneysville. It also housed a Washington family. To this day the property remains in the hands of the Washington heirs.

Charles and Fannie Lashorn came to the area seeking employment at the quarry. They were the parents of a son, Charles, and a daughter, Myrtle. Mr. Lashorn died sometime before the 1900 census, and Mrs. Lashorn then married William Cox, who also worked at the quarry. The couple had two sons, Edward and George, and a daughter, Ruth.

Plate 28. The second house owned by David Washington, built in 1883. Picture taken in 1995.

In October of 1918 a Spanish influenza epidemic raged through the community. Treatment resources were limited. The Board of Health of Jefferson County ordered all schools, churches, and moving pictures closed until further notice. Sadly, there were at least four flu victims of the community. Young Ruth Cox, Mrs. Capriotti, and Mrs. Bertha Creamer died. Also, Berkeley McDowell, the 18 year old son of Carrie and Will McDowell, who was a student at the Ramer School in Martinsburg, died.

In the 1920s, when the youth began sporting autos, young George drove his Ford Roadster to Martinsburg. An amusing story is told regarding one occasion when he was driving north on Queen Street. Suddenly realizing that he had passed his destination, he throttled the car more than necessary and neatly circled the Band Stand that was in the middle of the Martinsburg Square. An observant policeman on the corner waved and shouted, "Hey, Mister! You can't do that!" "Oh, I think I can," replied young George, and he tootled on down South Queen Street.

The Coxes maintained the original home that was built in 1880, one of the few in the area with an outside kitchen, known as a "summer kitchen." This house is still in excellent condition, more than a hundred years later. It stands on Route 9 near the B&O tracks, about a quarter-mile east of the intersection.

Someone has said when tracing our genealogy, we might find relatives among our neighbors. We should not be surprised, then, to

Plate 29. Jacob Lashorn house with summer kitchen, built in 1880. Picture taken in 1995.

find Foxes, Harts, Washingtons and Ropers related. Douglas Roper and his family lived in Mascena Hart's house in 1880 — possibly a duplex house. His son, Edward Roper married Lucinda Fox.

Ed Roper opened a small grocery on his property facing what is Route 9. The small store was a boon for those who lived within half a mile. No youngster would complain of being sent to buy a five-cent loaf of bread to make sandwiches for lunch. Far more important than the bread was the expectation that Uncle Ed would place a piece of candy in the hand that passed the nickle over the counter.

When Kip, Edward's son, took over operation of the store he added a restaurant to the rear. The last use of the building was as a home for Uncle Ed's maiden daughter, Theresa. The property is currently owned by Mr. Charles Fox; no one lives in the house.

Wilbur Thomas came into possession of one of the Burns's lots and built his home in 1880. Living at home in 1890 are his wife, Ann W., and three children: Bertha E., May C., who married Omer Whittington, a store keeper, and Edith, who married Ralph Young, a quarry worker. Older children who had already left home were Pearl, the wife of Jake Burhman, who worked for the State Road, and Mollie, the wife of Harvey Jackson.

Another son, Samuel Walter Thomas was 28 and employed at the limestone quarry that lay across the B&O tracks, just opposite his home. He had married Mary Smallwood. He and his wife were to become parents of ten children: Wilbur, Roy, Reba, Mary, Alton, Perry, Woodrow, Bill, Alma and Mildred. Bill was the only one who did not marry.

Plate 30. Wilbur Thomas house, built in 1880. Picture taken 1995.

Having been given an acre of land from his father's lot, Samuel Walter built a home in about 1889. He was to lose this to Mr. and Mrs. Charles Turner and lived in at least two other homes. When there was an opportunity to become foreman of a work gang on the B&O Railroad, he took it. Later Samuel worked at other occupations, and, after 1930 when he moved to Route 9, he opened a small grocery store. Samuel's original home in Hartstown was eventually purchased by Alton's widow, Edith Thomas.

Mr. John Clower, a B&O track hand, and his wife, Ellen, also bought one of the original Burns lots and had built a home there by 1880. They were the parents of one daughter, Bertha, and two sons, Robert and Wade. By the 1910 census, Mrs. Clower was living with her son, Wade, but Bertha had married one W.B. Horn. The couple owned a home on the Leetown Road and had two children, Mark and Dorothea. Mrs. Horn became well-known as a seamstress throughout the area.

Plate 31. Samuel Walter Thomas house, built circa 1900. Picture taken 1995.

Living two doors south of where Walter Thomas had moved on Route 9 was Aunt Sidney Dungeon, who came from the Shenandoah Valley. She was an important person in the eyes of some youngsters, who noted that "Aunt Sidney was a slave. She came from Shenandoah and smoked a pipe with Five Brothers tobacco." She was the oldest person in the village when she died on Sunday, February 28, 1937 at age 100. Her body was returned to Shenandoah, Virginia, where she was buried.

Aunt Sidney lived with her daughter, Henrietta Mason, who friends called "Rhett." Randolph Brown, an adopted son, also lived with them. He was almost blind and partly deaf. Residents may recall that every spring Randolph would purchase five pounds of sugar. "To make jelly," he'd say, but the villagers suspected it was for a batch of dandelion wine.

Near the Mason's, three of the Allen families had bought property. Annabelle Allen Ferguson was always quick to recite her genealogy, which goes as follows. Rebecca Mason, the "lady who wore 100 skirts", was her great-grandmother. Annie Mason Carter was her grandmother. Then there was Alice Bradford, a sister of Annie. Annabelle's Uncle Will and Aunt Nan Allen were the parents of Dave, Dan, Isaiah, Lillian, and Inez. The family came from Front Royal, Virginia.

Annabelle's mother was Bessie Allen. Since there were more opportunities for employment in New York City in the 1930s, Bessie moved to the City with Annabelle, Viola, and a granddaughter, Marjorie. A grandson, Andrew, was born later. Annabelle's other siblings, William, Chauncey, Daisy, and Hugh, remained in the village. As an adult, Hugh was remembered for bringing his white mule around to plow neighborhood gardens for spring planting.

Arthur Allen and his wife, Mabel Stubbs, were the last inhabitants of his parent's home. He was a preacher, and she a missionary. The house still stands, but is vandalized. This property and many of the others are owned by the Allen estate.

Intent on helping to support the family, Isaiah Allen, son of Will and Nan, quit school in the fourth grade and followed his father into field or orchard, wherever there was work. Both also worked at the Kearneysville quarry when employment was available. Eventually, Isaiah took a job at the Standard Lime and Stone Quarry in Martinsburg. He recalls that he was courting Grace Isadore Williams during the same summer — sometime in the

1930s — that Hunter Benner was courting Isabelle Marshall and Tyler Brown was dating Mary Hilda Banks. The three Kearneysville couples were married within a few months of each other.

Isaiah was originally a member of the Methodist Church. After he and Grace were married, he transferred membership to St. Paul Baptist, the church that Grace had belonged to since age 16. In typical community fashion, he with Bill and Fred Winston tackled a building project at the church. By breaking through a stone wall, they added a kitchen to the basement social hall. Local folks remember Bill's chuckling about "a big man to do a big job like this." In fact the Winston brothers stood over six feet tall, a size that could strike terror in the heart of a youngster who might encountered them near dusk on a summer's eve.

Isaiah and Grace lived in the home place of Mr. and Mrs. William Allen until Grace's death, almost sixty years after they were married. Grace had worked for Mrs. Mary Saum, who stood tall in Isaiah's memories, although she was quite a petite lady. It was typical for "Miss Mary", as she was known, to send Grace home with a part of a ham or some other foodstuff.

Miss Mary lived in Shenandoah Junction but was no stranger to Hartstown citizens. She had taken in Sarah Jane Bradley, which is another interesting story. Nelson Snyder, a county commissioner, visited the black orphanage often, and little Sarah was always the one to open the gate for him. And she always begged him to

Plate 32. William Allen's house, built circa 1900.
Note Boyd and Amelia Carter's home on the left.

take her home with him. One day he did, and brought her to live with Miss Mary. Years later, as Mary's hired woman, Sarah Jane would be sitting proudly in the back seat of the car when Mary drove to Kearneysville to buy strawberries.

William "Big Bill" and Martha Winston bought property on the south fringe of Hartstown and built a brick bungalow with a basement. Although the couple had no children of their own, they raised her sister's daughter, Juanita, educating her in local schools. I remember Bill as a big man — over six feet tall, but very gentle with children. The only vehicle he rode was a motorcycle with a side car, and it was a child's delight to take a ride with Big Bill. Martha also provided joy to neighborhood children, either as a baby-sitter or friendly neighbor. She read bedtime stories with vigor, and opened her parlor with its interesting old organ and large wooden keg of cool water.

Bill's brother, Fred, and his wife Sadie came from Virginia, probably for job opportunities. They built a two-story frame home beside Bill and Martha, and raised their three sons, several grand-children and even some great-grandchildren as well. Fred preceded Sadie in death. When she died at 98 years of age, a granddaughter was caring for her in the original home place.

Mr. James Head, or "Uncle Jim" was another neighbor in Hartstown. He lived in a house on a hill above Rutherford's Crossing that stood beside the Methodist Church. He and his first wife, Lucinda, had three children, but all of them died in infancy. After Lucinda died, he married a woman named Mary, and they adopted an orphaned baby. Uncle Jim had a horse and wagon and did farm work for himself and the neighbors. Aunt Mary kept house and took care of their son, Kelly. Years later, when the Federal Government built an Army hospital nearby — later to become the VA Medical Hospital — Kelly got a job there, as did many other men. The Head home was eventually sold to Harry Powell and Phoebe Washington. In time the house became vacant and was vandalized.

Israel and Laura Hunter came to Kearneysville sometime in the early 1900s. The couple lived on property later acquired by Ben Fox, on the north side of Grace Reformed United Church of Christ. While Israel used his horses and wagon for hauling loads of dirt as it was separated from the stone at the quarry, Laura was busy washing the laundry for Cliff Side Hotel in Harpers Ferry. At this point in time, their sons had left home and they had taken a boy, Bill, to raise, who was a great help to Laura. Bill drove a truck to the Hotel to pick up and return the laundry. He also helped to haul water, since there was no well on the property at that time. Cora Allen and Edna Morgan, nearby neighbors, may have assisted Laura in this back-breaking laundry venture. The linens had to be rendered snowy white without the help of commercial bleaches and then ironed with "sad" or flat irons.

Laura must have been a tireless woman; besides her laundry business, she was a self-taught midwife, and in the 1920s and 30s, also cared for small children in the neighborhood while their mothers were at work. Laura and her husband eventually purchased a twelve acre lot off Logie Lane, but were never able to build a home there.

As can be noted from the above stories, within a generation, sons and daughters of the original settlers of Hartstown were moving into other areas of Kearneysville and either renting or purchasing homes of their own. Hartstown seemed to have established an identity as a community within a community by intermingling the tangible and intangible; through land, homes, and churches, and through ideas, goodwill, mutual problem solving and neighbor affiliations. Outstanding contributions to the area were the achievements of various races, mostly black and white, living side by side as neighbors. Hartstown's population, like that of Kearneysville as a whole, became multi-ethnic and interdependent.

Plate 33. John Tucker's house, built circa 1876. Picture taken 1995.

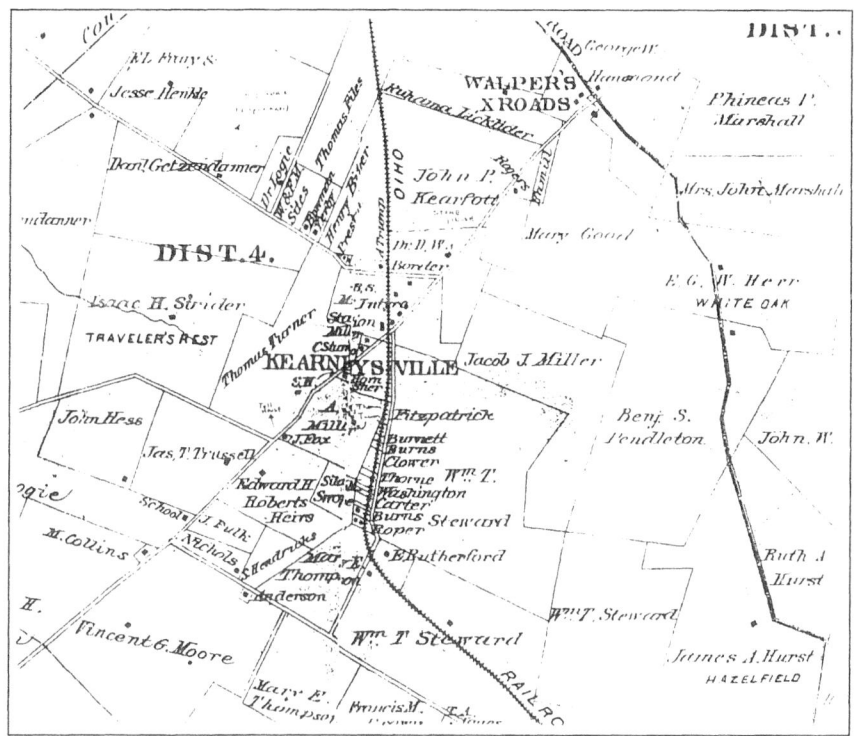

Plate 34. Hartstown: S. Howell Brown Map, 1883.

Economics

Economics

As with other early communities in the surrounding area, economic development of the Kearneysville community was based in rich natural resources, in this case the farmland and the geology. As noted earlier, the original settlers were drawn to the area by its farming potential. Farming did not remain a single source of development, however. Outgrowths were orchards and dairy enterprises that contributed to further employment and growth. The large limestone geology was a natural for the quarrying industry; for about 40 years this provided employment for skilled and unskilled labor in the community. Other factors were the amenable climate, the location, and ready access to railroads and roadways.

BAKER LIMESTONE QUARRY

Plate 35. Picture of one of the Kearneysville quarry holes, circa 1940.

The Baker Limestone Quarry contributed much to the economic and social development of the Kearneysville community. It stimulated ethnic diversity, small businesses, transportation, expansion of public utilities, and growth of personal income. But some tragedy and loss balanced the opportunities for gain.

The history of the quarry began in February of 1890, when A. J. Morris and Company of Avondale, Pennsylvania, bought from B.S. McIntyre 18 acres of land that lay north of the B&O. The purpose was to quarry limestone. The land quickly changed ownership again, however. By 1892 Daniel Baker, a member of the family who owned and operated the Standard Lime and Stone Company, had purchased the original acres from the Morris Company and acquired 81 adjoining acres. Records show the total cost was $7,000.

When families began arriving for quarry work, a series of houses was built opposite the grain elevator, not far from the train station. These houses were referred to as "Ten Row." Italian families occupied three of them; African Americans lived in the others. A larger house at some distance from Ten Row was constructed on quarry property for the superintendent. That property remains and is owned by Charles Ferguson, whose father worked at the quarry. The Standard Lime and Stone Company owners ran a semi-paternal company; that is they provided for the basic needs of their employees and families. As the Company began operations, a grocery store was set up on the southeastern part of the property, about a mile from the business center of Kearneysville. There is a record that a young girl, M. E. Williams, who lived with Mascena Hart and was possibly an orphan, worked at the quarry grocery store that was in operation as early as 1900. However, two new general stores near the center of town and within walking distance for quarry families soon opened. Most food and dry goods could be purchased at these stores, on a credit basis if one wished. By the turn of the century there were four general stores serving the community. Also, hog and chicken feed could be purchased at Hodges and Lemen Grain Elevator on Quarry Road, which opened in 1911. As a result of this competition, the quarry store became unprofitable and was closed.

Other evidence of the care given employees can be found in isolated instances, such as when Mrs. Capriotti died: Mr. Baker sent the three Capriotti sons to a private boys' school in Pennsylvania.

In addition to providing employment for local men and inadvertently supporting local general stores, the quarry also supported growth of the community in other ways. For example, Ellen Clower, wife of John, took in boarders who were quarry workers. Sometime around 1910, the Clowers lived in the house later occupied by Eugene and Edie Frith. For worship, families selected St.

Paul Baptist Church, Steward Chapel, the Presbyterian or the Grace Reformed Church. Or they attended one of the Catholic Churches in a nearby town.

Eventually, three sites were selected for limestone removal, resulting in the existing three large water-filled quarry holes. Blasting the stone was a delicate operation and brought many interesting, often frightening stories, to the Kearneysville community. On one occasion in the summer of 1895, William Cox was in charge of the blasting. During the Civil War, Mr. Cox was a member of the Rock Bridge Artillery and had been personally complimented by General Stonewall Jackson for his bravery. Loaded with this credential, he was certainly up to the quarry work and set about arranging to have twenty-one holes, each 10 feet apart and 20 feet deep drilled. Mr. Cox charged these holes with a total of 400 pounds of dynamite. The blast went off perfectly, although the ground shook with a mighty tremor, startling residents a mile away. Shortly after, Mr. Cox's work at the quarry ended. Within a week of this blast, he suffered a mild stroke. A second followed in July — perhaps the result of post-traumatic shell shock — leaving him quite feeble.

The number of workers fluctuated. In 1900, 26 people were listed in the census as quarry workers; in 1910 there were 70. These numbers reflect only residents who lived in Kearneysville. When the quarry was going full blast, in 1898, there were 150 employees, but many came from the surrounding areas. Sometimes the quarry was idle due to lack of orders. In these instances, a period of four to six weeks might elapse before operations would be started again. Such was the case in 1898, 1909, 1916, 1918 and again in 1922. During the less than 30 years of somewhat intermittent quarrying, several superintendents were hired. In 1910, Newton Kidwiler moved from Baltimore to Martinsburg to oversee the work. Henry Angelo and later a Mr. Prather also served in the superintendent capacity.

Since water continually flows through underground streams snaking along rock crevices, pumps were installed to keep the water from accumulating and impeding quarrying operations. In 1922, after the quarry had been idle for a few years, water was pumped out at a rate of 600 gallons per minute. This pumping lasted almost a month before stone could be quarried. As the quarry hole deepened from rock removal, a rail was laid to permit cars to descend and bring rocks to the top. A B&O siding that had been built for the shipment of apples was also used for shipment of stone out of Kearneysville.

Another important change that the quarry brought to the community occurred in 1909. In February of that year, a dispute arose when the Winchester and Washington City Power Company was granted a franchise to construct electric lines from Charles Town to Shenandoah Junction, thence to the Kearneysville Quarry. The telephone company sought to block these lines and questioned whether they might jeopardize their own telephone lines. The County Court, however, decided in favor of the power company, thus allowing Kearneysville residents access to electricity for their homes.

Quarry work was dangerous. There were no unions to protect the workers, nor were there government regulations for monitoring safety. As a result, simple mistakes became life-threatening, and people who worked for the quarry company sometimes died. Others were frequently hurt, and many spent the rest of their lives compensating for crippling injuries. In May 1894, Harvey Whittington's foot was crushed in quarry machinery. Under the skillful care of Dr. C.C. Lucas, the foot was saved, and Harvey was able to return to work by September. Harry Reed, a well-known conductor who had lived in Brunswick, Maryland with his wife and nine children was one of the many quarry casualties. In 1912, he was killed while operating the switch at a siding. Then, in August 1918, a severe electrical storm following a drought caused the electrocution of Boyd Splone, an electrician, as he was attempting to throw a switch. The full jolt of 22,000 volts came through killing him instantly. He was a grandson of Philip Lucas and was survived by a wife and child.

In January of 1920, another accident happened, this time to Earl Welsh, who was then 21 years old. His job was to run the drilling machine that was used to make holes in the lime rock in which dynamite could be exploded. In reaching across the machine to oil a part, his shirt sleeve was caught in a set of cogwheels. He was unable to stop the machine, and his left arm was drawn up to the shoulder. John Ferguson heard Earl's screams for help and rushed to assist. Although John was able to stop the machine, it had to be taken apart to extricate Earl's arm. Carl Fleming, who lived a short distance from the quarry, brought his car around and transported Earl to King's Daughters Hospital in Martinsburg, but the arm was lost except for a stub or 'nubbin' as Earl might have called it.

One never had a sense that Earl believed himself to be handicapped, however. He wooed and won his love, Bessie Shackelford. With her help, he supported a family of four sons: Earl, Jr., Wallace, Donald, and Richard (Dee). Anyone who visited Jefferson Orchards where he later was employed would marvel at the ease with which Earl managed the heavy wooden bushel boxes filled with apples.

Except in cases of extraordinary injuries, quarry workers in general made few calls to the local physicians, Dr. D.W. Border and Dr. C. Lucas. Vernie King or one of the Italian mothers would serve as midwife to deliver a baby or care for the sick. Other neighbors pitched in to help the sick when needed. Mrs. John Stanley for one was very busy during a serious flu epidemic in 1918.

While many families moved into the area to work the quarry, the activity among the Italian families will be related here through the story of Olga Angelo Paci. She spoke of the Italian community in general and her life during quarry times in Kearneysville during a recent discussion at the home of Margie Johnston. Her story as I recall it is told below.

> "I must start this account before my beginning. My father, Henry Angelo, and his betrothed lived in a small hill town of Tresungo, Italy. Aspiring to improve his opportunities and those of his future family, he emigrated to the U.S. in 1902 or 1903. He found employment with the Standard Limestone Company, saved some money and returned to Tresungo to marry his beloved Lucia.
>
> I was the first child of that marriage, and Father brought Mother and me through Ellis Island in February or March of 1912. Other quarry families living in quarry housing [Ten Row] were Rossi and Saladini. The Capriottis lived in a small house later removed by Wallace Welsh when he built a home for his family.
>
> I began school in Kearneysville in 1914 or 1915. At that time it was a two room school. However, within two years two more rooms were added. I think maybe Edna Seibert was teaching then. I also was fond of Mr.

Hendricks and Miss Bessie Bell, two other teachers. I quickly learned the language and got on well with most of the other students.

Sad to tell, I recall a hair pulling incident with Hattie Smallwood. Did our conflict begin because we were teased by Richard Tucker or because we both wanted Richard for a boyfriend? Whatever the case, I remember the two of us standing on the B&O Railroad tracks, each holding a hank of the other's hair and exchanging conditions for ending the fight. 'If you let go, I'll let go.' That may have happened at noon, since those who lived nearby went home to lunch, and the Smallwoods lived near the school, on the Shepherdstown Pike. Well, neither of us was hurt much.

But other memories remain also. I was given the lead in a school play *All On Account of Polly*. I played opposite Harry Tucker. Having the lead role in a school play evoked a wonderfully happy feeling, but my bubble was soon burst. Harry provoked me so that I stayed home from school and practice to spite him. Well, my parents would not tolerate such hookey, and I was returned to school, much embarrassed, since there was no legitimate or apparent reason for being absent. Miss Fannie Trump coached the play. (In 1923, Miss Trump was studying dramatic art in New York City and was one of the main performers in *Chicken Feed* at the Little Theatre). At the close of the school year, there were two nights of entertainment, and all grades from one to eight participated.

Often I stopped at the Stanley's on the way to school. Their home stood at the entrance to the school lane. I remember Mrs. Stanley as being kind to all the children. She stopped for us on her way to church and Sunday School even though we were not on a direct route. People walked wherever they wanted to go in the village at that time, so Mrs. Stanley would cross the B&O tracks with her children, Margie and Henry, and take us along. We would take our five cents for Sunday School that we'd set aside from trading eggs at Mr. Wilt's General Store, which stood near the railroad tracks. Mr. John Stanley, her husband, would go earlier to open the church.

Margie [Stanley] and I had some fun times when she gave me organ lessons. We also played records on their Victrola. I remember one of these records clearly; it was *In a Little Spanish Town* given me by Richard.

Special holidays for the Italian families were Christmas and Bafano (Epiphany). At Christmas, we hung our stockings to be filled with oranges, candy and nuts. We were also given clothes if we needed them. The Christmas Eve meal was traditionally spaghetti made with fish and accompanied by fritters. The fish were either squid (squabs) or dried codfish, which had been soaked a long, long time. The dish was called Baccalas. The fritters were made with apples and cauliflower. Polenta was another special food.

Hallowe'en was a prankish holiday when younger children — Cherry, my younger sister, for example — could be terrified by bullies such as Calvin Mason.

No doubt children today would consider our lives dull. But there was always something interesting happening, and we had lots of playtime. I remember our wonderful tea parties. We found a large flat rock for our table and carried our "tea" to it. Large pieces of glass and pottery that had been discarded in a dump heap served as dishes. The salad was made with chopped green onions from the garden, tossed with vinegar and oil. We took turns being hostess: Mary Rossi, Mary Saladini, and me. We were the older girls and would not let the younger ones, Cherry Angelo, Angeline Capriotti, and Crew Saladini, join our party. Those three were also pals themselves.

Hog butchering was a big occasion. Special foods were prepared to serve all those who came to help as well as those who came to watch and socialize. Nothing was wasted. One of the foods was blood crepes. Mother caught the blood when the hog had been hung by its hind legs and the throat slit. To this was added flour to make a thin pancake.

Another food was link sausage. One of the older women would scrape the small intestines of the hog, turn them inside out, scrape and wash and then lay them in salt water overnight. The next day when certain portions of the hog meat had been ground and seasoned, these intestines were stuffed, using a special piece of equipment. Then the sausages could be stored in a cold place during the winter months, since the meat was seasoned. Aging was supposed to improve the flavor. The stomach was cleaned and filled in the same way. This sausage "maw" was saved for special occasions.

The railroad and trains played a big part in our lives. Besides the hair-pulling incident I told you about earlier, I remember a game we played of walking on a rail, making a challenge to see who could walk the longest distance without toppling off. One foot had to be placed carefully before the other while trying to maintain balance. When freight trains, which had been stopped, impeded our crossing the tracks as we made our way to school, we climbed across the couplings between the cars. Then in 1917 when the U.S. became involved in World War I, we stood near the tracks and waved to the young men going off to training. Basil Chinto, a cousin who lived with us, fought in the war.

While a regular hand at the quarry, our father earned a dollar a day. But there were always a cow, chickens, hogs, and a garden to supply much of our food. Sometimes a chicken was sold for 25 cents. We could buy a bag of ginger snaps for 10 cents. Five or six pieces of candy could be had for one cent. Mr. Wilt, the storekeeper, gave a piece of candy if one stood in front of the counter long enough.

Most illnesses as well as infant deliveries were handled within the neighborhood. My mother with other women helped deliver Italian babies. During the flu epidemic, Cherry, Louis, and I became ill. Only Chris, my brother, stayed well. Mrs. Capriotti, who lived on the Shepherdstown Pike (Route 480) became ill and died. Neighbors helped Mr. Capriotti with the children: three boys and a girl, Angeline. When Mr. Capriotti died from a dynamite explosion, the Company paid for the education of the three boys at a private school in Pennsylvania. Angeline married my brother, Chris.

But I forgot to mention, Mrs. Capriotti was a most resourceful mother. The water supply came from the lower level of Ten Row. The energetic woman carried water in a tub cushioned by a towel on her head. She tucked her baby, Louis, on her back and carried a bucket of water in either hand.

For a brief time, my father was transferred to the Bakerton Quarry. When he returned, he was made superintendent at Kearneysville. In 1921, when orders for stone decreased, many men were laid off, including the timekeeper. My father, the superintendent, could neither read nor write. I kept the time for the workers, sending it to the main office in Baltimore. I was thirteen or fourteen at the time.

I'm sure Angie will never forget Mr. Hugh Allen's mule, which was tethered in a field near our house. Grabbing the animal's tail, she claimed possession: "My mule, my mule," she cried. But it wasn't easy to convince the mule. The animal kicked her severely in the side of the face injuring her eye.

When our father was moved to the Big Springs Quarry on Route 11 South, near Martinsburg, our parents agreed that Cherry, who was in the eighth grade, should finish school at Kearneysville. Chris made the trip in our own car twice a day. Usually, during the drive of eight or nine miles, they never met another car. There just weren't so many cars back then.

I stayed with the Prather's who had moved into the Superintendent's House for one year. I rode to Shepherd College with Henry and Margie Stanley and Minnie Tucker. But it was a much greater pleasure to take the train from the Kearneysville Station to attend a commercial course at Mrs. Brockton Winfrey's Business School in Martinsburg. Richard Tucker, who worked for the B&O could use a pass to Martinsburg in the evenings and accompany me home. I was the envy of some local belles."

When limestone quarrying ceased in Kearneysville, many of the quarry workers who were not Italian found local employment and remained to share in the growth and activity of the village. The Italian families of Rossi, Saladani, Capriotti, and Angelo moved to take up work at other quarries nearby. There are few residing in Kearneysville who knew them, but tangible evidence of the years the Italian families spent in the community can be found in what is known as the Italian wine berry. The families had brought this plant from Italy and cultivated it for making mild, sweet wine and jelly. Today it has become rather invasive.

Plate 36. Abandoned Capriotti home, 1966.

Before the Kearneysville quarry site was abandoned, three remarkable, enormous lakes had been created. These are identified locally as the big hole, which is the furthest north abutting the H.C. Miller property; the middle hole, more familiarly known as the Blue Hole; and the small hole, the most southerly of the three. The small hole had been abandoned first, and hence it is not as large as the other two. There is a shelf extending from the shore line with less than two feet of water. A minister of St. Paul Baptist Church frequently used that area for baptisms. Sarah Roper Walker was among those washed in holy water there.

The middle hole was reported to be 30 feet deep in 1918 while it was still being quarried. Sometime prior to that year, the quarry buildings nearby had been destroyed by fire, and a new plant was constructed of concrete and steel. Remnants of this plant still stand. Recently divers were searching for a car that was reported to be in the Blue Hole. They dove 40 feet and could see nothing. Little else is known about the depth, plant life or animals of the quarries. It had been rumored at the close of WWII that a German Company was interested in the quarry property. Residents were hopeful that the industry would once again bring employment, but this didn't happen. The quarry holes remain today as beautiful, unused, huge lakes with clear water. The last of the Ten Row houses stands in ruins, and modern homes have been constructed on quarry lands, which is now private property.

AGRICULTURE

During the early years of the village, farming was the chief occupation and has a rich and deep history in Kearneysville. Early crops were mostly wheat and corn. With the introduction of the steam engine to thresh wheat in 1868, wheat production increased. Within 10 years, records show that 26,000 bushels of wheat were shipped in the space of two months. During the years of World War I, raising wheat and corn must have been fairly lucrative. In March, 1917, wheat was $1.95 a bushel; by May it sold for $3.25 per bushel. Corn, which had been $1.05 per bushel in March sold for $1.65 in May.

Farming pulled together community members and made necessary the development of other enterprises that supported it. One example is divining (with a peach twig) and well drilling, a service offered by Charles Rutherford. It must have been a tricky business finding water, even with his divining rod. His records show that he sometimes dug 150 feet for an inadequate supply; at other times 35 feet was fine. Charles also had a blacksmith forge in the barn at his small farm to sharpen bits. Built before 1860, it stands at Rutherford Crossing (considerably altered), and is owned by Tom Bowers. Another supporting business was that of buggy construction. For some years before the turn of the century, Robert Rogers was kept busy constructing buggies at his place of business located about a quarter mile north of the village on the Shepherdstown Pike. Mr. Rogers gave up the buggy business when more and more people bought automobiles. The chief farming enterprises, dairy and orchards, continue today.

MILKING ENTERPRISE

In 1890, the Miller farm realized the sum of $285.67 in milk sales from eight cows during a 12 month period. Prices at that time ranged from 60 cents to $1.00 per 100 pounds. It is uncertain when Robert Roberts and Daniel Getzendanner conceived an idea for shipping milk produced in the area, but the enterprise became real when they secured a lot on the northeast side of the B&O from B.S. McIntyre. They constructed a stone building as a shipping station and sometime around 1913, established the Jefferson Creamery for shipping raw milk. Mr. and Mrs. John Stanley were hired to collect the milk from dairy farms locally and as far distant as Falling Waters. The cans held 11 gallons each. It has been said that George Thompson also worked at this job, and drove a truck with solid tires for it. E. Stanley Haller managed the operation of getting the milk on the train from the Depot in Kearneysville. The Jefferson Creamery business must have been short-lived. The stone building became the property of the B&O Railroad, was used for storage and then torn down about 1930 when the railroad underpass was constructed.

However, Mr. Bill Fulk and Mr. Herbert Miller (son of J.J. Miller) had large herds of Jersey and Holstein cows and needed marketing outlets for their milk. They found a large empty building which was also located on McIntyre property near the railroad tracks property (adjoining property of H.A. Trump) that had been abandoned after a failed cider plant operation. They expanded the building and established what became known as the Kearneysville Creamery. In an effective business strategy they acquired shareholders and organized with a Board of Directors and a charter to do business. The location was favorable to shipping the milk products. Information is scarce but reports in 1918 show that E. Stanley Haller was brought in from Pennsylvania as manager. Locally, milk sold for 24 cents a gallon, but more often was sold by one or two quarts. Five cents was charged for a short quart. Cream could be purchased for 85 cents per gallon. Products were delivered to local families by John and Blanche Stanley, and also by George Thompson.

The Creamery was one of the growing and progressive businesses in Jefferson County. In 1919 a new line was added — that of cheese processing. An expert cheese maker had been persuaded to come from New York State to make cottage and block cheeses. Mr. Haller was so proud of his wares that he sent a sample to the editor of the *Shepherdstown Register*. After a taste test, Mr. Snyder declared the product "sweet, rich, and appetizing."

Condensed milk was sold to ice cream factories in Hagerstown and Cumberland, Maryland. When electricity became available, the Creamery could make ice, and thus the amount of condensed milk was reduced and profits were increased. But milk was no longer raw: A boiler system was installed and used to pasteurize milk, so that fresh milk, cream and butter were also available. Another interesting development was an acid test for determining the amount of butterfat in the milk. Although some dairy farmers now concentrated on Jersey cows, others who were more interested in quantity of milk raised Holsteins.

I.D. VanMetre must have been one of the more progressive farmers in the area. At one point he spent two weeks in Wisconsin where he purchased a number of Guernsey and Holstein animals. Then in 1918 he installed automatic milking machines in his modern dairy barn. This machine would milk six cows at one time and was operated by a 4 hp engine.

Robert E. Fox was a well-known African American farmer dairy farmer in the area. Sadly, in 1920 he was forced to sell his dairy cattle, other stock and all farm machinery. He received $6,000 at this sale, but refused to sell his farm at $200 per acre. After the sale he returned to a sanitarium in Pocahontas County; his family moved to the County as well.

The Kearneysville Creamery had been paying an average of $20,000 per month for the milk of local farmers as the enterprise continued to grow. So encouraged was the board of directors that an apartment on the second floor was remodeled for the manager and his family. The board of directors now included: President, Mr. Fulk; Secretary, J.D. Muldoon, Treasurer, C.D. Wysong with E. Stanley Haller, Manager. In 1920 a few stockholders proposed increasing the business to handle 15,000 pounds of milk daily. There followed dissension between the manager and the directors.

By July of 1920, Mr. Haller resigned; H.R. Hoge became manager. In 1920 the plant was paying $142,000 to local farmers for milk. The next year it was rashly proposed, by some stockholders, to ship one car of fresh milk to Washington, D.C. and one car to Baltimore, Maryland. This was possible because ice was available for the cars, but it would further reduce the amount of condensed milk produced.

It should be mentioned that the Board of Directors had been increased. Added were C.W. Blue, H.C. Miller, John Y. McDonald, George Thompson, W.A. Higgs, J. Franklin VanMetre, Sr., S.M. Huyette and M.K. Bowers. So sharply divided was the board of directors over what direction the company should take that it was sold to three men: W.A. Fulk, C.D. Wysong, and C.W. Blue. Mr. Hogue left to accept employment with Farmer's Dairy in Martinsburg, and C.J. Reinsmith was hired as Production Manager. In April of the same year, 1921, Wise Brothers bought the business and closed it. However, the building found other uses in the next twenty years. It can be noted, though, that during the years the company operated, many local persons found employment: Richard and Mike Tucker, Frank Powell, John Stanley, Hugh Hill, and George Thompson.

ORCHARDS

The orchard industry gave an enormous boost to the economy and activity in Kearneysville. Perhaps the most important contribution of Dr. D.W. Border was his interest in orchards and in promoting the apple industry. Sometime prior to 1876 Dr. Border had visited the orchards of W.S. Miller in Berkeley County. Subsequently he planted forty acres in commercial apple trees, the largest orchard of any size being planted — not only in Kearneysville, but in Jefferson County as well.

He also started an apple tree nursery sometime during or before 1889, named Mendenhall Nurseries, and advertised 50,000 first class apple trees ready for fall and spring planting at a cost of ten cents each. The nursery idea was later abandoned as he concentrated on commercial orchards.

Between 1880 and 1900, at least five orchards were in production: Stewart, Robinson, Miller, Border, and Getzendanner (later to become the State University Experiment Farm).

At about this time, a charter was issued to the Jefferson Evaporating Company to cure fruit, store, pack, own, and cultivate orchards. Six shareholders held the charter with a capital of $10,000. During the period of operation it was commonly referred to as the "cider plant." (It is only speculation but surely Rothwell and Gatewell of Martinsburg had some influence on Jefferson Evaporating Company's going out of business).

The Hopper brothers started a barrel making shop near the B&O Station at about this time. The Hopper's cooperage was taken over in 1911 by the Rothwell Company of Martinsburg and moved to the completed barrel and box factory in Martinsburg. A concrete form to hold water for the soaking and shaping of barrel staves is all that remains of the shop.

To note the extent of the apple industry, in 1910 it was estimated that 30,000 bushels of apples were produced in all of Jefferson County. It seems likely that Kearneysville orchardists contributed extensively to this total based on records in subsequent years. For example, in 1911, the Border and Jones orchards alone sold 5,000 barrels of apples at $2.95 a barrel. In 1912, R.N. Steward shipped 5,000 barrels of apples to a firm in Olney, Illinois, priced between $2.50 and $2.75 per barrel.

Dr. D.W. Border contracted with W.M. Boxwell for a stable and large barracks on the Elkwood Farm in 1913, which is near Sunnyside on what is now Border Lane, for a cost of $1,000. The purpose of the barracks was to house the itinerant orchard workers. The stable was necessary to house the horses that pulled wagon loads of apples from the orchards to the packing shed. It's interesting to note that one of the Miller orchards was the first commercial cherry orchard in the Kearneysville area.

MERCHANTS

Many families raised a garden and a few small animals for food. In fact Uncle Will Ross came around in spring with his horse and plow, tilling small gardens. Mr. Hugh Allen, who owned a white mule, provided the same work. It was typical for community residents to share from their gardens; others sold eggs, butter, and chickens. Still, there was a great need for a place to purchase goods. Early stores, which were known as "general stores" until the middle of the twentieth century, provided a place to buy the basic needs of the household, including gardening tools, clothing, food, and other supplies.

The first store owners of record included Theodore Homsher and Alex Drawbaugh, who were in business by 1868. Their store was located near the railroad tracks on the McIntyre property. The following is a partial list of items offered in 1870, along with their prices.

Bleached cotton	10 to 15 cents per yard
Dress fabric	12 ½ cents per yard
Tickings	20 cents and up per yard
Crash	12 ½ to 20 cents per yard

Balmoral skirts and Dolly Vardens were also for sale. Notions included hosiery, gloves, corsets, and hoops. The store boasted a complete assortment of boots and shoes. Soon some ladies were complaining about the "fickle styles" in 1875 as short dresses were coming into vogue. From time to time, Homsher had clearance sales, boldly advertising that the present stock was to be disposed of at a low price. Frequently, customers needed to be reminded of "the time for paying up." In later advertisements, he urged all parties indebted to the store to please call and settle their bills. By 1879, having observed that some customers assumed credit would be extended indefinitely, Theodore changed his policy to "cash or barter — no deviation." When Mr. Homsher became postmaster sometime around 1885, Mr. Samuel Licklider took over. By this time, Mr. Drawbaugh had moved his share of the business to Bardane.

It seems that the building that housed Mr. Licklider's store, called the Depot, also housed the post office and train station. When it caught fire in 1897, a bucket brigade turned out but was unable to save the building; it was completely lost. However, since B.S. McIntyre owned the land, he contracted to have a two-story building constructed. In addition to the general store, the new building housed a comfortable waiting room and ticket office for passengers and a post office on the first floor. The second floor was available for dances or other

When S.L. Licklider took over the Homsher store in 1885, he advertised: "Quick Sales and Small Profit."

social activities and at some point came to be called "Trump Hall." This building was significant in the history and development of Kearneysville until it was destroyed in 1930 when the B&O Railroad and State Department of Highways built the under-pass.

Records show that Augustus Trump also ran a grocery store from his home in 1874, and F.O. Trump opened a butcher shop in 1898. In 1875, a Major Hamill was advertising fresh fish — shad was listed at 80 cents per pound, herring (probably salt) 30 cents, and potatoes at 40 cents per bushel, although I have not found the location of the store.

In addition to a grocery store on quarry property, there were two other general stores in operation that sold food and dry goods on a credit basis if one wished. One was owned by a Mr. Petrie, run from the Depot and purchased from Licklider; the other was owned by Lewis Wilt and run from his home, which was within 200 yards of the center of town on the Shepherdstown side. By the turn of the century there were four general stores serving the community. Also, hog and chicken feed could be purchased at Hodges and Lemen Grain Elevator on Quarry Road, which opened in 1911.

The Petrie general store was sold to M.M. Jenkins in 1915, and two years later he rented the John H. Fox farm and sold the store business to Walter Wilt and Carl Fleming. Then when Lewis Wilt died, Walter (his son) took over Lewis's business; Carl moved to the D.W. Border's Elkwood Farm and returned to farming. But the store continued. The business was sold to C.O. Whittington who moved his family to a four-room house beside the store. At this point, the quarry store had closed and there were three general stores in Kearneysville owned by Francis Miller, Walter Wilt and C.O. Whittington.

Mr. Whittington was particularly kind hearted to children, who called him Uncle Omer. But he had a head for business. Eleanor Powell told me that, as pre-teens in the early 1930s, she and Edna Tucker lived within walking distance of the store. When Mrs. Powell needed a loaf of bread, she would send the girls to the store. If she had looked over her statement at the end of the payment period, she would have been shocked to see she was using so much bread, as Uncle Omer would give the girls a dill pickle, for which they had a strong liking, and add another loaf of bread to the bill. He also gave sacks of penny candy when the monthly bill was paid.

The Whittington's store and house were moved about 25 yards to the south when the underpass was constructed in 1930-1931. Next, F.N. White purchased this store and lived in the small house nearby. Alas, there were no more sacks of penny candy when the monthly bill was paid or dill pickles, either.

Margie Stanley Johnston recalls her more than a decade as manager and head clerk of White's Store. Her advantages were that she knew the patrons from the community, since she had lived her thirty years within a few hundred yards of the store; she knew those who would come in on payday to "settle up," and she was a graduate of Shepherd College. But her nine years in the classroom at the Middleway graded school, both as a teacher and later as a principal, did not prepare her for the mountains of detail which confronted her when she accepted the responsibility of managing the store.

Her work hours were from 7 a.m. to 9 p.m. Monday through Friday, and until 10 p.m. on Saturday. There was no clerk except for Friday evenings and Saturday, and again on payday. Margie had no lunch or supper break. If she needed ten minutes off, the store was closed, and customers would wait until she returned. The situation was eased somewhat when part time clerks were hired. I worked, first as part time and then as full time clerk, from 1936-1942.

In 1932 when workers went on Social Security, Margie collected the one cent per dollar from the clerk's pay and marked two cents for the employer to pay. Each customer had a small book in which an account of charged items was recorded. There was no calculator. All monies were counted at night. The owner, Mr. Francis White, took most of the days intake each evening, leaving only enough to begin the next day's sales in the safe. When the State Legislature added a penny tax to any sale over five cents, this amount had to be kept separate. One customer, Mr. Ed Turner, was so outraged with the tax that he would buy a five cent article, such as a loaf of bread, pay for it, leave the store and return for the next article, repeating the process until his shopping was completed.

Margie remembers that fresh chickens were delivered whole. These were cut up on a meat block, the same one that Thelma Fleming Wall, a clerk, used to cut up a side of beef. She also remembers that Eugene Frith liked the sharp cheese which came in large blocks of 10 or 12 pounds. A sample was always given when asked for, and although the taste met his approval, the price drew a few profane exclamations. A warehouse in Charles Town was the supply source for each of Mr. White's three stores. It was necessary, however, to store extra cartons of milk (48 in number) and canned vegetables (24 cans) in the basement. These were brought to the first floor up a series of steps and through a trapdoor.

The store was a gathering place. Mr. Roland Hammond liked the walk of a mile or so from his home at Traveler's Rest, and wandered in to while away the time with any other loafer of the moment. Charles Rutherford and Roland Hammond happened to be in the store the day the gypsies came to town. Perhaps there were only eight or nine, but it seemed as if twenty had invaded the store. They moved everywhere, behind the dry goods counter, into the pop case, sliding back the door on the candy case, all the while chattering and engaging the attention of Margie. Their visit served for lots of conversations long after they had left. But the most excitement came the night the store was robbed.

That was in 1941 when a lone robber entered the store about 9 p.m., the usual Saturday closing time. Only a few customers were in the store as the manager, Margie Johnston, and I finished with last minute activities. The corner filling station had been robbed a couple of times, but only when it was closed.

On this occasion, Margie was counting money to put in the safe and I was behind the counter on the opposite wall. The unmasked intruder approached the counter as any customer would, but Margie knew he didn't come to make a purchase when the gun appeared. Mrs. Johnston coolly handed him what money was in the register, and he was out of the store before the rest of us realized what had happened. Within several months, by careful sleuthing of the State Police, the man was captured, tried and convicted.

F.N. White remained a merchant for several decades and acquired several more stores. What I remember about him is that he paid his help very low wages and asked them to work 12 or more hours each day. Mr. White was the last owner of this general store; it went out of business, probably from competition of the general store and filling station next to it owned by Norval and Margie Johnston. Today, the house has been converted to a gift shop, and the store building has been demolished.

For a period of time, beginning in 1911, Mr. C.H. Cook operated a meat shop at the stone house formerly occupied by Israel Hunter. (The building is now a home remodeled by Larry Crouse, located near Walper's Cross Roads). F.O. Trump's meat shop was probably discontinued when he began his construction business after the turn of the century.

There were some choices in buying clothes. While fabrics of various kinds could be purchased from the general stores, not all ladies could sew their dresses. Some seamstresses would come into the homes to repair and sew new garments. Mrs. Nodie Welsh sewed for her neighbors to supplement her husband's income. Also, peddlers would bring threads, needles, scissors as well as fabric for selections from the lady of the house.

M.B. Miller advertised his Boot and Shoe Shop at the Depot in 1874. His expertise was "stitched boots and ladies shoes." He moved his business to his home in 1879. Tom Briscoe set up his barber shop in his home as well. In 1917, he charged from 15 cents to 25 cents depending on the age of his client. The price was raised to 35 cents in 1929.

Many personal needs were met by other individuals. Charles Dorsey, a cobbler, repaired shoes. He had suffered a birth defect or crippling disease and his legs never grew from the knees down to the normal length. He made small buttoned shoes for his tiny feet. He never stood upright, but when the day's chores were over, he would propel his body into the porch swing with his powerful arms and wave and smile, having a pleasant word for those who walked along the road. It was Charlie who bowed his fiddle for square dances at Cox's Hall.

> **BOOT AND SHOE SHOP AT KERNEYSVILLE.**
>
> THE undersigned would inform his friends and the public generally, that he has opened a shop at the above named place, and will manufacture to order Boots, Shoes, Gaiters, &c. Special attention given to STITCHED BOOTS AND LADIES' WORK. None but the best material used, and all work guaranteed. Repairing neatly done, and at moderate rates. Orders filled promptly.
>   M. B. MILLER.
> June 6, 1874.   1y

Plate 37. Notice of Shoe Shop opening by M.B. Miller. June 6, 1874.

Mr. Arrington operated a blacksmith shop on the north side of Mr. Dorsey's home. When he no longer shoed horses to pull buggies, he continued shoeing horses for farm and garden work. One of his customers was Uncle Will Ross, who made the rounds with his horse and plow, tilling small gardens for spring planting.

Another important place of business in Kearneysville was the Grey Goose, which Tabb Janney opened sometime in the 1920s, at about the same time automobiles came into use. Not only was this an important social gathering place for local residents, but people from nearby towns came to the Grey Goose, especially for the sugar cured ham sandwiches. Although these were popular, Mr.

Plate 38. Tabb Janney in foreground; McIntyre barnyard and roof of home behind. Picture taken 1961.

Plate 39. Grey Goose transitioned to grocery. Used as storage space in 1961.

Janney was never accused of being generous with the ham: It was said that he sliced the ham so thin, one could see through it. Neither was Mr. Janney generous with payment to his teen-aged help: Once he gave Eleanor Powell a box of shoe polish for washing the windows and wiping the tables. Nevertheless, the Grey Goose provided work for local teen-agers.

Much later, Henry Burnett and Tyler Brown operated the Grey Goose as a grocery store. Its last use (before complete disuse) was as storage space for Margie and Norval Johnston's operation of the Esso Station. It was razed, along with Mrs. Wilt's home, when the Kearneysville Branch Bank of Charles Town was built recently.

Automobiles brought a bit of economic development to Kearneysville. By 1920, there were 131 cars in the Middleway District. For all of Jefferson County, between December 1925 and five years later, the number of autos had doubled, from 1,856 to almost 4,000. As a result, local entrepreneurs built filling stations, sometimes adding a minimum of service. Sometime in the 1920s, the Kearneysville Auto Company, owners William B. Horn and H.W. Wagely, rented a small frame building across the Pike from the Elementary School built by F.O. Trump.

F.E. Miller's first general store was a two-story beside the Auto Company. The top floor was let out to a local African American youth, Gilbert Brown, who saved the store when a fire broke out one night in 1922. The story goes that he dreamed of driving an auto through hell in high gear. When flames leaped at his windows, he awoke and realized an urgent kind of reality.

In fact, the fire had started at the Kearneysville Auto Company next door. The source of the fire was two oil barrels from which customers filled their containers. The Company burned to the ground, partially because someone in the bucket brigade accidentally doused the fire with a bucket of kerosene. The general store was saved, however, but F.E. Miller gave up on that location anyway. The Kearneysville Auto Company was rebuilt nearby.

Although F.E.'s general store survived the fire, he moved to a two story building northeast of the B&O Railroad, along the quarry road and added Magnavox radios to his business. Unfortunately, the store in this new location also caught fire on a night in early winter, 1930. This fire was discovered by a night watchmen employed at the railroad underpass, who sounded an alarm that summoned fire equipment from both Charles Town and Shepherdstown. Mr. And Mrs. Wesley Cline were living in the

Kearneysville Store

Saves You Money.

Five Bros. tobacco, 3 pkgs, 25c.
Duke's Mixture tobacco, 6 pkge, 25c.
Sensation tobacco, 3 pkge, 25c.
Piedmont cigarettes, 3 pkge, 25c.
Brown's Mule tobacco, plug, 25c.
Red J. tobacco, plug, 25c.
Half pound Prince Albert tobacco, 89c.
1 lb. jar Prince Albert tobacco, $1.59.
Camel cigarettes, pkge, 17½c.
Early Bird tobacco, 17c.
Piedmont cigarettes, pkge, 17½c.
Honest Scrap tobacco, 3 pkge, 25c.
My Maryland tobacco, plug, 42c.
Union Leader tobacco, 3 tins, 25c.
Small Piedmont cigarettes, 3 pkge, 25c.

Bishop's Flour 80c Sack

Salmon, can, 10c.
Seeded raisins, pkge, 22c.
Hecker's oatmeal, pkge, 12½c.
Puffed wheat, pkge, 12½c.
2 lbs Army corn beef, 25c.
Currants, pkge, 21c.
Soup beans, 3 lb, 25c.
Arbuckle's coffee, lb, 25c.
Carnation milk, 2 cans, 25c.
2 lbs soda crackers, 25c.
2 lbs ginger snaps, 25c.
3 pkge Armour's macaroni, 25c.
Triangle salt, box, 7c.
Caraja coffee, lb, 27c.
Corn meal, 10 lb sack, 25c.

Pay Cash—Cash Pays

Black pepper, lb, 10c.
Linseed oil, gallon, 98c.
Gillette safety razors, each, 98c.
Alarm clocks, each, 98c.
Watches, each, 98c.
25 lb fine salt, 45c.
4 bars Woodish soap, 25c.
Chocolate drops, lb, 19c.
4 lbs self rising buckwheat, 25c.
Ivory soap, cake, 7c.
Carter's O. N. T. thread, 6c.
Eagle milk, can, 25c.
Gun shells, box, 95c.
Lanterns, each, 85c.
Large galvanized tubs, each 98c.
Sweet-Orr cord pants, $4.50.

Men's Work Pants $1.98

Men's Sweat shoes, $1.98.
Dark green window shades, 50c.
Men's heavy union suits, $1.39.
2 pr men's work hose, 25c.
Men's heavy underwear, 69c.
Men's blue work shirts, 75c.
Dress gingham, yd., 15c.
Cretonne, yard, 25c.
Men's dress shirts, 98c.
Mens' dress hose, 2 pr., 25c.
Ladies' silk hose, 49c.
Women's dress shoes, $2.98.
"Stawell" corsets, $1.50.
Goodyear raincoats, $3.98.

Large Oysters 55c qt.

Lunch boxes, each, 15c.
Canvass gloves, 10-15-20-25c.
Men's overalls, 98c.
Men's jackets, 98c.
Borden's caramels, lb, 24c.
Ny-Ko milk, can, 10c.
Dreting swinging lamp, $1.98.
Fancy cakes, lb, 25c.
Army gum boots, $2.98.
Dog chains, 25c.
Shoe tacks, 6c.
3 pkge chewing gum, 10c.
Dress cambray, yd., 15c.
Men's heavy drawers, 69c.
Boy's cord pants, $1.39.
Men's dress shoes, $3.95-4.95.

Nice Oranges 39c dozen

Collar pads, 59-69c.
Salted peanuts, lb, 15c.
New toweling, yd., 9c.
Corduroy pants, $3.49.
Grey outing flannel, yd., 22c.
Safety pins, pkge, 5c.
Nema peas, can, 18c.
Crochet cotton, 10c.
Jazz ties, each, 29c.
Men's work shoes, $2.98-3.48-3.98
Men's work suits, $5.98.
Men's heavy coats, $3.98.
10 qt. galvanized buckets, 29c.
Men's dress suits, $16.75.
Men's caps, each, 98c.

Men's Army Boots $2.98

Sardines, 2 cans, 15c.
Canned milk, 2 cans, 15c.
Small sacks flour, 40c.
Wire nails, lb, 6c.
Mail Pouch tobacco, 3 pkge, 25c.
Half pint vanilla, 39c.
Coal hods, 48c.
Fire shovels, 10c.
Sole leather, lb, 98c.
Stud tobacco, 6 pkge, 25c.
Canned corn, 2 cans, 25c.
Alabastin, pkge, 75c.
Flashlights, 89c-$1.19.
Curtain scrim, yd., 15c.
We pay 60c a dozen for eggs.

Wire Nails 6c a lb.

Women's dress shoes, $3.98.
Country lard, lb, 15c.
Sliced pineapple, can, 29c.
Canned sweet potatoes, 18c.
Army baked beans, 2 cans, 25c.
Fairy soap, cake, 7c.
20 oz. can Bob White powder, 25c.
Large lamp globes, 15c.
$3.50 men's wool sweaters, $2.48.
Chesterfield cigarettes, 3 pkge, 25c.
Brown sugar, lb, 6c.
Jumbo peanuts, lb, 25c.
Prince Albert tobacco, can 15c.
Syrup, qt., 15c,

These prices good until the next issue of this paper.

Miller's Store

FRANCIS E. MILLER, Proprietor.
Kearneysville, W. Va.

Plate 40. Miller's Store ad, 1921.

upstairs apartment with their small infant. They escaped safely, but with only the scant clothes they were wearing. In spite of an heroic attempt, a fireman was unable to retrieve a gold watch and $200 that Mrs. Cline begged for.

As a practical matter, when the store was deemed too far gone to save, the fireman turned their efforts to saving the store of Walter Wilt and the building in which it was located owned by Irene Brown. Had this building burned, it would also have destroyed a dwelling house belonging to Joseph H. Trout. Not a single thing was saved from F.O. Miller's store. Taking no more risks in Kearneysville, Mr. Miller established a Magnavox sales and service store on Martin Street in Martinsburg, which is still operated by the Miller family on North Queen Street.

Mr. And Mrs. Walter Wilt owned a filling station building (later to become the Esso Station) that was on McIntyre property. It was operated as the Kearneysville Garage in 1924 by Robert (Bob) Seibert. Margie Johnston relates that there were four kinds of gasoline to be purchased: Gulf, Richfield, Texaco, and Esso; there was only one grade, however.

Plate 41. View of Kearneysville Service Station, circa 1920. Note that road appears unpaved.

In 1932 Harvey Tabler was running the business. In 1939, he remodeled it, conforming to Standard Oil plans without the large workshop. Later the business was named the Kearneysville Esso Station, and Norval and Margie Johnston became the owners. This building was torn down recently and a Sheetz station was built in its place.

HOUSING AND CONSTRUCTION

One of the needs of this growing population was housing, but details of how this need was met are sketchy. What is certain is that at least four dwellings were built in 1873. E.H. Roberts caused a house to be built about three-quarters of a mile south of the Depot. James T. Trussell had a dwelling built on his farm that was 15 feet by 24 feet and two stories high. This house, constructed by D. Wagely, still stands near the corner of Bower Road and the Shepherdstown-Middleway Pike and is owned by Juanita Anderson. Mr. Weddle was commissioned to build a log dwelling for Thomas Turner, Esquire in 1883 that was 18 feet by 24 feet. This house is currently owned by Thomas McDowell and has been enlarged. Weddle also had a contract to build a small house for Charles Clower near the B&O Railroad at Hartstown. It has been replaced by a more modern home.

The small building boom continued. In 1875 a log dwelling was built for Mr. League. Records show that another two homes were built in 1879. The first belonged to Mr. C.M. Stump, who had purchased a lot from Mr. Thomas Turner. Years ago Mrs. Leila Grantham said this is the original section of the Carrie McDowell house that is located on Route 480. A second house was built by Mr. Lawson Weddle, who also bought a lot from Mr. Turner. This house was constructed on the east side of the Pike. In 1884 Mr. Jones contracted to build a large home for T. Homsher opposite the Presbyterian Church. This home was inhabited by Walter and Virginia Wilt well into the 1900s, but was destroyed when the Bank of Charles Town Branch was built recently. Other houses were also built on what is now Route 9 for Harvey Whittington, C.O. Whittington, and John Tucker late in the nineteenth century, and in 1929 for Frank Powell.

Plate 42. Harvey L. Granigan house, built 1906-1908. Picture taken 1995.

Before the turn of the century, L.G. Brotherton and H.C. Motrin were advertising as carpenters. John Stanley was a community carpenter, also, well-known for careful attention to detail. F.O. Trump began a lumber business around the turn of the century, but then moved into construction. A

Plate 43. C.O. Whittington house, built 1908-1910. Harvey Whittington house at left. Built 1910-1912. Picture taken 1995.

construction job for T. J. Clapham shows that four carpenters were hired for a certain piece of work that lasted from March until October. In 1906 three men were paid one dollar per day, the fourth received 75 cents. Accurate wages were noted if less than an hour was used. Mr. Trump built three houses off Kearneysville Lane. These were double units, one of which has been remodeled.

Changes in residence were usually planned for springtime. In 1928, records show that these changes occurred: Mr. And Mrs. T.A. Everhart purchased the former home of Dr. C.C.Lucas; Mr. And Mrs. J.C. Burhman, who had lived there, moved into the home owned by Mrs. James Whittington. The George Johnson farm at Leetown left vacant by the Everharts was taken by Frank Pennington, who moved from the Frank Gardner farm now rented

Plate 44. One of the unremodeled Trump units. Picture taken 1995.

by John F. Ware.

When Mr. Ercel Basore and his family moved into the area in the late 1930s, he bought the former property of Mr. Rogers, the carriage maker, when it came up for sale. Wishing to enlarge the house and make it comfortable for his family, he found a source of lumber that required only manual labor to acquire. This was the Presbyterian Church in Shenandoah Junction, which had been standing idle for some years. He made good use of the timber to enlarge his home, which stands today much as it did many years ago when it was remodeled.

When Ben Fox purchased the small lot and house beside the Reformed Church, he was taken to the Charles Town courthouse to have the paper notarized and receive his deed. When asked if he could write his name, he replied, "Certainly, but you won't be able to read it."

Mr. Arrington's house was recently owned by Mrs. Fannie Hazelton. Mr. Allen's house burned and Mr. Ross's house fell into disuse.

The boom times following the Armistice in 1918 briefly brought a strengthened economy. It was of short duration. Even before Black Friday on Wall Street in 1929, jobs that could be found in cities after 1918 were being phased out. As a result, strangers — who came to be called hobos — were knocking on doors in the community. But they weren't asking for a hand-out: Their first question was, "Do you have any work in exchange for a meal?" Seldom was anyone turned away. Even when there were no odd jobs, a sandwich would be freely given.

However, for some reason there was a sense of suspicion and distrust associated with the arrival of the gypsies sometime in the 1930s. In the brief time they spent in Kearneysville, there was no sign of gainful employment. That is, they simply were passing through, appearing one day, camping out on the south end of the village in a field and moving out after a few days.

Nearby neighbors questioned one another: "What are they doing here? Who gave them permission for the camp site?" Celina Carter remembers her mother shooing the children indoors when the gypsies arrived, although she also remembers the adult gypsies sitting on her front porch in the evenings, peacefully talking with her parents. In fact, it was Charles Rutherford's field that they camped in, and they had his permission to do so. Only a few days later, the field was empty, no children were missing, flocks of chickens could be accounted for, and no house break-ins were reported. But stories of the visit of the gypsies remained the topic of conversation for some time.

TAXI SERVICES

As early as 1868, transportation to Kearneysville was offered by James Adams. He advertised that anyone wanting to go to Kearneyvsille in either of his hacks must procure a ticket for cash only at the depot or any store.

By 1878, Mr. Powell Licklider was advertising the "Overland Express" to convey travelers from the B&O and others who wished to go to Shepherdstown. Until other arrangements were made, he carried mail bags to and from Shepherdstown, also. Later Mr. F.O. Trump also provided service for any passenger who wished to travel to Shepherdstown, Charles Town, and any other place within the area. Local citizens received a discount. Since buggies were popular, Mr. Rogers was busy making several designs during the last 20 years of the nineteenth century.

Education

Education

There are two strands related to schools in the Kearneysville community. The first has to do with private schools, which started early in the community's history; the second has to do with public or "Free" schools which opened in 1872. Private schools continued at least until 1911, overlapping the public schools.

PRIVATE SCHOOLS

The first schools in the community were private, and were sponsored by different families at various times. Only one private school was operating at any point in time. Neighboring children were invited to attend for a fee. The earliest school that I could identify was one recalled by Leila Bitner Grantham that had begun at Willow Hill, the home of her parents, Mr. and Mrs. H.C. Bitner. Miss Della Coburn (who later married Will Seibert), came to live with the family as governess for the three Bitner children, Blanche, Ernest, and Leila, and then took on the extra responsibility of school teacher; in addition to the Bitner children, her students included the McIntyre children, Ralph Border, and Bertie Clower.

The next teacher at Willow Hill was Miss Lizzie Barnes. As Blanche and Ernest Bitner moved into higher education, the school moved to Traveler's Rest where Mayberry McKee resided. Miss Mildred Marshall and in turn, Miss Bertie Patterson, were hired to tutor the children. These students included Bessie, Hugh, Guy, and Walter McKee; Jim and Mary Trussell, Campbell Blue, Mabel Miller and Leila Bitner. Although in need of repair, the one room schoolhouse may still hold evidence of these scholars.

About 1902, Mr. Kearfott persuaded Miss Effie McIntyre to teach at Rock Dale. Mary and Jack Lucas, Phil Campbell, Lige and Ruth Miller attended this school with the Kearfott children. Later still, Miss Blanche Bitner started a private school in a building owned by Mr. Casper Stump, who supervised the Hodges and Lemen Grain Elevator. This class included: Jim and Mary Trussell, Clarence Thompson, Leila Bitner, Catherine and Walter McKee, Virginia Homsher, and Irvie McIntyre. Leila Bitner recalled an unfortunate incident regarding this school taught by her sister. Mr.

Stump was not noted for keeping sanitary conditions. The school was held on the first floor — Mr. Stump's bedroom was on the second. One day his chamber pot overflowed and began dripping through the ceiling, Miss Bitner became shocked and confused and her not-too-attentive class was overcome with laughter. It did not take much persuasion for the Episcopal minister, Rector A.J. Willis, to convince Miss Bitner to relinquish private tutoring for a position in the public school at Bardane. This seems to have ended private schools in Kearneysville.

Plate 45. Private school moved to property of Lige and Jane Miller.

BEGINNING OF THE PUBLIC (FREE) SCHOOLS

The construction of two buildings in Kearneysville in 1872 marked the beginning of public schools and advanced the education of all the children. One which Motrin Collins helped Dr. Logie establish was a log, one-room school for colored children opened on Dr. James Logie's farm on the west side of the Smithfield-Shepherdstown Pike, opposite the Jacob Fulk farm. (See S. Howell Brown map, 1883). The contract to build was given to Mr. Samuel Fowler of Smithfield for a cost of $230.00. An eight month school term was post-

Plate 46. Cornerstone of Kearneysville Masonic and Temperance Hall, 1872.

ed and the average daily attendance was 15 pupils.

The second building was a two story brick building on a small lot owned by Theodore Homsher, opposite the Presbyterian Church. A board of directors was formed from stockholders of the

> *Shepherdstown Register*, November 2, 1872
> Kearneysville is a small but thriving place, and its progress is of a healthy character, and we commend it to other places, where permanent prosperity is aimed at. The citizens of this model village have a neat and pretty church, built about three years ago, and are now just completing, in conjunction with the Board of Education of Middleway school, and Masonic and Temperance Hall, that for the purposes for which it is intended, will have no superior in the County of Jefferson.
>
> The building is located between the B&O Railroad and the Turnpike, and nearly opposite the Presbyterian Church. The lot has a front of 60 feet with a depth of 150 feet, costing $40. The building is of brick, two stories high, with a cornice projecting fifteen inches on all sides.... The bell to be placed upon the building is a fine toned instrument, and was purchased by private subscription, will be heard a distance of several miles. The front door and window have segmented heads, and a marble slab is inserted in the front wall bearing the inscription "Kearneysville Masonic Temperance Hall, 1872." The window sashes are all suspended by weights and the blinds are provided with patent fastenings. The schoolroom is well ventilated, and is furnished to accommodate about forty pupils. The inside trimmings are painted brown, outside white, window blinds green, walls painted and penciled, and the whole appearance of the building is attractive. The entire cost of the building will be $1500; of this only $825 is borne by the taxpayers of the Township

Plate 47. Article on Kearneysville public school, 1872.

building to be used as a Masonic and Temperance Hall[1] on the second floor, with a school room on the first.

Dr. James Logie was treasurer of the board, his son, John H., was secretary, and C.T.Butler, president. The Board of Education owned the small lot, having exchanged property with Mr. Homsher, as shown on the map below. Then in 1888, the Board bought out the stockholders of the Masonic and Temperance Hall.

John Hess, a Kearneysville resident, was Superintendent of Jefferson County Schools in the fall of 1878. Not much is known about how teachers were selected. Records do show that some certification was required. For example, E.R. Turner, John Quigley

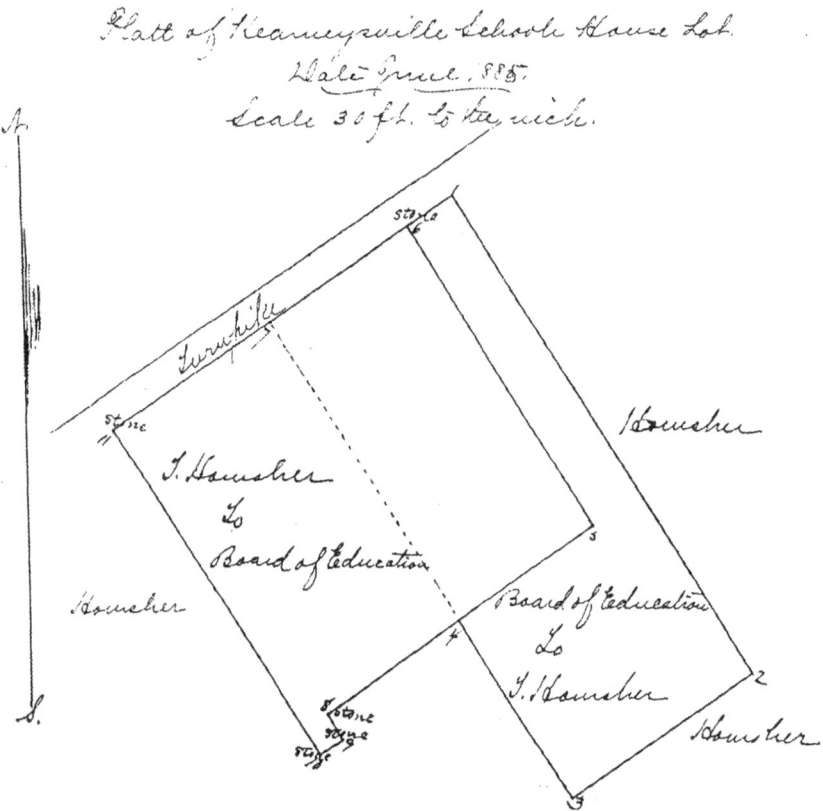

Plate 48. Plat showing exchange of property for school, June 1885.

---

[1] In later years, after the 18th amendment had been added to the U.S. Constitution, there were rumors of bootlegging in the neighborhood. At this period in local history no application had been made to the court for a liquor license, but, preemptively, when the Temperance Movement began in 1868, a local unit was formed.

and W.A. Arter attended the first Teachers' Institute held at the Stone School in Charles Town on April 6, 1878. There were no grade levels until August 1887. At that point, courses were designated for grades one through seven. High school students, grades eight and nine, matriculated at the Leetown School. For the first couple of decades after the school was built, there were two teachers at Kearneysville. In the fall of 1888, records show that Miss Edith Lloyd and John Trussell endeavored to enlighten those who desired basic education. These two teachers were followed by Ada Brotherton (1889-1890), Florence Snyder and Meta Shirley (1890-1891) and Alice Grantham and Mary Hoffman (1897). Later, in 1917, records show there were three teachers employed at the school: Mr. Ed Turner (also principal), and Misses Ada Knode and Beatrice Rogers.

In 1877 a new school law was enacted that allowed trustees to close a school if attendance in the school district fell below 35% of the total enrollment. This included students between ages six and 21 years old. Enrollment record for February 1879 show average daily attendance of 35 students. This probably reflects a general trend of poor attendance, since there was talk in

Plate 49. Hints for teachers, 1884 from Shepherdstown Register. Note suggestion to form professional association at end of article.

[For THE REGISTER.]
SOME HINTS TO TEACHERS.

BY AN OLD TEACHER.

Teachers in the public schools are often sorely puzzled how best to economize the time of the children at school and give them the greatest amount of instruction in the several branches that they may study, as many children only attend a few months in the winter and many more cease to attend school at the age of fourteen years, and their whole educational training must be crowded into a very brief term. How then can they gain the most knowledge in this short time?

1. As soon as the child can readily call the words in reading, or as soon as he can read easily in McGuffy's Fourth Reader, discard the reader and put him to reading the history of the United States, either Cook's Sketches of the Old Dominion (which includes West Virginia), Miss McGill's History of Virginia, or some of the child's histories of the United States. A very good one is the "Eclectic Primary History," published by Van Antwerp & Co. These books are written in an easy style and in familiar language, so that children can soon gain a good knowledge of United States history, and will be encouraged thereby to read larger works on the same subject.

2. As soon as the pupils are familiar with first lessons in geography, skip the second book and take up the third book in geography and confine their attention to those parts that will prove most useful to them. Use the geographies as a reading book and let at least one reading lesson a day be out of this book.

3. Have all the classes to read one lesson a day either out of the speller or dictionary; that is, pronounce the words without spelling the syllable. This will prove a wonderful help in training pupils to divide words into syllables by the eye in their reading lessons.

4. In teaching English grammar, train the pupils to give brief but concise definitions, allowing them to substitute words of their own synonomous with those used in the text. Dwell more upon sentence making and analyses in the grammar than upon memorizing definitions and rules. Teach them how to find out what the sentence means and why one arrangement of the words is better than another.

5. After they become familiar with the principles of arithmetic, let their lessons in it be confined to practical examples, introducing frequently such as occur daily in business circles and in mechanical and farming operations.

Attention to these things will save time, money and labor.

A SUGGESTION.

It has been suggested that the teachers of this district form an association and meet once a month on Saturday afternoons to discuss such matters as pertains to their school work. They could meet regularly at some convenient place, or go from school-house to school-house, as teachers may prefer.

Plate 50. Rock-faced concrete, two room Kearneysville school.

Kearneysville and elsewhere of compulsory education.

In 1906 the rock-faced concrete, two room school was built off of what is now Stanley Lane. An engraved stone was placed above the porch on the west side of the building. The names of Jesse Engle, County Superintendent, M.E. Trussell, President of the Board of Education, and F.O. Trump, contractor are cut into the stone, along with the dates 1872-1906. On the face of it, these dates are confusing, since the first public school was in the Temperance Hall in 1872. My theory is that since F.O. Trump was born in 1864, he probably was the contractor for the 1906 building. The 1872 date simply recognizes the first public school built in Kearneysville (part of the Temperance Hall), and, other than that, has no bearing on this building.

Somewhere between 1914 and 1916 the East portion was added to the school building. There is speculation that the Temperance Hall School was torn down and the bricks were used for this purpose. More resources were allocated to the school across time. A furnace was installed by Janney and Baldwin in 1924. Before there was running water in the building, water was brought in buckets from the Stanley's house next door. After a well was drilled in 1926, an indoor pump was installed in the hall. Hot lunches were added during the winter months of 1938, although they were subsidized with federal funds because of the Depression. There were three teachers in 1923: T. VanMetre, Jo Seibert, and Olive Athey, but by 1927 attendance had grown to warrant four teachers, those being Cornelius Carter, Laura Thompson, Joe Clipp, and Mrs. Russell White. Teachers were welcomed into the family homes. Reva White recalls being invited with two or three other teachers to the home of Mrs. MacGruder, who had two foster daughters, Ruth and Frances, and lived at Locust Grove. Supper was often served at a long table on a screened-in porch. Ruth and Frances would serve a bounteous meal and occasionally the teachers were invited to spend the night. Reva also recalled an evening meal with the Paul Miller, Sr. family, who lived near the school at Rellim. It turned out to be a dizzying affair. She wondered why the room was spinning until it became clear that someone had spiked the punch. There were three young men in the house who were her students. She never found out who pulled the prank — one or all.

Although the school required tax support, it also added to the economic base of the community. In addition to providing construction opportunities, teachers and principals found employment. Salaries in 1916 were $75 per month for principals, $45 for teachers holding a No. 1 certificate, $35 for those with a No. 2, and $30 for those holding a No. 3 certificate. By 1921, salaries had increased to $150 for the principal and $85 for teachers.

Schools provided other employment opportunities. Mr. John Stanley, who kept meticulous personal bookkeeping records, noted that he was "putting benches in the school house that were brought from Leetown, putting up blackboards, placing wire on tower windows, and tearing out partitions" on October 10, 1914. The job was completed by August 5, 1915. Perhaps this was when the folding doors were installed between the middle and upper grade classrooms.

Audrianne Seibert Parkins remembers how she eagerly anticipated the beginning of school. Even before she was six years old, she waited at the end of her lane at Rocky Ridge for Miss Ruth Miller, who taught at the VanMetre School. When she did start school, she considered herself lucky to be seated at a double desk with Reva Copenhaver. Transferring to Kearneysville for the next two years, Audrainne recalls shared memories of other students, namely Margaret Trussell, Dorothy Horn, Juanita and Irma Whittington, Alice Hopper, Eula and Harry Turner, Max, Tracy and Lucille Brown, and Henry and Margie Stanley.

Students who lived a mile or less from the school, usually walked, reporting for the 9 o'clock handbell. In later years, safety patrols were necessary at the intersection, and students filled this capacity, which was considered an honor. Gilbert Miller, Harry Dillow, Harry Powell, Russell Fowler and Marvin Thomas were trusted with this duty.

Students who lived further from school and had a pony cart for transportation were considered fortunate. "Not always," said Lillian Flagg Shipper. Her parents owned the Flagg Farm, where Memory Gardens are now. After the VanMetre School closed, Lillian said that she attended school at Kearneysville. Not only was she obligated to arrive at school on time, but she had to deliver the milk to the creamery on her way. The ten gallon can was placed on the floor of the pony cart and the five gallon can on the seat beside her. Lillian had to pass by a bull in J.C.Bitner's field who may have caused her trouble. As it turned out, he fell into a routine of placidly following along inside the fence as she passed for school, and then meeting her in the afternoon to do the same as she returned. It wasn't the bull who added excitement. A certain David Talbott liked to joy ride on his motorcycle, and the pony took an instant dislike to the commotion, turning around and hastening back to the safety of the barn. The milk was delivered a day late, and Lillian missed a day at school.

Typically, the school day started with chapel. After about 1916, folding doors separated two of the rooms, making it possible for all students to gather in these rooms for the opening exercise. Everyone sang a song together from paperback songbooks, then repeated the pledge to the flag followed by the Lord's Prayer. There were frequent breaks in the daily routine of school. Often the last half hour on Friday would be used for a game of the students' choosing. A favorite of both boys and girls in the upper grades was Clap In, Clap Out. Valentine's Day provided an opportunity to exchange cards with a special friend.

Subjects taught in the upper grades included spelling, geography, history, civics, reading, English, oral and written arithmetic and health or hygiene. Parents followed closely what their children were taught in school in this small community. Newton McKee was sanctioned when he explained puberty in his health class for the upper grades. Mr. and Mrs. Benner, parents of Lena, were quite offended by this discussion that had occurred before more than twenty students of different ages and both sexes. Newton was reassigned elsewhere in the county, and the health curriculum was revised.

Many activities linked the school and the community. For example, apparently there was an organ in the school, because an article from 1911 notes that friends of the Kearneysville School held an oyster supper to finish paying for the new organ. There are other examples. After President Woodrow Wilson joined our forces with those of the Allies in 1917, students supported the war effort by buying Savings Stamps sold in school. Spelling bees, although intended to raise money, were also an important community activity. These were held at Trump's Hall, which was located where the railroad crossed the Turnpike. The best speller in the upper grades was awarded $2.50 in gold; the best in the lower grades was awarded $1.00. Besides an admission fee of ten cents, ice cream was sold to earn money for necessities at the school. Paper and pencils were purchased for children whose parents could not afford them; when school money ran out, school teachers pitched in for these and other needed articles.

Christmas programs were also presented by the children for parents and friends. These were a two evening affair, as was graduation in the spring. For each of these events, a stage was erected, the folding doors were opened, and a folding chair was set up in every available space in the two rooms[2]. Even then, many supporters needed to stand along the walls. About 1934, the Bardane Public School was closed and the students transferred to Kearneysville. This enlarged the number of children who participated in school events, and it expanded the community that was interested in school activities.

It must have been a rather formal school community at times. Helen VanMetre remembered hearing her classmates say "excuse me" often while playing Prisoner's Base. Possibly this was the result of Miss Olive Athey's insistence that her students observe good manners at all times.

For a number of years, the county schools held a Field Day near the end of the school year. An accounting of this special event that was held in May 1, 1925 relates how, as the day drew near, students and teachers spent many hours preparing for the competition. On the day of the event, the opening processional was led by the County Superintendent and members of the Board of Education. Those attending joined in the salute to the flag and sang "America" and "Hail to West Virginia." Edgewood School won the most events for a one room school. Kearneysville students won thirteen scholastic awards, including five firsts, and were congratulated by

---

2 These folding chairs were stored at the school when Trump Hall was demolished to make space for the underpass.

Following is an example of the entertainment that might fill a typical two-night event. This particular performance was held on December 19-20, 1935.

Primary grades presentation: "A Strike in Santa Land"

Santa — Bill Cline
Mrs. Santa — Frances Shifflet
Books — (seven girls)
Brownie — Jack Boyd
Tin Soldiers — (four boys)
Top — Catherine Southard
Jumping Jack — Harry Blackford
Doll —- Eleanor Thompson
Fountain Pen — Madeline Thomas
Tree — Catherine Clemmons

Intermediate grades presentation: "Behind the Scenes"

Fairy — Alma Reinhart
Six Elves
Six Helpers
Two Brownies
Weather Man — Irving Hall
Boy Doll — Harry Blackford
Santa Claus — Donald Heinz
Old Mother in the Shoe — Tessie Stokes (and children)
Dr. Fester — Paul McCarty
Chief of the Household — Mildred Byers
Dream Man — Bill Bradley

Upper grades presentations: "Red and the Christmas Whopper"

Red Sims — Bruce Albright
Mother Sims — Josephine Ambrose
Father Sims — Harry Dillow
Ione Sims — Anna Belle Stokes
Jack Adams — Marshall Blackford
Bobby Adams — Marvin Thomas
Carol Clark — Grey Bradley
Aunt Etta Briggs —Anna Herndon
Uncle Phil Briggs — Benny Johnson
Bebe Briggs — Betty Barrett
Cousin Susan — Elsie Dillow
Deacon Dunn — Elwood Buracker
Hilda — Mary Frances Bradley

"The Doll's Dolls"

Anna May Painter, Virginia Costello, Virginia Lee Thompson, Helen Clemmons, Ruth Blackford and Eileen Southard

"The Christmas Holly"

Louise Kite, Alice Shackelford, Grey Bradley, Mary Frances Bradley, Goulder Frith, and Mida Southard their teachers.

Beginning in 1928, eighth-grade students returned to the classroom after this fun day to prepare for the Uniform County Examination. This was a two day affair and determined if students were eligible for graduation. Following the exam, preparations began for the end-of-school Exercises, which, again, were held on two successive evenings. Recitations and plays were presented on the first night; on the second night students who were graduating were awarded their very important certificate as the President of the Board of Education recognized each graduate. A clipping from the Spirit of Jefferson Advocate (right) shows a list of all students black and white, who passed the exam in 1935.

A description of the 1936 graduation was found in a local paper. This was the year Josephine Ambrose, second highest in the County, gave the valedictory address; Anna Herndon, the salutatory address; and Dorothy Chapman, the class prophecy. In addition Marshall Blackford delivered the Class History and Mary Frances Bradley read the Class Will. Oscar Jones, Principal, with Mary Frances Morrison and Laura Thompson, teachers, smiled with pride as each student performed. The 1935-36 year had come to a close and celebrations were in order. This called for the

---

24 Students Successful in 8th Grade Elementary Diploma Test 1935

Twenty-four students were successful in the eighth grade elementary diploma tests for Jefferson County held by County Superintendent I. N. Bonham here on May 9th, and 10th. Miss Rena Belle Brown, of the Leetown school, led the county with an average of 86.6%, while Miss Elsie Genevieve Heinz, of the Kearneysville school, was a close second with a mark of 86.2%. Mr. Charles C. Kretzer is principal of the Leetown school and Mr. Oscar Jones is principal of the Kearneysville school. The successful applicants were:

Dorothy Virginia Thomas, Shenandoah Junction, 84.9%; Helen Louise Ware, Kabletown, 84.2%; Burten Lee Frith, Kearneysville, 83.6%, Blanche Ellen Harden, Leetown, 82.8%; Dorothy Elizabeth, Shen. Jct., 81.9%; Robert Maurice Whittington, Shen. Jct., 81.5%; Katherin Elsie Clinton, Eagle ave., col., 81.%; Harold Banks Wintermoyer, Shen. Jct., 80.5%; Anna Virginia Whirley, Shen. Jct., 80.3%.

The following also passed the tests: James Warren Meade LaRue, Summit Point School; Lyndon T. Morrow, Jr., Middleway; Mary Virginia Broyles, Shenandoah Junction; Selden Furtney Darr, Shenandoah Junction; Clyde Wilmer Foster, Shenandoah Junction; Charles Wesley Creamer, Kearneysville; Mary Agnes Edelman, Shenandoah Junction; Emma Oneda Farmer, Summit Point; Edward Henry Thornton, Eagle Avenue, colored school.

Promoted conditionally: Mary Katherine Roberts, Summit Point; Phyllis V. Naylor, Summit Point; Marvin Bailey Farmer, Summit Point; Merle Cooper, Shadyside, colored.

Plate 51. Successful eighth-grade graduates, 1935.

annual picnic in the old orchard of Herbert Miller, once farmed by his grandfather, J.J. Miller.

I remember these picnics as being significant community events. Each family brought a complete meal that was shared with all others. Children and adults alike played a variety of games, such as softball and prisoner's base. When picnics were held in the Miller's orchard where cows pastured, games became more challenging. Younger children played drop-the-handkerchief, ring-around-the-rosy, red light, and Mother, May I? Parents came to the picnic even when they no longer had children who attended the local school. It was a time to share fun and conversation.

At one time during the 1920s, there were three school baseball teams of different age groups. Henry Stanley, Rex and Jacob Smallwood, Herb Everhart, Frankie Trump, and Zack Fleming played on the older team. Often this team competed at Leetown or Shenandoah Junction. Mrs. Stanley encouraged and supported this activity by driving the boys to their games. Henry recounts a game against the Leetown School. Kearneysville was leading 11-0 while Lefty Willis was pitching for Leetown. But when the coach sent in

Plate 52. Miss Bessie Bells' intermediate grades class, 1920-1921. Left to right, first row: Piney Hammond, Frankie Trump, Jessie Whittington, John Heinz, Eula Rose, Mary Rossi, Lynn Grantham, unknown, Hattie Smallwood. Second rose: unknown, three Italian girls — names unknown, Amy Campbell, Emma Hammond, Mary Saladina, unknown, Olga Angelo. Back row: Grace Whittington, Frances McKown, Garland Frith, Oscar McAllister, Lena Benner, Hester Hammond, Mabel Lee Hammond, Norman (Coo) Benner, two unknown children, Tyler Brown. Teacher Miss Bessie Bell at top of picture.

Plate 53. Miss Olive Athey's class, possibly 1921-1922. Can you identify the children? (I couldn't).

Plate 54. Thomas VanMetre, Principal, with students, circa 1923-1924. Left to right, front row: Henry Stanley, Herbert Everhart, Dorothy Horn, Lucille Brown, James Trump, Jacob Smallwood. Second row: Preston Hopper, Margaret Martin, Zack Fleming, Gladys Frith, Margie Stanley, Virginia Grantham. Back row: Mary Fowler, Margaret Milburn, Alton Thomas, Verona Frith, George Cox, Rex Smallwood, Amy Campbell. Thomas VanMetre, top.

Lefty's brother, Herman (who later became a professional baseball pitcher) Kearneysville scoring stopped.

There was a limit to community spirit with these baseball games, however. No doubt Mr. Henry Stickel regretted that his fenced-in garden lay in a direct line with home plate of the school baseball diamond. Many of the boys, including Burrell Frith, could land a home run by hitting the ball high in the air so that it fell in Mr. Stickel's garden, and eventually his fence was trodden down. When his patience was at an end, Mr. Stickel began collecting balls. But since he was also honest, the balls were returned at the close of the school year.

A discussion of early schools would not be complete without also describing discipline. Punishment for the greatest offenses, such as skipping school, could involve being strapped with the teacher's belt. Of course, only male students were so disci-

Plate 55. Three faculty members: 1937-1938. Left to right are Virginia Hawn, 1st and 2nd grades; Oscar Jones, 5th, 6th grades and principal; and Laura M. Thompson, 3rd and 4th grades.

Plate 56. Primary grades, 1937-1938. Left to right, front row: Robert White, Ethel Henderson, Jimmy Blackford, Mary Wilson, Junior Shackleford, Julia Mae Brown, and Doris McCarty. Back row: Betty Lou Thomas, Elizabeth Wilson, Emmerson Stokes, Boyd Henderson, and Lenora Meadows.

plined, and only a male teacher would administer such punishment. It seems that girls were more likely to be given demerits. At least one student failed a grade because she could not complete a demerit in time. (A demerit could be writing "I will not talk in class" one hundred times or working a lengthy problem in mathematics). The smallest punishment could be depriving a student of recess time.

I am reminded of a conversation with Reva Copenhaver White. She spoke openly and lovingly of her experience as a teacher in the middle grades, but one incident concerning Bill Thomas bothered her to the end of her life. Each schoolroom at the time was heated by a pot-bellied coal stove. Bill had a compelling hobby of collecting baseball cards. Perhaps they came in boxes of look-alike cigarette candy. At any rate, the cards were his treasures, and he knew all the players and the teams they played with. The cards were also a distraction for Bill, however. When he should have been paying attention, he sometimes took the cards out of his pocket to look at them. Reva became so frustrated one day she opened the stove door and told Bill to put all the cards inside. In her 96th year, shortly before she died, Miss Reva recalled the incident with sadness and regret. She wished it had not happened.

One tragedy that had a big impact on the community occurred one spring day in 1917. Miss Ada Knode, a teacher of the lower grades, led some children on an outing to the quarry hole. Each child hoped to catch a gold fish that occupied the water along with other fish and frogs. The children were permitted to walk out on the ledge where the goldfish were darting. One small girl walked too far out on the ledge and slipped into deeper water. As Ada saw her go under, she immediately went into the water without removing her shoes or sweater. She was able to reach the child and push her back to safety, but her soaked clothes dragged Ada under. Young George Cox pushed a pole across the ledge, hoping his beloved teacher could grasp it. Meanwhile, Margaret Trussell (later married to Fred Shaeffer) ran for George Thompson, the Constable. She thought he could be found at the Kearneysville Station Store, but both attempts to save Ada failed. Then young Cox, knowing that John C. Heinz owned a boat, hurried to the Heinz home nearby. The rescue effort was too late to save the life of this brave teacher. It was an event that brought the community together. The funeral was held at the Methodist Church in Shepherdstown. In a heartbreaking procession, school children followed the coffin to the cemetery, carrying floral arrangements.

FREE SCHOOL FOR BLACK CHILDREN

Actually, before the first free school for black children was opened, Mrs. Emma Hart Brady had opened a school for children in her home. This was in 1869, and between 60 to 90 students were enrolled for two terms, although daily attendance was probably much lower than these numbers suggest. Then in 1871, Miss Sallie Fox also taught children in her home. No mention was found of tuition payments.

Mr. Motrin Collins and Dr. James Logie were patrons of a school for black children. Dr. Logie gave the land about one mile south of the B&O Station. Mr. Samuel Fowler was hired as contractor. The school was of log construction and has long since disappeared. It was one room, built at a cost of $230, and completed on October 10, 1875. The school term was eight months; average daily attendance was fifteen students. This school was abandoned in 1911.

Black teachers taught in black schools. It seems that they were paid the same as white teachers for a No. 1 certificate at least. They were given a qualifying teacher exam at the Baptist Church in the West End of Charles Town, and, as mentioned previously, Mr. A.W. Arter attended the first Teachers' Institute held at the Stone School House in Charles Town.

During 1912 and 1913, black children attended the Woodbury School, which was located midway between Kearneysville and Leetown. This was after the Leetown School was enlarged and white students had been transferred there. In 1914 the Linwood School opened for black children. It was built on a lot purchased by the Board of Education from G.T. Hodges of Shepherdstown. The lot cost $150; a wooden two-room building was constructed at a cost of $700. Pot-bellied stoves provided heat, and children carried water from the well at the foot of the hill. This property was owned by Hodges and Lemen Grain Elevator, and Mr. Arthur Trussell was manager.

In 1925, black parents petitioned the Board of Education for an addition to the school and the implementation of a two-year high school program. The argument was that Leetown already had a high school and white students from Kearneysville could attend there; black students could not. According to an article released by the Board of Education the petition was denied. The Board noted that a new building was already under construction at Middleway (for whites), and that consideration was being given to moving the old Middleway School to Kearneysville to avoid congestion. Although the move was not made immediately, young Henry Burnett assisted his father, Clarence, and Mr. George Thompson in adding this school to the existing Linwood School. Hot lunches were added in 1938; Lilian Mason was in charge of the kitchen.

A number of current Kearneysville residents, such as Juanita Stella Eggleton, Irene King, Ethelene Clinton, Celena and Sarah Roper and Sam McDowell, share memories of this school. Some jolly times included recess and lunch hour. Juanita Eggleton liked to slip off to Mr. Wilt's store nearby to buy a candy bar — Mr. Goodbar was her favorite. At Christmas time, school children presented entertainment for their parents with Santa Claus and elves as well as religious plays, recitations and singing. Field Day, sometimes called May Day, was held on the grounds of Storer College in Harpers Ferry. This was an all day affair when schools competed in sports events similar to Olympics. In 1938-39 Juanita recalls, there was flag pole singing while children wove paper streamers; then the children played ball games and enjoyed other activities.

Kearneysville residents fondly remember many teachers from Linwood, such as W.A. Arter, Amelia Carter, Elsie Clinton, Daniel Johnson, Richard Jackson (a principal), Elizabeth Green, Lawrence Taylor (a principal), Margaret Arrington, Arianna Johnson, Arianna Fox, and Lucy McDaniel Saunders. One teacher, Reverend Thomas, was not so fondly remembered. He was from the West Indies, was particularly strict and kept a narrow strap handy with which he whipped the children. On one occasion, after giving a Bible quiz, he ordered all students who failed to stand in a line. They knew what was coming. Reaching in his desk drawer, he retrieved the strap and went down the line. Irene King was hit so sharply, the wound bled. She took her plight to her mother, Vernie King, who immediately sought help from Herbert Miller, President of the Board of Education. The problem was resolved appropriately: Mr. Thomas lost his teaching position at Kearneysville. Still, after 60 years, Irene's voice held a tone of outrage at Reverend Thomas's cruelty when she told this story.

Although I wasn't able to follow the academic careers of all Linwood graduates, one graduate stands out. Miss Lucinda Estelle Fox, grand-daughter of John H. Fox, graduated from Storer College in June, 1936 with academic honors. Her Salutatory Address was "The Problems of Leisure."

Linwood School was closed in 1948 when the Kearneysville students were transported by bus to Eastside School in Shepherdstown or to Eagle Avenue in Charles Town. The old school was sold and torn down. When the white school closed in 1971, there was no longer a public school for village children. In spite of the benefits promised in a new and larger school nearby, some parents objected to the removal of the school which had brought families together. No longer was there a neutral place for meetings, such as literary and religious groups, or the Farmer's Alliance; nor was there a compelling reason for the traditional inter-generational picnics and sports. The village lost a center of interaction and with it a path to community spirit.

Social Activities

Social Activities

In a sense, Kearneysville social life reflected what was happening in larger towns. With access to roads, travel by train, newspapers, and other resources, people were able to keep up with new inventions and social trends in the nation, such as movies, electronic devices and automobiles. Some activities were unique to the community. That is, social clubs were formed to meet specific needs; community outings came into being because of access and opportunity.

The Kearneysville community had its news collectors who filled in the details about what was happening socially. Early on these people used pseudonyms, such as Mary Beau and The Templar, so it's difficult to identify who these individuals were. But what is of interest here is that their reporting was a source of understanding social activities and interests of the community. Sometimes even small details are recorded, such as when people moved through Kearneysville — a frequent springtime occurrence. For example, one item notes that P.N. Brillhart and his family passed through Kearneysville with eight large wagons of furniture on their way from Timberlake Farm in Middleway to Shepherdstown. This was in 1911. Another item from 1932 notes that young people were driving to see their favorite stars at the Charles Town Theatre: Norma Shearer and Robert Montgomery in "Private lives," Kim Maynard in "Texas Gunfighter," and Buster Keaton, Jimmy Durante and Molly Moran in "The Passionate Plumber." Adults paid 25 cents while children were charged 15 cents. A cheap date could sit with his girlfriend in the balcony for 15 cents each. A few other miscellaneous details that I found in newspapers are included below.

The community kept up with the styles of the times. Perfume and Chalfont Balm could be purchased at Hutchinson and Burnett in Shepherdstown. Hoop skirts, however, had to be ordered from Baltimore. News items indicate that some ladies complained of the fickle styles in 1875, as shorter dresses were coming into vogue, and that some were having difficulty getting a size 6 foot in a size 4 shoe!

Various social activities could be held at the churches and the school. Square dances, spelling bees, ice cream festivals, and community suppers were held at other community buildings, such as the Patriotic Order Sons of America Hall, YMCA Hall, and Trump Hall. Music and plays were an important part of community life also. The Kearneysville Minstrels presented concerts from time to time before the turn of the century, one of which was on May 22, 1875 at Railroad Hall. Other troupes performed at local churches.

Chatauquas came through the area, too. In 1900 William Jennings Bryan (who unsuccessfully ran for President in 1896, 1900 and 1908) spoke in September. An enormous crowd of 15,000 thronged the Fountain Rock Property, what is now Morgan's Grove Park. Lige Miller recalls that his father, Herbert, attended this event and had high praise for the speaker.

Often children made their own fun, and because the area was rural, spending time with friends might involve a walk of two miles or more. Sarah Roper Walker told me recently of her Sunday visits to Johnsontown. When she was about ten years old, she would be joined by the Washington girls, Dorothy, Helen and Alice and by Essie Campbell and her sister, Mary. After church, the girls would walk down Route 9 to Bardane, a distance of about a mile. After a fresh drink of water at the Kite's home, they would continue down Wiltshire Road another mile or so to play with Dorothy Taylor, John Fox, a cousin, and whoever else was visiting at the time. Late in the afternoon, the girls would walk back home. Sarah remembers these occasions with pleasure.

There was always a warm place of business for loafers on a wintry evening or for gabbing on a hot afternoon. A favorite was the Grey Goose, opened in the 1920s. This was a corner store across from the Presbyterian Church, a favorite of young and old alike, owned and run by Tabb Janney. Strangers to the community were curious about the name of this restaurant. Simply put, it was named for the goose that was penned up in the barnyard across the road.

A tragedy stands out in the minds of those who can recall the afternoon of September 15, 1925. As usual, a few locals had gathered at the Grey Goose for a cool drink on a sweltering afternoon. Among them were Harold Burhman, Garland Frith, Freddie Smith, and Preston Hopper, and Mr. Janney, along with a few people from Martinsburg. At about 5 p.m., thunder roared, lightning flashed, and the rain began to pour. The young men moved toward the windows at the front of the building to gauge the fierceness of the storm. Suddenly a bolt of lightning hit the screen covering the windows. Preston Hopper was burned about the chest and arms, although not seriously. Garland Frith, standing under a conductor pipe through which wires led to the building, received a direct hit. He was taken to Seibert's garage across the road as soon as the adults recovered, and Dr. J.L. Myers of Shepherdstown was summoned. But he had died before he hit the floor, according to Dr. Myers. Garland was buried in the Presbyterian Church Cemetery.

Other fierce thunderstorms contributed to the history and legends of the Kearneysville community. In 1923 a storm accompanied by a howling wind blew off the porch roof of the home of Mr. and Mrs. Fowler. At the same moment, the B&O engine that was passing nearby blew an unearthly shriek. The story goes that Mrs. Fowler declared, "It's judgement day. That was Gabriel's trumpet." The two arose from their beds, dressed, and sat waiting for what was to come. This particular storm was especially severe in the Kearneysville and Leetown areas.

Sometime after Trump Hall was demolished in 1930, George Cox had constructed a building on his property to use for car repair. He quickly discovered that it was more profitable to rent it for social functions and religious revivals in the 1930s and early 1940s. When square dances were held, local musicians, such as Albert (Shewby) Whittington and Charlie Dorsey were called on to play the fiddle. Later Burrell Frith might have played the autoharp or a mouth organ. George called the figures or squares as he swung his partner to a "do-si-do."

Earliest county fairs were held in Shepherdstown and known as the Morgan's Grove Fair. As today, the fair was a week-long occasion of rides, exhibits and vendors. Families took tents that provided shelter during the day and allowed them to stay over-night if they chose. Many from the village were among the 12,000 reported at the Morgan's Grove Fair on one day in September 1894. Rose and Alva Lashorn were judged finest twins and received the prize of $2.50 in gold. In 1916 at the September 7 County Fair, William White Hammond, infant son of Mr. and Mrs. Bates Hammond won second prize for prettiest baby boy.

SPORTS

The earliest sporting events of record seem to have been tournaments that were held as early as 1866, in which men on horseback rode under a ring that was hanging from a pole. The object was to remove the ring with a blunted lance. The women sought to be designated Maids of Honor. Tournaments were often held more than once a year, and the public was invited. On occasion, tournaments ended with dancing accompanied by a band, sometimes from Summit Point. The men came as knights with creative titles. In May 1871, when Virginia Blue Bells and May Apples were flowering and apple blossoms added their fragrance to the air, a tournament was advertised for Kearneysville. Chief Marshalls were William G. Butler, James A. Hamill, and Grover Henkle. Judges included Dr. W.F. Alexander, John W. Allen, and Casper Stump. J.S. Bragonier gave the charge to the knights. The tournament concluded with coronation speeches followed by contestants crowning their favorite belles. A news article shows that Scott Lemen used the title of Knight of the Wildwood in this event and crowned Miss Jessie Henkle as the second Maid of Honor. Other participants and their titles are shown below. Mr. Darnell photographed the queen and her court.

Knight of Peru	William Koven
Knight of Flying Cloud	J. Whittington
Knight of Wildwoods	Scott Lemen
Knight of Jefferson	Daniel Oden
Knight of Crimson	Sash W. Blackford
Knight of Old Domino	Robert Turner
Knight of Clarke	W. Locke
Knight of Willow Well	H. Rinehart
Knight of Shenandoah	Jacob Kinkle
Knight of Frederick	Charles Carter
Knight of Red, White and Red	David Flanagan
Knight of Potomac	James Kearney
Knight of Cabin Run	John Kinkle
Knight of Arabia	George Watson
Knight of Blooming	Rose W. Lewis
Knight of Potomac Mills	J. Osborn
Knight of No One to Love	H. Rogers
Knight of Fair View	C. Whittington

But the format had changed by 1894. When W. H. Kearfott held a semi-annual tournament on his shooting ground, instead of crowning the ladies, prizes between $90 and $110 in merchandise and trophies were given.

Baseball was a popular sport as early as 1887. Teams from neighboring towns competed and continued doing so for many years. A game between Shepherdstown and Kearneysville, September 1887, was noted in the *Register*. Most games were played in friendly rivalry, but this particular game ended abruptly in the sixth inning when an umpire called a local player safe. Angry Shepherdstown players refused to continue play. By the rules of the game, Kearneysville won 9-8. A return match was held the following Wednesday; the score was 9-8 once again. And once again Kearneysville had 9.

Baseball remained popular throughout the coming years. Various organizations usually sold refreshments, turning the occasion into a gathering of families where children played together, and people caught up on community news in between cheering for their favorite teams. Even WWI could not extinguish the sport. The men laid out a baseball diamond on the quarry ground that soon came to be known as "Quarry Diamond." Both black and white teams played there, although at separate times. Some teams also had a ball diamond in a corner of Miss Effie McIntyre's field, adjoining the filling station. In 1932, there is a record of a Grey Goose Wonders Baseball team. Its members were Herbert Everhart, Lige Miller, Bud Turner, Perry Thomas, Rex Smallwood, Jacob Smallwood, Mike and Harry Tucker.

Many local young men excelled in certain positions on baseball teams, including Bill Hammond, Perry Thomas, and Raymond Tucker. Richard Tucker, a brother of Harry, played with the Martinsburg Blue Sox; it is said he could pitch so accurately, he could knock a squirrel from a tree at 90 yards. (He was not going to waste a baseball apparently). Ercel Boyd also was a local baseball pitcher known for his fast ball and curve who successfully tried out for the Martinsburg Blue Ridge team. All three of Paul Miller, Sr.'s sons gained a spot on a team. Charles Miller went on to Buffalo to play with an international team and his brother, Gilbert, joined a western Double A league in Lincoln, Nebraska.

During the Depression, the equipment was cared for by Max Brown and Paul Miller, Sr., who coached the team. Eventually, as money became more scarce, the men used tar tape to hold their baseballs together. There weren't enough gloves for the players either. Baseball competition was interrupted when many young men went off to serve in World War II and was not resumed for some time.

Informal Sports

The community enjoyed many informal sports, too, as occasion and weather permitted. Winter activities included ice skating on local ponds and on the Potomac River. Sleigh riding was another pleasant social activity. It being fine weather in March of 1887, the Marshall ladies ordered the family sleigh to be made ready for a sleighing party. Mary and Leila Marshall, Leila Boteler, Nannie Herr, and Jacqueline anticipated an outing both pleasant and exciting. Unfortunately the horses became frightened and panic followed. One lady fell out, one jumped out, two fainted, and one lady's hands were rubbed raw from holding the reins. Fortunately none was seriously hurt. Deep snows that occasionally fell on the community provided opportunity for other kinds of informal sports. Bill Thompson told me a story of a time in 1936 when the Kearneysville-Leetown road was snowed in with drifts five to seven feet high; the Barron boys dug a path that was about a half-mile long to Kearneysville to get to the Night Owl, a local beer hall.

Probably many of the winter sports were suspended during the winter of 1911-1912; records show that temperatures dropped to between 10^0 and 14^0 below zero on January 18, 1912.

Indoor games that adults played included various kinds of cards; bridge was a favorite. Children's favorites may have been Monopoly, card games or a favorite "Mother May I?" For this latter game, players stand at a starting line, facing a leader or "Mother" who stands a number of feet away. The leader makes requests of individual players, such as "Take two skips forward" or "Make three steps to the side." The player must first ask, "Mother, may I?" Failing this, the player returns to the starting line. Articles from local papers indicate that in the 1920s and 1930s young men found amusement in hunting with BB guns or 22-rifles, which seemed to have been the weapons of choice for hunting rabbits. This was probably a year-round sport.

Trips

There are many news items from the early years about trips both near and far that residents took. Apparently people traveled freely to places such as New York City; Hartford, Connecticut; and Illinois. One item mentions that in 1912 three women spent ten days in Atlantic City.

Within the region, the Baltimore and Ohio Railroad provided excellent transportation to Harpers Ferry and back. Residents traveled there to a circus as early as June, 1853 and to Island Park.; outings there were popular until the bridge to the island and the thrill rides washed away in the flood of 1936.

Kearneysville residents could also make a trip by hack or horse and carriage to attend a circus with a menagerie in Shepherdstown as early as 1867. For 50 cents one would be admitted to the "zoological, ornithological, and equestrian tents" — the main features of the circus.

TOYS FOR ADULTS

New inventions provided much entertainment and opportunities for social interaction. It's not clear when the first autos were owned in Kearneysville, but Dr. Lucas purchased one in 1911; shortly thereafter A.E. Trussell and C.E. Jones could be seen tootling along in a Ford. Today's auto "buff" may find the price of new Ford vehicles in 1927 of interest: A two-door sedan was $495, a four-door sedan was $570; the coupe was $495, the sport coupe was $550.00. A roadster was $395.00 and a Phaeton was $395.00. Trucks were more expensive: A half-ton chassis with cab and express body was $600.00. Advertisements boasted that each vehicle could get 20 to 30 miles per gallon.

In addition to the purchase price, there were a number of other costs associated with owning an automobile in 1925. Licenses had just changed from 30 cents per hundred pounds to a flat rate of $13.00 per ton or less and 60 cents for each 100 pounds over. A certificate of title was $1.00, with a fine of $25 to $100 for driving without one. Gasoline tax was 3.5 cents per gallon.

During the 1920s, the community became more focused on automobiles as a means of travel as well as fun. In the local paper, some prankster chided brothers Charles and Gene Frith for planning a trip in their car to New York City to see if the "sky scrapers worked."

As with other communities, cars provided service, pleasure, but sometimes pain and even tragedy. In March of 1923, during his last year at Leetown High School, Locker Miller was allowed to drive the family car to school. He felt quite pleased to be behind the wheel with his friends, Lucille Brown, Dorothy Horn, and Zack Fleming — until the return trip, when he lost control of the car, tore down several rods of Mr. Bill Fulk's fence, and damaged the car. His passengers were frightened but unhurt. On other occasions mentioned elsewhere, cars became stalled on the railroad tracks, resulting in serious injury or fatalities.

Radios came to Kearneysville during the early 1920s and were the source of fun for some. One Joe Trout claimed that his radio would receive news from Key West, Kalamazoo, Bremenhaven, and Hong Kong. The Templar also reported that Joe had received two valentines by radio but (playfully) wouldn't let anyone see them.

CLUBS

Kearneysville residents have formed and participated in many social clubs throughout the years. These were usually organized around church or civic activity. The Young Men's Christian Association was active quite early in the history of the community, offering a variety of social activities, such as suppers and lectures, although it's not clear where they operated from. In 1878, the Y.M.C.A. held a three-day convocation. By 1885, the group was planning to build a new hall. As usual, suppers were held to help pay for it. By December of that year, the building had been completed. Members of the Y.M.C.A. held an oyster supper for several evenings until the New Year at their new building. It was dedicated in February 1886 with W. H. Morris, Secretary of the Baltimore Association in charge, assisted by E.E. Sheldon, Secretary of the Association. Meetings were held on Saturday and Sunday of the dedication week-end with "good speaking and good singing."

In July of the same year, records show that a series of twelve lectures had been scheduled at the Y.M.C.A. with a prominent person to address each session. The first speaker was Dr. James A. Wiltshire of Baltimore, Maryland. His topic was "The Eye and How to Care for It." A modest admittance charge of two for 50 cents was asked. The group also printed a monthly newsletter called *The Messenger*, sometimes with the help of the Shepherdstown Register Publishing Company. Occasionally, weekend activities were planned as in 1889, when several meetings were scheduled in both the Presbyterian and Reformed Churches for the week-end of February 16. In 1895, "The King's Daughters," a group of players from the Kearneysville vicinity presented a charming play, "Among the Breakers" for a fee of 25 cents at the Y.M.C.A.

The Temperance Union was another organization open to membership of various economic levels. The intent was to preserve the community from alcoholism. It was organized in the County in 1868; branches were formed soon after in Kearneysville and Leetown.

Community activism by the Templars (as Temperance Union members were known) was evidenced in other ways in Kearneysville's early days. Those loafing at Homsher's Cash Store in the evening of March 1872 were in for an impressive sight. The Reverend Jacob Hawkins of Shepherdstown was invited to address the membership at the Presbyterian Church across from Homsher's. About 35 men from the Leetown and Kearneysville Temperance groups met at the Depot, which was nearby, and marched from there to the church with Snowden H. Watson, Esquire of the Leetown Lodge serving as chief marshall. The Leetown reporter for the Shepherdstown Register, who goes by the by-line of "Templar," reported that "the large audience was attentive to the address which was well-delivered."

New officers of the Friends of Templars of Kearneysville were elected in July of 1872. Letters of the alphabet were used sometimes to designate position of each as follows: W.G. Butler, P; T.W. Hammond, A; J. Hamill, R.S.; T.P. Licklider, E.S.; A. Trump, Treasurer; J.V. Moore, Chaplain; C.E. Ruckle, A.C.; J. Smallwood, I.S.; J. Gageby, O.S.; D.W. Border, Ex- President. The same month, Kearneysville Council No. 11. Sons of Temperance attended the annual picnic at Balch Grove in Leetown; Dr. D.W. Border led the procession. Other men who served in an official capacity at different times included: Samuel Licklider, J.H. Logie, Alex Butler, W.C. Byers, W.T. Rutherford, W.H. Burnett, Thomas Tucker, J.H. Bruner, and J.W. Clower.

By 1876 the Temperance Movement was growing. There was a conference held at the Temperance Camp Ground in September of that year, perhaps at Balch Woods. About 7,000 people from the surrounding area were reported to have attended. The Kearncysville group was well-represented. During the week, services were held twice each day for the Templars by the Y.M.C.A. The Reverend John Logie opened the camp meeting with prayer each day. The next year, the Templars organized a "cold water" group for juveniles.

No news is available from newspapers in the intervening years, but mention of the Templars is made again in 1909, indicating that the group was still active. In 1911, a law went into effect that there would be no licensed saloons in Jefferson County. Although Mr. John Frith of Leetown held a license to sell liquor, Kearneysville remained dry except for the bootleggers. Little of the Temperance Movement was reported in the succeeding years as locals became involved in aiding the Allies from 1914 through 1918 and afterwards. The 18th Amendment was ratified on January 29, 1918. This prohibited the sale of liquor but was repealed by the 21st Amendment in 1933. It is not clear how these amendments affected the Kearneysville community.

The Grange was a national movement to promote better farming practices. By 1877 a local Grange had been organized in Kearneysville, and members met in July of that year to help organize the Pomona Grange in Charles Town. Apparently there were a number of existing Granges in the county. A notice shows that the County Council Patrons of Husbandry (or Grange) held their September 16, 1876 meeting at Kearneysville and were urging full membership attendance for the session, which was to begin at 10 a.m.

Another social group was the Kearneysville Kummunity Klub; early in 1919, members were preparing to debate the Shenandoah Junction Team on the topic "There should be a tax placed on absentee lands such as the absentee ownership of land would become unprofitable." No further information was found about this club.

Little is also known about the purpose or activities of the Patriotic Order Sons of America. As reported in the Advocate, January 20, 1925, the Washington Camp No. 30 had a meeting to elect officers. These names reflect residents who were prominent in the community: Past President, T.O. Everhart; President George H.Cox; Vice President Max Brown; Master of Forms S.W. Thomas; Recording Secretary A.E.Trussell; Right Sentinel R.E.Tucker, Treasurer John B. Hopper, Conductor Charles Turner; Inspector C.H.Fleming; Guard R.M.Everhart, Jr.; Chaplain C.E.Rutherford; Left Sentinel J.F. Amey; Trustees John H. Hopper, J.P. Amey, W.F. Wilt, and Vice President State Camp P.O.S of A, W.F. Wilt. The article notes that W.F. Wilt attended the state camp on August 19,

1925. Another item from the same paper, shown below, indicates that P.O.S. of A. group could be made up of people from throughout the eastern part of the State.

P.O.S. of A. Officers

At the State convention of the Patriotic Order Sons of American at Towlesburg last week the following officers for the ensuing year were elected: P.R. Under, of Morgan county, president; W.X. Arey, of Charles Town, vice-president; Herbert C. Miller, Kearneysville, State master of form; D.C. Dolly, of Charles Town, secretary; I.G. Gale, of Terra Alta, conductor; I.T. Johnson, of Levels, inspector; C.E. Harden, of Berkeley Springs and W.R. Wable, of Rowlesburg, guards; and I.H. Irvin, of Charles Town, Trustee.

Each officer is moved up one seat from the position he occupied last year. The retiring president is O.B. Schokey of Berkeley Springs. It was decided to hold the 1933 convention in Charles Town.

Plate 57. Article from **The Advocate.**

The first 4-H Club that I was able to find from my research was formed in the early 1920s. Margie Stanley, who was a member of this club, the Cheerful Workers, recalls that Reva Copenhaver was the leader and Heath Holden was the County Extension Agent. The club members met at the grade school after 4 p.m. Lige Miller was a member, and recalls that other members were Betty and Edward McKee (cousins), Louie Angelo, Floyd Kemp, and Anna R. Hammond.

By 1933 the active 4-H club was named Rocky Glen. Heath Holden continued as county agent; the local leader was Betty McKee and members included President Nancy Miller, Josephine Ambrose, Elsie and Donald Heinz, Gilbert Miller, Edward Moore, and Virginia Miller. When I belonged to the club, we met in the homes of various members. After the business of the group was completed, we played games and had refreshments. Projects did not include the variety of later years, but were limited to sewing, cooking, canning, wood crafts, and specific farm learning activities. Members were urged to enter projects as exhibits in the county fair. The County Extension Office does not have records of these early years. Fannie Boyd and I, with the help of others, organized the Evergreen 4-H Club in 1945. The club recently celebrated 50 years of growth.

POLITICS

Jockeying of power is a theme throughout all human interactions, and politics played a part in each chapter of Kearneysville's history. Residents participated in local, state and county initiatives. A few highlights of political activities are included here.

Because of Civil War activities, the court records had been moved from Charles Town to Lexington (Virginia) and then to Rumsey Hall in Shepherdstown in1861. In 1871 a new building to house the functions of the County Court was to be constructed in Charles Town. The Kearneysville residents who lived north of the B&O along the Turnpike joined Shepherdstown residents in protesting this move — to no avail.

The Democratic Conservative Party was active early in the existence of the community, as shown in the news item below from the *Shepherdstown Register* of 1874. Later, in the primary election of May, 1876, the Party chose Isaac Strider as Delegate, with James H. Grove, alternate, to the Charleston convention. These men paid nothing to ride the trains. This didn't sit well with local citizens

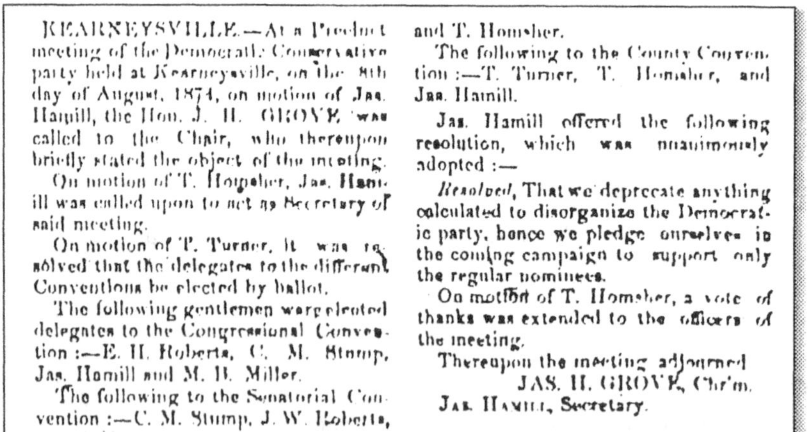

KEARNEYSVILLE.—At a Precinct meeting of the Democratic Conservative party held at Kearneysville, on the 8th day of August, 1874, on motion of Jas. Hamill, the Hon. J. H. GROVE was called to the Chair, who thereupon briefly stated the object of the meeting.

On motion of T. Homsher, Jas. Hamill was called upon to act as Secretary of said meeting.

On motion of T. Turner, it was resolved that the delegates to the different Conventions be elected by ballot.

The following gentlemen were elected delegates to the Congressional Convention:—E. H. Roberts, C. M. Stump, Jas. Hamill and M. B. Miller.

The following to the Senatorial Convention:—C. M. Stump, J. W. Roberts, and T. Homsher.

The following to the County Convention:—T. Turner, T. Homsher, and Jas. Hamill.

Jas. Hamill offered the following resolution, which was unanimously adopted:—

Resolved, That we deprecate anything calculated to disorganize the Democratic party, hence we pledge ourselves in the coming campaign to support only the regular nominees.

On motion of T. Homsher, a vote of thanks was extended to the officers of the meeting.

Thereupon the meeting adjourned.

JAS. H. GROVE, Chr'm.

JAS. HAMILL, Secretary.

Plate 58. Record of Democratic Conservative delegate selection for Conventions.

who felt over-charged on their farm products by the B&O. Mr. John Grantham, a Middleway activitist and member of the Democratic Party, stepped into the fray declaring no free passage would be given officials. The B&O railroad resolved this dispute by rescinding the free rides. Also of significance in this election was the candidacy of Mr. Rogers, the carriage maker, who had lived in Kearneysville for twenty years; he entered the race for Jefferson County Magistrate but lost.

Local Democrats began early in the year to plan for the Presidential election of 1876. Isaac Strider, Vice-President of the Democrat Executive Committee presided at the meeting in support of the Tilden-Hendricks ticket for President/Vice President. A club was organized, and a committee was appointed for raising a pole with a banner. Mrs. Drawbaugh, wife of the merchant Alex Drawbaugh, and her committee designed a small blue banner with "Reform" at the top. Another committee was appointed to send invitations to the speakers.

J.C. Bitner, Secretary, was named pro temp for the ceremony with the Charles Town Band invited to play. Willliam B. Daniels, Esquire, introduced V.M. Firor, Esquire, the speaker. Other speakers were Mr. C.G. Faulkner and R.S. Eighelberger of Martinsburg. Thirty or forty members were present, including the ladies. Democrats for Tilden and Hendricks who thought their candidates had won in November with 184 votes were disappointed in March when the House of Representatives declared Hayes and Wheeler winners with 185 votes.

Although there have been women serving in the background in political campaign controversy, the name Mary Beau, correspondent for the *Shepherdstown Register*, takes a position early in the presidential race of 1884. Senator Blaine's name had been proposed in 1876 for Republican presidential candidate. He was bypassed in that race but became a candidate in 1884 with General John A. Logan, Vice President. The Democrats appointed several Kearneysville residents to their election committee including John P. Kearfott, Caspar Stump, Frank Homsher and James Trussell. E. Willis Wilson was invited to speak. Sentiment ran high among locals on both sides in this presidential election. Ms. Beau's pledge was to garner 150 votes. Perhaps she was successful, but Grover Cleveland won the most electoral votes. Cleveland lost the following election in 1889 to William Henry Harrison.

In October of 1887, President Cleveland designated November 25 as Thanksgiving Day.

Cleveland was notorious for his numerous vetoes. When he left the White House in 1889, wags wondered if he left his veto behind.

Other wags noted, "The (new) President Harrison won't find many rascals to turn out. But it's also reasonable that he won't find many rascals to turn in."

Still others opinioned, "Mrs. Harrison is quite put out that Congress won't enlarge the White House. Still she is not mad enough to move."

When electric lights were installed in several Kearneysville homes and businesses, there was talk of incorporating the town, electing a mayor and lighting the principal streets. That idea did not seem to take root. Some community-minded residents conceived the idea of a Village Improvement Society in 1917, however. Unfortunately in that year the U.S. became involved in WWI; establishing a Red Cross unit seemed to take precedence.

Kearneysville was a large enough community that some legal services were provided locally by county officials. For example, a record from February 23, 1878 noted in briefs that when Judge Rogers held court in Kearneysville, he hung the prisoner first and tried him afterwards. Another record shows that by October 17, 1884 the Kearneysville Justice of the Peace was Mr. J.P. Kearfott. Yet another record shows that on October 14, 1918 the Sheriff of Jefferson County sat at the Depot to collect real estate taxes from 9 until 12 noon.

CHURCHES

Presbyterian Church

As early as the 1830's, the Reverend Dr. John Matthews and the Reverend Henry Matthews served as ministers for the Presbyterian population of Kearneysville. But it wasn't until 1869 that a plan for building the church was formed and land obtained. In that year Henry Bitner, then of Cumberland County, Pennsylvania, gave a deed for the sum of one dollar to the trustees of the Kearneysville Presbyterian Church. The trustees were J.J. Miller, B.S. McIntyre, and James V. Moore. Relatively few facts are known about these early church years.

It's not clear how large the congregation was at first, but it was joined by Sarah, Abraham, and Solomon Miller and his second wife, Catherine. Records show that Reverend James A. Armstrong was serving as pastor in 1876 at a salary of $150 annually. At that time George T. McIntyre and Thomas Hammond were trustees. Services were usually held at 3 p.m. on Sunday, to accommodate the minister's schedule at another church. In 1881, $33.00 in land and fencing money was donated by Henry Bitner; he later petitioned the Superior Court to open a road west of the church in 1883, which was accepted. The road was to be 30 feet wide and simply consisted of clearing a path and putting down stone.

The congregation voted to redecorate the interior of the church, a task that was

Pranks FOR THE Memory

February 1889 At a "hugging bee" to raise money for a local church, a blindfolded gentleman hugged his wife for several minutes before he realized who she was. When he found out, he asked for his 15 cents back.

One Hallowe'en during the 1920's, Lige Miller rigged a "tic-toc" to the door of Stella and Douglas Morgan's home. He hid in a nearby bush and pulled a string so that it kept time with the player piano music coming from the house. Stella knew what was happening and called out, "Where's my knife?" Lige ran for his life without retrieving his tic-toc..

Lige Miller knew how to — and did — play an autoharp while riding a horse.

Fred Smith thumbed his way to Florida in 1932 and rode his bike to Chicago in 1933. The bike ride took ten and one-half days. In January he was contemplating a trip to Panama. Instead, in August of 1936, he joined the National Guard Infantry.

completed in 1885. Reverend Charles Ghieslin, who was the minister at the time, held a dedication service marking the occasion.

By 1900 there were 70 members. In 1903 Dr. Ghieslin resigned his commission, although he returned in 1908 and held the charge until his retirement in 1927. Apparently membership waned, because in 1939 there were sixty communicants and 53 children on the Sunday School roll. R.A. Hammond served as Superintendent.

A number of men church members held leadership positions for extended periods of time as shown below. Most of these last names are still familiar in the community.

Name	Office/Length of Service (Years)	Death Date
H.C. Marshall	Elder/Trustee (years unknown)	1938
Walter Thomas	Deacon/Sexton (years unknown)	1937
G.W. Seibert	Ruling Elder 36 years	1927
Thomas Hammond	Elder & Superintendent 22 years	1928
Milton S. Miller	Ruling Elder 29 years	1916
Joseph Hess	Sexton (years unknown)	1912

Upkeep of the church seems to have been a consistent challenge. In 1912 the original paling fence was replaced by a wire one with metal posts and a gate in front. The church was repainted inside and out in 1923, and the floor was refinished and stained. At some point in time, inside shutters were added. The community supported the church with gifts outright. One example is the silver offering plates that are still in use, given by Miss Effie McIntyre in 1926, in memory of her sister Mary Irvie McIntyre.

The community also supported the church by giving and attending fund-raisers. For example, the Girls Society held an ice cream festival in June, 1895 at the home of Thomas Hammond, Walper's Cross Roads, to which the public was invited. That same summer, the Presbyterians held a lawn party from 5 to 10 p.m. on two consecutive days. Supper could be purchased for 25 cents with cake and ice cream extra. The money collected was used to pay for a new organ.

There was an active Missionary Society which began in 1883. The Society supported needs of other churches, especially in foreign countries. A Christian Endeavor was active from 1922-1933, mostly for outreach purposes. Youth of the Reformed Church joined with Presbyterians during the years 1923 to 1927.

Sometimes meetings were held at one church; sometimes at the other. Socials were a place to chat with friends while members of an organization sold refreshments for a particular project. Records show several of these that were held by groups in the Presbyterian Church. For example, finding it necessary to supply the church library, the women of the Church held a lawn festival, or social, on July 23rd and 24th, 1886. Everyone was invited to attend.

The building was also a place for other, non-religious community events to be held. Records show that frequently concerts were held at the Presbyterian Church. A small fee of 25 cents or 10 cents was charged, depending on an adult or a child. On one occasion, music was provided by young people from Martinsburg, Shepherdstown, Harpers Ferry, and Kearneysville.

Although little information was found regarding the cemetery, some unmarked graves were covered during the construction of Route 9 in the 1920s, including that of Thomas W. Rutherford. A list of names on existing tombstones is included in Appendix A.

One last story associated with the Presbyterian Church was told to me by Audrainne Seibert, who attended there with her parents and Lillian Flagg, a neighbor before they moved to Martinsburg. She recalls no sermon but can describe in detail the Sunday-best hat worn by Mrs. Kearfott. It was black, quite small without a brim, and came to a point in front, where it was adorned with a

Plate 59. Presbyterian Church, built in 1869. Picture taken in 1995.

Plate 60. St. Paul Baptist Church, built in 1883. Picture taken in 1995.

large jeweled ornament. The pin wobbled each time Mrs. Kearfott moved her head — an enormous distraction for a six-year old!

St. Paul Baptist Church

According to an article in the *Shepherdstown Register* of February 28, 1880, a Free Will Baptist Church was begun with a foundation planned for thirty-two feet long by twenty-one feet eight inches wide. The deed shows that land was acquired from Benjamin Carter in 1879 by Trustees John H. Fox, George Mason, and George Johnson. In October of 1883 Trustees John H. Fox, George W. Johnson, Lewis Sommer and Harrison Morgan purchased a quarter acre of land from George Watson and another trustee (perhaps Ben Carter) for $172. This was probably land for the cemetery. At that time Pastor Reverend Rawson and several Christians gathered as the first congregation of what is now known as the St. Paul Baptist Church. Early ministers included Reverend Nickon, Reverend Carter, Reverend Rody Butler, Reverend Thomas Jackson, and Reverend Coleman.

The black church was also a center of community social interaction. There was an annual summer festival with food and refreshments served at moderate rates. I was able to find a record of one of these as early as June, 1896. Also, St. Paul Baptist Church hosted a concert by native-born Africans on June 13 and 14 of 1890.

Although little information was found regarding the cemetery, a list of names on existing tombstones is included in the Appendixes. In addition to carefully keeping the cemetery neat, congregations across the years have maintained the church in good repair. Originally the edifice had a gabled front. In 1912, a front section with a tower and a side gabled section with poured concrete foundation were added. The original building is still used for services today.

Grace Reformed Church

About six families made up the first congregation of the Grace Reformed Church: the Borders, Roberts, Osbornes, Getzendanners, Hoffmans, and Trumps. Before the church was built, the parishioners met at the local schoolhouse. The land was donated by Clara Getzendanner and Dr. Daniel Webster Border in the summer of 1884. The lot adjoins property once settled by Robert Lemen, an early Kearneysville settler. On September 19, followers of the Reformed faith broke ground for their new church, having hired James P. Conley as the builder. Records show that in October, 1884, Allen Cole fell from the roof to the ground during construction; fortunately he was not seriously injured. But this seems to indicate that the building was rising quickly. However, an early winter set in and work was delayed.

Finally in the summer of 1885 the nearly-completed church was dedicated at a service officiated by Reverend B.F. Bausmann, the first pastor. The building was 27 by 50 feet with a pulpit recess, belfry, and interior vestibule. The ceiling and all other interior woodwork were of yellow pine, and finished with oil. The entire cost, including furniture, was $1,650. At the dedication a debt of $200 remained, which members of the community and congregation contributed during the service.

No major structural changes were made to the church until after 1950, although periodically repairs and minor changes were made, as noted in the church records. In 1914, the interior and exterior walls were repainted; electric current was installed and electric bulbs replaced the candles in the two chandeliers in 1919. Originally the sanctuary was heated by two pot-bellied coal stoves. These were replaced in the 1930s by two oil-burning stoves as noted in the Ladies' Aid Society minutes. The final payment on the stoves was made in 1937. The belfry stood vacant for many years, and no one today seems to know where the bell came from or when it was installed.

Plate 61. Grace Reformed Church, built 1885. Picture taken 1995.

A chapel organ with brass pipes was purchased from A.M. Ordway and Company of Hagerstown, Maryland in February of 1911. Youngsters would compete to pump the organ; the trick was to make sure that enough air entered the chamber before the hymn was to begin. I recently talked with Margie Stanley Johnston, who has been a member of Grace Reformed Congregation for 78 years, about her memories of the church and the organ. Margie was born in 1909, and she and her brother, Henry, were taken to the church at a very early age by their parents, Mr. and Mrs. John Stanley. She clearly recalls images of Miss Leona Obsourn seated on the organ bench, fingers on the keyboard and feet on the peddles. Young Ed McDowell was behind the organ, pumping air into the bellows. He was given 25-cents each Sunday for performing this task.

Lillie Stanley, Margie's aunt, followed Leona as organist. But this was also a position that Margie aspired to: having taken lessons in Shepherdstown and showing some aptitude at age thirteen, Margie was allowed to play the organ one Sunday as a substitute for Lillie — possibly without Lillie's complete consent. Margie remembers feeling great pleasure in leading the congregation in singing with the organ music in the background, and she was proud to be filling an adult role. Unfortunately, Aunt Lillie took exception, and immediately withdrew her membership from the church. Margie faithfully continued as organist for more than 60 years.

Across the years, pumping the organ became an adventure for children, although sometimes they would fall asleep during the sermons. Then Margie would need to rouse them gently when it was time for the last hymn. This magnificent old organ was replaced by an electric one sometime in late 1957.

Some of the early recorded religious activities reflect great diversity in the use of the church. In 1887 the Missionary Society of Grace Reformed Church held a service of recitations and music and an address by Reverend A.S. Weber of Westminster, Maryland. The public was invited. By the following year a Sunday School had been organized and children presented an Easter Service on Monday, March 31 at 7 p.m. Then in April of 1888 a concert of sacred music was held at the church. Youth from Martinsburg, Shepherdstown, Harpers Ferry and Kearneysville performed vocal and instrumental pieces. Admission was 25 cents and 10 cents for children.

On a lovely July day in 1891, Miss Sevilla Trump became the bride of Clifford Roach of Baltimore, Maryland. The ceremony, held at Grace Reformed Church was conducted by three ministers: Reverend Charles Trump, Reverend George G. Everhart, and Reverend Charles Ghieslin. The wedding march was played by Miss Daisy Yantz. Miss Trump was attended by four ladies. Local guests attending the wedding and the reception afterward included: Mr. and Mrs. Daniel Getzendanner, Phoebe, May and Frank; Mr. and Mrs. George Hoffman, Mr. and Mrs. J. P. Kearfott; Dr. and Mrs. Daniel Border; Dr. and Mrs. Lucas; Mr. and Mrs. Vincent

Moore, the Misses McIntyre; Mrs. Homsher and daughter, Virginia; Miss Laura Hammond; Miss Jessie Henkle; Mrs. H.A. Bitner and daughters, Leila and Blanche. This was the earliest recorded marriage that was held in the church.

In January 1910, the Reformed Congregation joined in the celebration for the 50th wedding anniversary of Reverend and Mrs. David Miller. It was reported that among the gifts was a good sum of money, and one parishioner showed his admiration for the Reverend with these words: "He is remarkably well-preserved."

Through the years a number of pastors have served the church, as can be seen below.

Tenure	Pastors	New Members
1884-1889	Benjamin Bausmann	Information Unavailable
1889-1901	George Everhart	Information Unavailable
1902-1905	Joseph Guy	Information Unavailable
1906-1912	John David Miller	Information Unavailable
1912-1913	Charles Freeman	Eliza Amey, Fanny Cox, Margaret Getzendanner, Mr. & Mrs. G.H. Hoffman, Mrs. G.L. Hoffman, Myrtle Lashhorn, Mr. & Mrs. D.L. McGruder, Laura Osbourn, Leona Osbourn, Florence Owens, Lila Powell, Mrs. C.J. Roberts, Cora Smallwood, Bell Stanley, Mr. & Mrs. John Stanley, Mr. & Mrs. F.O. Trump, Mrs. Thomas VanMetre, Mr. & Mrs. Edward Whittington, Della Wyndham
1914-1915	Guy Bready	Information Unavailable
1916-1925	Stephen Flickinger	Ruth Cox, Lelia Smallwood, Ethel Stanley, Dayton Stanley, Margie Smallwood, Mrs. Newton VanMetre, Mary Fowler (and mother), Floyd Owens, Frank Owens, Thomas VanMetre Jr., Ben Whittington and family, Ralph Border, Blanche Foster, Henry & Margie Stanley, M.M. Stanley, Elisabeth Trump, Alice VanMetre, Marjorie Lyons, Emma Osborne
1928-1938	Joseph Guy	Information Unavailable
1939-1943	William Solly	Information Unavailable

In February 1898, an awfully touchy woman brought suit against a newspaper for printing that her husband had gone on to a happier place.

Efforts to upkeep the church began early in its existence, were held in various halls, and resulted in many community projects for its members, who contributed resources of time, effort and money. But projects were also social, and in this sense helped to build bonds among residents of Kearneysville. Grace Reformed Church sponsored a magic lantern exhibition and selections of choral music at the Young Men's Christian Association Hall in early December 1888. A small admission of 5 cents and 10 cents was charged. The Ladies of the Church held a mid-winter festival at the Y.M.C.A. Hall in February of 1896 to raise money. This event featured oysters and continued for three evenings. Perhaps these were annual events, since another article was found that cited Trump Hall as the location of a sumptuous supper served by the Ladies of the Reformed Church on February 10 and 11, 1911. Sixty dollars were netted but cost of the meal was not reported.

The Ladies Aid Society tracked financial efforts on behalf of the church. An example between May 1937 and March 1938 — when the membership was 25 — is shown in the table below.

Debit		**Credit**	
Labor for church	$4.07	Festival	$48.85
Final payment on two oil stoves	$73.27	Men's fund on stoves	$48.00
Expense for soup sale	$5.05	Surprise box	$4.25
200 gallon fuel oil	$14.50	Sunday School on stoves	$5.00
Expense for quilt	$2.48	John Stanley on stoves	$38.00
Flowers	$2.53	Soup Sales	$35.36
Card for Rev. Guy	$0.25	Christian Endeavor on stoves	$10.00
Total	$102.15		$188.46

Individual memorials have also sustained the church across time. The most recent contribution before 1950 was that of L.D.

Getzendanner bequeathed $500 in cash in 1944 to the Reformed Church in memory of his parents, Mr. and Mrs. Daniel Getzendanner. A condition of the bequest was that a plaque be purchased as a memorial and the church could keep the remaining funds. A plaque was purchased for $100.

Methodist Episcopal Church

The land for the Methodist Episcopal Church was bought from William Stewart in 1890. Sometime between then and 1906, the Church was built. It is bounded by the John C. Heinz house and the Stewart farm and orchard on Quarry Road. Only the name of Alan Cole, Trustee, is available. Isaiah Allen, a former member, told me that when the congregation became too small to support the church, it was closed, probably in the 1940s. Some people changed their membership to St. Paul's in Kearneysville; others joined a church in the neighboring towns.

Mr. Stewart gave the deed to the church trustees for a cemetery lot. The cemetery does not abut the church property but lies a short distance away, along a dirt road to the orchard. It is still being used. The tombstone of William Goens, who died in 1919, is the oldest marked grave in this cemetery. Other names on gravestones are included in Appendix A.

In the early 1940s, a Methodist Episcopal Meeting House was constructed on the site. Both the Church and the Meeting House are no longer used and have fallen into disrepair.

Old School Baptist Church

One other church affiliation will be mentioned although exact dates are not available. Lige Miller told me that the Old School Baptist Congregation met at the home of his great uncle, Abram Miller, several times a year. Elder Lefferts conducted the service. As a youth in the 1920s, Lige, a son of Mr. and Mrs. Herbert Miller, said he found it unfair that he should be kept in for the services while his cousins, Paul Jr., and Charles were permitted to play ball outside. The property is now known as "Rellim" and is owned by Mr. and Mrs. Charles Miller.

"When I die," said a married man, "I want to go where there is no snow to shovel."

Said his wife, "I presume you will."

War Years

War Years

Kearneysville residents have responded to war efforts across time in various ways. As mentioned previously, Robert and Nicholas Lemen served in the Revolutionary War. Robert Lemen also served in the War of 1812 with Captain Cockrill's company under Colonel Griffin Taylor. Then, in 1848, Private Thomas Turner served with Battery C, 4th Regiment Artillery. Little is known of the activities that supported these early wars.

CIVIL WAR

Expansion in Kearneysville was slowed between the years 1861-1865, when much of the nation was engaged in mortal conflict. Drawn into the War for States rights, either by kinsmen or friendship, locals joined the Confederacy since Kearneysville was within the boundaries of the State of Virginia. It is known that some area farmers owned slaves. In the 1930s, slave quarters were still visible at the property that Minor Hurst had owned in 1860. Also, the Dandridge's had slaves; there may have been others.

For whatever reason, when the Confederate States sent out the call for mobilization, some local young men responded. A partial list of these men is included below.

Company A
Second Infantry Stonewall Brigade
Sgt. Thomas McIntyre
Sgt. Charles C. Trussell
Pvt. Henry C. Hunter
Pvt. James T. Trussell
Lt. James A. Hurst

Company H
Second Virginia Regiment
Capt. J.H. Hunter
Pvt. W.T. Rutherford
Pvt. J.A. Rutherford
Pvt. Milton B. Miller

Company A
Twelfth Virginia Regiment
J.P. Kearfott
Hugh McKee
Mayberry McKee

One of the ways that the War Department tried to prevent the Rebels from disturbing transportation of any sort by rail was to build block houses along the lines. One of these was located at Kearneysville.

The presence of Union soldiers caused great concern for local Rebs, who had leave to visit their families. Anna McKee told me of an ancestor who had lived for several generations on farmland bounded by the B&O. Having spent his leave with his family, Mayberry McKee wore his farm clothes to the barn at dusk, changed there to his uniform, and when darkness was complete, slipped out and returned to his contingent.

A more charming tale reveals the courtesy extended Southern belles by the Union soldiers amid the violence of war. This story comes from Leila Bitner Grantham, a direct descendant of the Kearneys. The Kearney home stood within twenty feet of the B&O Station and fronted the tracks. The watch regularly patrolled the area.

A Reb had spent the daylight hours in the Kearney home, visiting his kinsman. He felt obliged to leave this safe haven as soon as dark fell in order to report to his unit on time. A plan was revealed by a lovely lady in the home. When she made a trip to the outhouse (which stood behind the home), the watch moved to the opposite side of the home to give her privacy. At this point, of course, the Reb slipped out the rear door and safely made his escape. Another story of John H. Fox, told by his son, Dewey, is included elsewhere in this history.

Two skirmishes have been reported that occurred along the Smithfield-Shepherdstown Pike in the Kearneysville vicinity. On July 16, 1863, a contingent of Federal Cavalry left Shepherdstown and advanced toward Kearneysville. They were met by mounted Confederate forces. Due to the uneven terrain, both sides dismounted. The Confederates could congratulate themselves that the Federals retreated to Shepherdstown. The second engagement occurred on October 22, 1864. In this instance, Lt. General Jubal Early's forces repulsed the Union Cavalry under Major General

T.A. Torbet.

Because of the intensity of engagements in the Shepherdstown area, facilities there were hard pressed to care for all the wounded. Thus, field hospitals were used in Kearneysville to care for those who could be moved. Since there were no churches here at that time, homes or tents were put into service. The Kearfott's secluded front lawn might have been an ideal place to care for the wounded, but I couldn't find any record of this. St. Bartholomew's Episcopal Church at Leetown was made available.

Finally the war ended, elections were held to organize the Federal government, and Congress settled in to make restitution to citizens for damage incurred during the War. An Act of Congress in 1871 is explained by "The Templar" in the text below, which was taken from the *Shepherdstown Register* in 1872.

> The U.S. Claims Commission sat at Kearneysville some weeks since. I understand that claims to a large amount were handed in. They will convene at Charlestown[1] in the latter part of July. For the purpose of informing those who have been misinformed I would say that by Act of Congress of 1871, these claims are for the benefit only of those States that were under insurrection, including the counties of Jefferson and Berkeley, the remainder of West Virginia excluded. The Commission pays damages only for property actually used by the Union army, and not for property lost or destroyed, either purposely or accidentally.

On April 29, 1872, the Claims Court held a session at Kearneysville with Judge Thomas H. Hargest presiding. Evidence was taken in some thirty cases of war claims against the United States involving between $30,000 and $35,000. Since all claims were not settled at that time, plans were made for another session to be held later. Colonel G.W.Z. Black of Frederick, Maryland prosecuted the claims. The Templar, a Leetown columnist, reported in the *Shepherdstown Register* that "the gentlemen composing the court made many friends during their brief stay, and their manner of conducting business was generally commended."

Regretfully, news of activities in the Kearneysville homes during the Civil War years is quite limited. I did find one item,

---

[1] This refers to Charles Town. The name was changed when Charleston became the state capitol.

however, that involves an Afro-American and Miss Hannah Hurst's carriage. Miss Hurst's carriageman saddled her horse, hitched it to the carriage one morning in 1857 and rode off to Frederick, Maryland, where he sold the carriage. It was of such fine workmanship, however, that it was easily identified and reclaimed. The driver was captured.

It wasn't until June 10, 1909 at a meeting of the Sons of the Confederacy, that J.B. VanMetre urged members to erect markers at the 25 engagement sights in Jefferson County. Donations were accepted and John C. Heinz was awarded the contract to make the concrete obelisks with the logo of the Confederacy on them. The one shown below originally stood at the railroad underpass in Kearneysville. Recently, due to vandalism, it was restored and moved to the property of James Welsh.

Plate 62. Civil War marker.

WORLD WAR I

Perhaps editors or the *Shepherdstown Register* didn't realize the impending significance of World War I, because when President Wilson was on the verge of declaring war on Germany in February 1917, the news didn't make the front page of the newspaper. And even when the President signed a declaration of war, the *Register* included it on the second page of the April 12 issue. However, villagers had telephones and would have known of these national events in spite of the fact that national radio did not come into general public use until 1920.

June 5 came quickly that year — the date that all males between 18 and 25 had to register for military service. Many from

Kearneysville served, as can be seen below. Note that African Americans and Whites served in different units. Dr. Ernest H. Bitner served in the Medical Corps in France in 1918.

World War I Enlistees 1917-1918[2]

Robert Earl Dorsey	Walter Hugh Hill
Paxton Jones	Wilbur Bushrod Thomas
John W.F. Whittington	Samuel C. Heinz
Paul Miller, Sr.	Thomas Briscoe
Paul B. Goens	Angus Carter
James McDaniel	John Ferugson
Marion Hite Lucas	James Goens
Allen Washington	Henry T. Carter
Tom Campbell	Kip Roper (deferred)

NOTES: African-Americans and whites served in different units. Major John Lucas was wounded and received the Purple Heart. Dr. Ernest Bitner served in the Medical Corps in France in 1918.

Few stories of these men have survived. However, John Ferguson, who died in 1995 a few days before his 100th birthday, shared his memories of this war with me. He was 21 when he made his first trip away from home, which was also his journey into the war. He recalls leaving by train with Angus Carter, Thomas A. Briscoe, James Goens, Randolph Brown and Allen Washington that day. After Boot Camp, John was assigned a different unit from the other men and was sent to France. He spoke to me of the trenches, the mud, the cold, and the frightening sound of shells.

Farmers were not deferred from war efforts in WWI as they were in later wars. Hugh Hill served his two years of U.S. participation at Camp Meade, Maryland. As a youth, his father called him "little man." Years later, he told his daughter, Elizabeth, that when he returned home he weighed 155 pounds, more than he weighed at any other time in his life.

Samuel Heinz had been married six months when he enlisted in 1917 — in spite of the fact that both his parents were German born. In addition to the Army uniform, the only other tangible reference to his year spent in France were the letters he received from

---

2 Source: Bushong, Millard (1941), *A History of Jefferson County.*

Genevieve, a paramour that he met in Europe, after he returned home. In these letters, she continued to praise the American efforts in repulsing the German army from French soil.

Those on the home front shared in the war effort as well. Early in 1918, women in the village organized a Red Cross Chapter in cooperation with the Shepherdstown Branch of the Red Cross. In February of that year, the women met to elect officers. Although the meeting place was not reported, one might surmise the group met at the home of Mrs. Bates Hammond. What local individual would be better informed of the Red Cross efforts than a registered nurse? Twenty-seven members came together to elect officers and make their plans. Mrs. Nannie Kearfott was elected president; Mrs. Bates Hammond, Secretary; and Mrs. Joseph Trout, Treasurer.

The first contribution to the Red Cross was $40. As a working goal, everyone in the community who raised chickens was asked to give the money from the sale of eggs collected on the last Sunday of each month. In March, $25 was collected and in April $44.71. Later that year, at a benefit lawn party at the home of Mrs. J.P. Kearfott, $145 was given to the Red Cross. This event was advertised in the local newspapers, and visitors from Shepherdstown and Charles Town areas supported the effort. Another organization committed to raising money for the war was the United War Activities Fund Drive. Miss Annie McDonald, Mrs. H.C. Marshall and Mrs. G.P. Morrison worked through this organization.

The Federal Government programs touched everyone's life. In the fall of 1917, the Post Office sold War Savings Stamps at 25 cents each. James Grantham of Middleway visited the schools and urged the children to buy these stamps. Also, in an attempt to save gasoline, the government issued statements to reduce travel: "Unlimited joy riding will not be tolerated." On March 29, 1918, Daylight Saving time went into effect as a measure to save energy. As late as October of that year, research had proven that gas masks could be made from charcoal obtained from burned coconut shells and fruit pits. The government was asking all households to begin saving the pits immediately and the Red Cross to arrange for pick-up.

During the war years, men's hair cuts were between 15 cents and 25 cents. A year's subscription to the *Shepherdstown Register* was $1.50. Sugar sold for 8.5 to 9 cents per pound and was rationed. Turkeys sold for between 12 and 18 cents per pound. An interesting note is that corn meal and flour had to be purchased in equal amounts.

By November 7, 1918, the war was practically over, and on November 11 the Armistice was signed by all warring parties. It was estimated that it would take two years to demobilize. With the Great War ended, the draft was cancelled by General Crowder at the order of President Wilson.

The war was over but the effects continued to be felt. Some commodities were still limited: Two pounds of corn meal had to be purchased with each five pounds of flour; certificates for the purchase of sugar were in effect, although they were gradually phased out. The effort to assist in rebuilding of Western Europe was enormous. Under the direction of Herbert Hoover, North America gave generously. Twenty million tons of grain or 60 percent of the total needed was provided during the first year of U.S. involvement. This locality as well as all of West Virginia felt the need to help. When C.W. Blue, on behalf of the Federation of Farm Bureaus called on our farmers, they generously sent seed by the bushel to assist the farmers in Serbia.

No fatalities of local servicemen have been discovered. However, Major John Lucas, son of Dr. and Mrs. C.C. Lucas was wounded in France in 1918 and awarded the Purple Heart. At the conclusion, the Federal Government promised $60 to each veteran of the war who had been honorably discharged. When the promise was not kept, there was a march on Washington in 1919. It is not known if any local veterans participated.

Activities that supported the war efforts of World War II extend beyond the scope of this history. However, a list of those who served is included below for the reader's information.

Chauncey Allen	Frank G. Powell, Jr.
Thomas W. Campbell	Harry Powell
Arthur Carter	Walter E. Rodgers
Benjamin F. Carter	John C. Roper, Jr.
Charles E. Clemmons	Charles Ross
Garland Demory	Moselle Ross
Charles L. Ferguson	James H. Smith
Edgar Goens	Marvin E. Thomas
William W. Hammond	Perry G. Thomas
E. O. Hamstead	William J. Thomas
D. Heinz	Frank O. Trump, Jr.

John S. Heinz	Carl F. Wall
Louis L. Hilliard	George Washington
Burhman Cline	Thomas Welsh
Charles H. Miller	Boyd L. Widmyer
Paul E. Miller, Jr.	Jack M. Widmyer
Paul D. McCarty	Irving C. Widmyer
Benjamin F. McDowell	Gilbert J. Willingham
Edgar Hammond	Herbert Hoover Ross
Henry Washington	James W. Winston

Conclusion

Conclusion

The research has been a pleasant ten year journey. Each time some new information was discovered, new questions arose that required a search for even more information. For example, when I found out that several general stores operated at the same time, I wanted to know where each was located, and then how the community could support the duplication and if the businesses were successful enough to support the owners and their families. As the history of the Grace Reformed Church unfolded, I wanted to know the names of the organizers and who its first members were. And the early social organizations were ubiquitous: Did the local members of the Masonic Order go to Shepherdstown or Shenandoah Junction when they stopped meeting in Kearneysville? And why was the Patriotic Sons of America formed here anyway? Why did it close?

Other questions were the result of accounts with differing information. For example, two local newspapers recorded two different birth dates for Robert Lemen. Where could more evidence be found, or which should I use?

Looking back on the formation of the community, there were a number of turning points that set a course for Kearneysville. Dissension among board members of the local creamery led to its demise. Although it started as a farming community, the major sources of employment shifted to the B&O and quarry work. From 1842 when the B&O Railroad first made its appearance until the 1920s, there seemed to be continual growth. Houses were built to accommodate the influx of workers. New organizations came into existence. Citizens talked of forming an Improvement Society to install street lights and enact measures to eliminate accumulated trash.

When the quarry closed in the 1930s, and the B&O work waned locally after WWII, many of the sons and daughters in the community found employment in welcoming villages elsewhere. The automobile precipitated freedom to choose other venues for shopping and social activities. Social organizations of various sorts grew and declined across time.

Through the years I have come to appreciate the villagers' willingness to move through conflicts in forming a community of economical, political and societal interests. It couldn't have been easy. And it's clear how personal or collective decisions along the way made significant differences in shaping Kearneysville and setting its direction. My work on this history has provided a lens through which to notice the personal impact that each of us continues to have as we share our one small community.

Appendix A: Cemeteries

Cemeteries

EXISTING TOMBSTONES AT PRESBYTERIAN CEMETERY

Cunard, Blanch Viola, daughter of G. & Amy	1880-1880
Fox, Ralph Lemuel	D. Oct. 7, 1918 2yrs.
Frith, John G, son of E. G. and E. M.	Jan. 14, 1909-Sept. 13, 1925
Granigian, H. L.	Dec. 8,1866
Granigian, Francis J., wife of H.L.	Dec. 7, 1867-Nov. 28, 1909
Granigian, Mary Albertha	D. Sept. 28,1905
Granigian, Isaac T.	D. Dec. 23, 1911 20yrs.
Jackson, John H.	1860-1919
Jackson, Mary D, wife of John	1867-1923
Jackson, H. Russell	1900-1902
Medler, Donald E. Buddy	July 15, 1933-Dec. 19, 1936
Owens, A.E.	D. July 8, 1899, aged 59 yrs.3mo.9da
Price, Richard	1922-1951
Price, Mary Amelia	1900-1953
Tharpe, Flossie Frith	Sept. 20, 1898-Dec. 31, 1932
Tharpe, Ruby M.	1916-1918
Thomas, S. W.	Jan. 28, 1872-Mar. 31, 1931
Thomas, Mary D.	Aug. 2, 1875-Sept. 18, 1940
Thomas, Willliam J. B. Pvt. WWII	June 21, 1908-Mar. 10. 1971
Thomas, Roy E., W.Va. Wagoner S. Calvary, WWII	Mar. 1896-Aug. 27,1950
Thomas, Elsie Marie, mother	1904-1957
Thomas, Alton W.	1904-1955

Thomas, Edith E.	1910-19__
Tucker, Melvin R.	D. Nov. 2, 1909, aged 29 yrs.
Tucker, Samuel R.	D. Sept. 12, 1882, 60yrs. 8mo. 26da
Tucker, Thomas E., son T.W. & Jane	D. June 25, 1879, 3yrs. 2mo.
Tucker, Gertrude M., daughter of T.W.& Jane	D. Nov. 24, 1880, 3yrs. 2mo.
Tucker, Emma A., daughter of T.W. & Jane	D. Dec. 25, 1880
Turner, Catherine W.	D. 1921, aged 9mo.
Whitelock, Bette E., daughter of H. & I.W.	D. June 12, 1928 infant
Whittington, George Wm, son of G. W. & L.G.	D. Sept. 22, 1898 5mo. 12da
Whittington, Lucas	Oct. 14, 1898-Oct. 28, 1898
Whittington, Nina Bernice, daughter	D. Nov. 20, 1902 8yrs. 5mo. 26da.
Whittington, Adrian Charles, son of C.O. & M.C.	Mar. 8, 1909-June 19, 1911
Williams, John C.	D. Mar. 28, 1900, 35yrs. 6mo. 14da.
Wyndham, James E.	1899-1955
Wyndham, Alma B.	1914-1975
Wyndham, James E., Jr.	1938-1939
Cane, John, son of Mr. and Mrs. George Cane	D. 1911, aged 2yrs., no tombstone

ELMWOOD CEMETERY, SHEPHERDSTOWN

Bitner, John Calvin	Aug. 21, 1845-March 2, 1926
Bitner, Bettie Henkle	Sept. 6, 1848-Sept. 25, 1928
Bitner, Sarah	July 27, 1872-March 12, 1892
Border, Ralph Winebrenner	Feb. 3, 1882-Aug. 10, 1960
Border, Anne Etheridge	Dec. 5, 1882-Dec. 9, 1967
Border, Daniel Webster, M.D.	June 18, 1850-May 17, 1914

Border, Clara Getzendanner	Dec. 14, 1850-March 27, 1934
Border, Daniel Worth son of D.W.& Clara	Jan. 14, 1881-May 1, 1881
Border, Margaret Getzendanner, D.W. & Clara	Oct. 23, 1880-July 30, 1887
Burhman, Jacob E.	1870-1947
Burhman, Pearl E.	1874-1947
Burgman, infant son of Henry C. & Anna McKee Burgman	d. Dec. 2, 1937
Bumett, Clarence H., Sr.	March 25, 1880-June 30, 1965
Bumett, Sadie S.	Jan. 1, 1876-May 9, 1931
Campbell, Rebecca Struder, wife of John T.	June 24, 1870-March 23, 1930
Campbell.John T.	1905-1958
Campbell, Sarah P.	1911-
Clemmens, Albert E.	1874-1948
Clemmens, Bessie	1883-1964
Clemmens, Clarence E.	1907-1944
Cline, John Wesley	
Cline, Wesley Burhman	Feb. 12, 1897-Dec. 29, 1945
Glower, Wade Hampton	Sept. 2, 1926-Apr. 17, 1946
Glower, Rose Ellen	1881-1938
Constant, Mary E.	1853-1936
Cox, David E.	Nov. 17, 1906-Dec. 5, 1962
Cox, George H.	July 24, 1868-Oct. 18, 1900
Cox, Mary T.	1879-1933
Cox, Ruth	1863-1946
Cox, Daniel, son of G.H. & Fannie Cox	Oct. 17, 1902-Oct. 3, 1918
Drawbaugh, Alexander C.	Nov. 30, 1905-Sept 23, 1906
Drawbaugh, Emma S.	Aug. 31, 1833-Apr. 28, 1909

Drawbaugh, Edward D.	Mar. 12, 1848-Jan. 30, 1913
Drawbaugh, Rose	1871-1953
Entler, Sallie G.	1873-1945
Fulk, Prof. Jacob	July 22, 1859-Oct. 27, 1939
Fulk, William	d. Dec. I, 1899-37yrs., 6mo., 4days
Fulk, Catherine L.	Oct. 19,1829-July7,1903
Fulk, Katie	Apr. 5,1839-March 4,1917
Fulk, Charles H.E.	Aug, 3, 1866-Oct, 7, 1888
Fulk, William A.	Oct, 13, 1871-June 18, 1900
Fulk, Mary E. Entler	Oct, 20, 1864-July 1, 1942
Getzendanner, Daniel	Dec. 17, 1864-Dec. 14, 1948
Getzendanner, Margaret E.	Sept. 26, 1829-Feb. 18, 1900
Getzendanner, Louis D.	Jan. 26, 1837-March 29, 1914
Getzendanner, Phebe E.	Dec. 28, 1862-Dec. 6, 1942
Getzendanner, H.C.	July 21, 1867-July 17, 1964
Capt. to W.Va. Infantry Sp. Am.	Jan. 14, 1861-March 12, 1941
Getzendanner, Anna Morgan, wife of Henry Clay	1861-1944
Getzendanner, Charles C.	Dec.28,1855-Nov. 18,1913
Hamill, James	1845-1914
Hamill, Laura	1856-1931
Hammond, Edgar M., Sgt. WWII	1917-1978
Hammond, Stella	1920-1966
baby boy	1955-1955
Hammond, Rowland A.	July 3, 1878-Feb. 10, 1949
Hammond, Hester I.	March 15, 1911-Sept. 11, 1975
Hammond, Charles E.	1890-1967
Hammond, Leah J.	1893-1976
Hammond, Mabel L.	Dec. 11, 1878-Feb. 10, 1949
Heinz, Samuel	1894-1957
Heinz, Catherine M.	1896-1972
Henkel, Daniel Grove	Jan. 29, 1815-June 21, 1884
Henkel, Eliza J.	d. on 85th birthday, Nov. 13, 1898

Henkel, Mary Jessie	July 2, 1852-Jan 8, 1944
Hill, Walter	
W. Va. Prt. WWI	Sept. 10, 1893-July 15, 1973
Hill, Nellie Fulk	May 28,1903-
Hill, William H.	Aug. 26, 1852-Aug. 19, 1937
Hill, Martha A.	June 17, 1859-Sept. 20, 1950
Homsher, T.	Feb. 16, 1828-Feb. 22, 1904
Homsher, Letatia Reed	Feb. 13, 1832-July 15, 1903
Homsher, Frank C.	1861-1927
Homsher, Belle	1857-1930
Horn, Bertha G.	Aug. 29, 1872-Aug 29, 1955
Jewett, Aaron	d. Sept. 17,1822
Jewett, Elizabeth, wife of Aaron	d. June 30, 1864, 78yrs.
Jewett, John M.	d. Sept 13, 1862, 47yrs.
Kerney, James A.	May 30, 1792-May 30, 1849
Kerney, Ariadna, wife of James	June 8, 1794-July 27, 1863
Kerney, Uriah	d. Dec. 27, 1859, 62yrs.
McKee, Bessie M.	Aug. 25, 1876-March 5, 1957
McKee, Walter L.	May 4, 1880-Apr. 30, 1959
McKee, Nannie, L.	Sept. 28, 1884-Jan. 19, 1961
McKee, John Howard	1870-1942
McKee, Blanch Bitner	1874-1946
McKee, Mayberry	Feb. 3, 1843-Oct. 21, 1915
McKee, Annie M.	July 20, 1844-Dec. 12, 1908
Magruder, David Lynn	Apr. 28, 1861-Dec. 31, 1937
Magmder, Jane L.	March 3, 1867-Apr. 14, 1940
Miller, Herbert C.	Apr. 27, 1880-July 20, 1941
Miller, Nannie W.	Sept. 20, 1883-Jan. 10, 1974
Miller, Jacob R.	June 20, 1976, 26yrs., 7mos, 3 days
Miller, J.J.	Nov. 12, 1886, 69yrs., 2mos., 22days
Miller, Catherine	

Miller, Milton S.	Dec. 11, 1844-Nov. 9, 1916
Miller, Ruth A.	Dec. 16, 1886-Dec. 5, 1964
Miller, M. Fred	1890-1962
Miller, Mabel	1898-1951
Stanley, Blanche M.	1880-1971
Stanley, John	1877-1968
Stephens, Charles H., Dr.	d. Nov. 21,1883
Stickel Henry B.	March 11, 1878-aug. 12, 1942
Stickel, Mary C.	Apr. 7, 1872-Nov. 8, 1919
Strider, Isaac H.	Dec.25, 1915, 74yrs, 11 mo.
Strider, Sarah E., wife of Isaac daughter of Philip Reich ofMD	d. Jan 28, 1929
Trump, A.	Nov. 20, 1837-Dec. 27, 1907
Trump, Julia S.	Nov. 1, 1839-Dec. 2, 1928
Trussell, A.	1877-1953
Trussell, Edith H.	1880-1956
Turner, Harry M.	Nov. 30,1927, 71yrs.
Whittington, Clarence L.	Apr. 1, 1879-Jan. 14, 1926
Whittington, Lula R., wife of Clarence	Apr. 8, 1888-Sept. 17, 1957
Widmeyer, Abram M.	1845-1904
Widmeyer, Ellen U.	1840-1927
Widmeyer, Charles E.	1874-1961
Widmeyer, Lenora M.	1881-1963
Widmeyer, Boyd Lucas	Jan. 22, 1917-July 23, 1976
Wilt, Walter F.	1874-1943

St. Paul Baptist (Kearneysville)

Bradford, Daisy Bell   d. Aug. 28, 1897 aged 17yrs.
    Daughter of Alice Bradford   5mo. 13da.

Campbell, Edgar Bernard
    Sgt. Air Force WWII   June 15, 1926-Oct. 17, 1956
Campbell, Thomas H.   Aug. 16, 1888-July 18, 1970
Campbell, Nellie L.   Feb. 10, 1896-Nov. 2, 1975

Carter, Boyd   b. Sept. W, 1888
Carter, Amelia Monroe
    wife of Boyd Carter   July 10, 1891 -July 27, 1945
Carter, Herbert W.   1888-1963
Carter, Lucy L., wife of Herbert   1890-1962
Carter, Norman D.   1879-1956
Carter, Essie C., wife of Norman   1883-1974
Carter, Benjamin   1840-1910
Carter, Mariah L., wife of Benjamin   1844-1906
Carter, George   1852-Jan. 11, 1922
Carter, Annie, wife of George   Apr.2,1854-Apr,8,1943
Carter, Alice, Zeine, Lula,
    Lucinda Mason   (no dates-probably children)

Dixon, William H.   1880-1974

Fox, Bertha E.   Aug. 8, 1873-Mar. 17, 1895
Fox, Nellie A.   Sept. 12, 1893, aged 6yrs.
    daughter. of J. H. and Lucy E.   6mo. 22 da.
Fox, Georgie E.   d. Apr. 24, 1899 l0yrs. 1 mo. 2 da.
Fox, Lemuel D.   June 12, 1891-May 14, 1896
Fox, Mary E.   d. Dec. 12, 1916
    aged 60 yrs. 1 mo.

Fox, John H.   Nov. 27, 1845-May 19, 1911
Fox, Lucy E., wife of John   Feb. 2, 1853-Apr. 14, 1892
Fox, Rusco F.   d. Sept. 24, 1899 aged 18yr.
    son of J. H. and Lucy E.   4mo. 2da.
Fox, JohnH.   d. June 24, 1897 aged 15yr.
    son of J. H. and Lucy E.   4mo. 13da.
Fox, Carrie A. E.   Feb. 6, 1900-Aug. 17, 1901
Fox, Joseph   d. Sept. 1909 aged 66yrs.

Fox, Robert E.	Oct. I, 1877-Mar. 29, 1921
Fox, Charles Kynnes	
adopted son of Robert and D.	d. Mar. 24, 1911 2 yrs.
Fox, John William	
son of Robert and Idellia	Dec. 26, 1906-Jan. 23, 1908
Fox, William Kynnes	
adopted son of Robert and Idellia	d. Apr. 24, 1913 aged 7yrs.
Frazier, Thomton	d. May 12, 1837, aged 56yrs.
Frazier, Louisa	d. Apr. 15, 1893, aged 55yrs.
Goens, Sarah A.	d. Feb. 8, 1886, aged 75yrs. 10 mo. 7da.
McDaniel, James W.	d. Jan. 31, 1936, aged 74yrs. 4mo. 3da.
McDaniel, Maria Ellen	d. July 12, 1909, aged 50yr.
wife of James	7mo. 16da.
Reed, Alice Carter	1881-1949, aged 67 yrs. 8 mo.
Rock, Travis Coy, II	1903-1970
Roman, Mary R.	1886-1954
Roper, James D.	Jan. 9, 1837-1908
Roper, Frances Virginia	Dec. 28, 1837-Mar. 30, 1902
Roper, Nancy Clara	d. Feb. 16, 1880, aged 1 yr.
daughter of James and Frances	3mo. 13da.
Roper, George W.	
son of James and Frances	May 13, 1861-Dec. 7, 1896
Roper, Martha E. Smith	
daughter. of James and Frances	Nov. 10, 1875-May 18, 1900
Roper, John Clifton	1893-1969
Roper, Nannie E.	1899-1977
Roper, John Clifton, Jr.	
U.S. Navy WWII	June 24, 1924-Nov. 22, 1971
Roper, James Douglas	Oct. 4, 1902-Aug. 3, 1967
Roper, Sarah A.	d. Aug. 24, 1897, aged 78yrs.
Roper, Ruth Elizabeth	Apr. 18, 1900-July 16, 1980

Saunders, Lucy M.	Oct. 28, 1895-Oct. 21, 1976
Strider, Elizabeth	d. Dec. 1893, aged 76yrs. 4mo.
William, J. Robert	1894-1961
Washington, Myrtle U.	d. Jan. 6, 1937, aged 30yrs. 4mo. 14 da.
Wilkins, Martha E.	Nov. 7, 1883-Jan. 1, 1974

STEWART CHAPEL METHODIST CEMETERY

Alien, Harry H	1888-1949
Alien, Helen E.	1893-1968
Brown, James	1885-1925
Burden, Nimrod	1865-1927
Campbell, Abraham G.	1887-1948
Campbell, Sarah M.	1879-1919
Campbell, Carter	1886-1927
Campbell, Lilliam	1888-1936
Carey, Jesse	
Carey, Kenneth L.	July 30,1947-Feb.13,1993
Carey, Robert Lee	1899-1987
Ferguson, Charles H.	1870-1965
Ferguson, Alice R.	Aug. 15, 1900-Jan. 13, 1967
Ferguson, Jessie	Apr. 15, 1928-Sept. 22, 1948
Ferguson, John	Jan. 2, 1895-Dec. 3, 1994
Ferguson, Edward	Aug. 18, 1927-March 17, 1990
Fredericks, Alice	Feb. 24, 1925-Oct. 28, 1949
Ford, Sarah	D. June 14, 1924, age 46 years
Goens, William	1861-1919

Goens, Harriet	1865-1927
Goens, Paul	March 4, 1890-May 8, 1937
Goens, Edgar	May 11, 1911-Aug. 3, 1963
Head, James W.	1870-1935
Head, Mary E.	1885-1935
Jackson, James A.	Aug. 3, 1922-Oct. 15, 1942
Jackson, Infant son	1957-1957
King, Herbert	
King, Sarah Rebecca	1924-1975
King, Theodore R.	1903-1975
Lockley, Jr.	Oct. 16, 1927-Oct. 18, 1927
McDowell, Carrie	1879-1968
McDowell, William	1879-1935
McDowell, Ronald	1945-1966
McDowell, Vincent	1954-1964
McDowell, (illegible)	Feb. 19, 1922-March 23, 1974
Splown, Jefferson	1853-1905
Splown, Jennie	1866-1911
Strother, James	(No dates)
Stubbs, Benjamin	1904-1966
Ross, Herbert Hoover	
CS3. U.S. Navy WWI	Nov. 14, 1927-Sept, 4, 1956
Ross, Edmund Moselle	
U.S. Navy WWII	March 7, 1922-Oct. 18, 1971
Ross, William A.	1899-1989
Ross, Estelle L.	1895-1871
Twyman, James N.	1896-1947
Twyman, Sarah E.	1878-1959
Twyman, Frank	1870-1947
Twyman, Harry	(buried ? 1984)

Walker, Sarah	1901-1957
Walker, Elizabeth H	
Warren, Fannie	1880-1966
Winston, Floyd Beverly	June 18, 1907-Jan. 4, 1961
Winston, Frederick	Apr. 27, 1887-July 17, 1955
Winston, Sadie Frances	Sept. 1, 1890-1988
Woodfork, William G.	1883-1953
Woodfork, Clara	1889-1957

HART GRAVEYARD

Brady, Randolph, Father	March 20, 1841-Dec. 7, 1914
Brady, Emma Hart, Mother	Aug. 31, 1846-March 19, 1911
Brown, Martha Hart	July 26, 1850-Aug. 17, 1932
Brady, Mabel Susie	Aug. 19, 1877-May 8, 1965
Bird, Howard James	Sept. 22, 1897-Dec. 13, 1941
Bird, Elizabeth Brady	March 9, 1880-Jan. 14, 1969
Wilkins, Martha E.	Nov. 7, 1883-Jan. 1, 1974
Goens, Delphia	1895-1983
Goens, James Elmer U. S. Army WWI	Aug. 10, 1895-May 17, 1983
Ross, Paul Alfonzo AIC U. S. Air Force	May 30, 1931-Nov. 1, 1991
Hart, Mascena	June 5, 1839-Sept. 5, 1905
Hart, Sarah Roper, wife	Jan. 17, 1841-Dec. 28, 1895
Hart, Emma Virginia	1864-1929
Hart, William Osbourn	1866-1917
Hart, Howard W.	March 28, 1872-March 24, 1956
Hart, Arwilda M., wife, daughter of Joseph and Lucy Goens	June 13, 1875-April 25, 1930

Jackson, Julia Ann wife of David Jackson	Jan. 21, 1850-Aug. 28, 1929 at rest in Heaven
Lucas, John Edward	Feb. 12, 1888-July 28, 1904
Lucas, Alice Louise, wife of John Lucas; dau. of Sara Hart	Sept. 3, 1861-May 13, 1908
Lucas, Delia Virginia, daughter of Philip and Alice Lucas	March 26, 1884-March 12, 1889
Lucas, Martha dau. of Philip and Alice Lucas	Jan. 22, 1901 -Dec. 22, 1901
Lucas, Sallie	March. 19, 1898-Sept. 5, 1925

Plate 63. Hart-Lucas Cemetery.

Appendix B: Selected Names from Federal Census

Selected Names from Federal Census

Selected from Federal Census of Jefferson County 1850

Name	Race/Sex		Age	Occupation	Appraisal
Hurst, William	W	M	56	farmer	36,500
Hurst, Mary	W	F	53		
Hurst, Stephen	W	M	25		
Hurst, Ruth	W	F	23		
Hurst, James	W	M	20		
Hurst, John	W	M	15		
Hurst, Jannetta	W	F	12		
Hurst, Julia	W	F	10		
Lemen, Willoughby	W	M	44	farmer	16,000
Lemen, Esther	W	F	50		
Lemen, Martha	W	F	18		
Lemen, William	W	M	15		
Lemen, John	W	M	10		
Lemen, Thomas T.	W	M	7		
Lemen, Newton	W	M	5		
Coonty, Emily	W	F	19		
Quigly, Sarah	W	F	56		
Hamil, Elizabeth	W	F	32		
Quilgy, Hariet	W	F	28		
Quilgy, Julia	W	F	12		
Ruckle, Samuel	W	M	56	farmer	5,000
Ruckle, Mary	W	F	47		
Ruckle, Greggs	W	M	19		
Licklider, Thomas	W	M	25	merchant	
Licklider, Mary	W	F	25		
Licklider, Alexander	W	M	3/12		
Miller, Jacob J.	W	M	33	farmer	4,000
Miller, Catherine	W	F	34		
Miller, George W.	W	M	12		
Miller, Susan E.	W	F	11		
Miller, William H. H.	W	M	9		
Miller, Milton S.	W	M	6		
Miller, Abraham S.	W	M	3		
Miller, Jacob R.	W	M	8/12		

Name	Race/Sex		Age	Occupation	Appraisal
Rutherford, James	W	M	38	laborer	
Rutherford, Elizabeth	W	F	32		
Rutherford, Thomas	W	M	10		
Rutherford, Sarah E.	W	F	9		
Rutherford, John A.	W	M	7		
Rutherford, Samuel D.	W	M	2		
Butt, Margaret	W	F	13		
Walper, John C.	W	M	32	farmer	5,000
Comegys, Elizabeth	W	F	61		
Walper, Margaret	W	F	30		
Walper, Catherine	W	F	59		
(Illegible), Mary	W	F	30		
Baldwin, Minerva	W	B	19		
Hurst, Minor	W	M	45	farmer	12,000
Hurst, Sarah	W	F	40		
Hurst, Mary	W	F	16		
Hurst, Sarah	W	F	14		
Hurst, James G.	W	M	3		
Moore, James	W	M	34	farmer	12,500
Moore, Phebe	W	F	30		
Moore, Elizabeth	W	F	9		
Moore, Vincent	W	M	7		
Campell, John	W	M	53	overseer	
Campell, Nancy	W	F	30		
Campell, James	W	M	15		
Campell, Susan	W	F	13		
Campell, Annie	W	F	12		
Campell, Jacob	W	M	10		
Campell, John	W	M	8		
Campell, Octavius	W	M	7		
Carey, Henry	B	M	38	laborer	
Carey, Lucinda	B	F	35		
Carey, Susan	B	F	7		
Carey, Evelina	B	F	5		
Carey, Marshall	B	M	3		
Carey, Edmund	B	M	1		
Goens, Thomas	B	M	50	laborer	
Goens, Lucretia	B	F	50		
Goens, William	B	M	18		
Goens, George	B	M	16		
Goens, Mary	B	F	13		
Goens, John	B	M	11		
Goens, Arthur	B	M	9		
Goens, Betsy	B	F	7		

Name	Race/Sex		Age	Occupation	Appraisal
Goens, Ann M.	B	F	5		
Goens, Charles	B	M	3		
Johnson, George	B	M	35	laborer	
Johnson, Maria	B	F	40		
Johnson, John	B	M	12		
Jackson, Norman	B	M	35	laborer	
Jackson, Louisa	B	F	36		
Jackson, William	B	M	10		
Newman, Anthony	B	M	7		
Newman, Harriet	B	F	5		
Newman, Charlotte	B	F	1		
Johnson, John	B	M	35	laborer	
Johnson, Sarah A.	B	F	36		
Johnson, John Jr.	B	M	7		
Johnson, Betsy	B	F	5		
Johnson, Lavinia	B	F	3		
Robinson, Hannah	B	F	15		
Turner, Ehud	W	M	31	farmer	
Turner, Lorena	W	F	28		
Turner, Ann L.	W	F	4		
Turner, Thomas	W	M	1		
Samuel, Manuel	W	M	25	laborer	
Fulk, Jacob	W	M	35	farmer	8,750
Fulk, Lorena	W	F	64		
Fulk, Ellen	W	F	19		
Spears, James	W	M	14		
Hess, John	W	M	42	teacher	
Hess, Elizabeth	W	F	30		
Hess, Joseph A.	W	M	8		
Hess, Charles W.	W	M	6		
Hess, Nancy E.	W	F	4		
Hess, John P.	W	M	1		
Maddox, Hannah	B	F	17		
Hart, Edward	M	M	47	farmer	
Hart, Eliza	M	F	45		
Hart, Thomas	M	M	25	farmer	
Hart, James	M	M	20		
Hart, Joseph	M	M	18		
Hart, Harriet	M	F	16		
Hart, Mary	M	F	14		
Hart, Mascena	M	M	12		
Hart, John	M	M	10		
Butler, Ann	W	F	70		75,000
Butler, Ann	W	F	45		

Name	Race/Sex		Age	Occupation	Appraisal
Stephens, Elizabeth	W	F	35		
Hart, Joseph	M	M	38	laborer	
Hart, Elizabeth	M	M	28		
Hart, Joseph	M	M	5		
Hart, John	M	M	4		
Hart, Robert	M	M	2		
Hart, James	M	M	1		
Cox, William	W	M	38	laborer	
Cox, Harriet	W	F	19		
Butler, William	W	M	32	farmer	
Butler, Lucinda	W	F	33		
Butler, William	W	M	9		
Butler, Mary A.	W	F	7		
Butler, James	W	M	5		
Butler, Nancy	W	F	3		
Butler, Lucy A.	W	F	1		
Kerney, Uriah	W	M	30	farmer	19,000
Kerney, Maria	W	F	34		
Kerney, John K.	W	M	20		
Kerney, Sarah	W	F	18		
Hunsucker, Maria	W	F	8		
Henkle, Daniel G.	W	M	35	manufacturer	
Henkle, Eliza J.	W	F	32		
Henkle, Bettie	W	F	1		
Jervett, Eliza	W	F	64		9,525
Jervett, John M.	W	M	35	lawyer	
McElroy, Ann	W	F	65		
Blue, Michael	W	M	41	farmer	6,000
Blue, Susan	W	F	31		
Blue, Emily M.	W	F	8		
Blue, Susan C.	W	F	6		
Blue, Mary A.	W	F	5		
Blue, Samuel	W	M	5		
Blue, Ellen J.	W	F	2		
Quigley, Capt. John	W	M	36		
Frary, Jesse L.	W	M	39	A.S.P. minister from Mass.	5,100
Frary, Mary A.	W	F	42		
Frary, Eliza L.	W	F	10		
Helm, (illegible)	W	M	15		
Blue, Henry	B	M	45		
McDaniel, James	B	M	47	laborer	
McDaniel, Nellie	B	F	43		
McDaniel, James	B	M	22		

Name	Race/Sex		Age	Occupation	Appraisal
McDaniel, Naomi	B	F	21		
McDaniel, Robert	B	M	13		
McDaniel, George	B	M	12		
McDaniel, Harrison	B	M	10		
McDaniel, Samuel	B	M	7		
McDaniel, Mary	B	M	4		
Brady, Henry	B	M	50	laborer	
Fulk, Jacob	W	M	65	farmer	
Fulk, Sarah	W	F	67		
Fulk, Frederick	W	M	23		
Fulk, William	W	M	18		
Fulk, James	W	M	13		
Rogers, Isaac B.	W	M	34	blacksmith	
Rogers, Lucinda	W	F	32		
Rogers, Margaret A.	W	F	6		
Rogers, Mary E.	W	F	4		
Rogers, Ellen V.	W	F	2		
Rogers, Georgetta	W	F	3/12		
Blakemy, George	W	M	23		
McElroy, Charles	W	M	17		
Nicely, Catherine	W	F	60		

Selected from Federal Census of Jefferson County 1870

Name	Race/Sex		Age	Occupation	Real Estate	Personal Property
Logie, James	W	M	47	physician	24,000	2,000
Logie, Mary C.	W	F	38			
Logie, William J.	W	M	7			
Logie, Benjamin P.	W	M	3			
Logie, Francis W.	W	M	7/12			
Atkinson, Emma	W	F	14			
Turner, Justina	B	F	13	domestic servant		
Trump, Henry A.	W	M	32	store keeper	3,000	3,000
Trump, Julia	W	F	31	housekeeper		
Trump, Frank	W	M	7			
Trump, Fanny	W	F	5			
Trump, George	W	M	3			
Trump, Sevilla	W	F	8/12			

Name	Race/Sex		Age	Occupation	Real Estate	Personal Property
Kranby, Fanny	W	F	20			
Sullivan, David	W	M	13			
Rutherford, Elizabeth	W	F	64		300	
Rutherford, Thomas W.	W	M	28			
Rutherford, Samuel	W	M	22			
Rutherford, Charley	W	M	8			
Rutherford, Annie	W	F	6			
Rutherford, Mary J.	W	F	3			
Rutherford, Emma C.	W	F	1			
McDowell, Catherine	B	F	32	domestic servant		
McDowell, Robert	B	M	7			
McDowell, Rose	B	F	1			
McDowell, John	B	M	3/12			
Fulk, Jacob	W	M	58	retired farmer	1,400	1,000
Fulk, Charles	W	M	17			
Fulk, Mary	W	F	13			
Fulk, Edward	W	M	11			
Fulk, Martha J.	W	F	42			
Fulk, Ida	W	F	6			
Conin, Ellen C.	W	F	16	servant		
Bitner, J.C.	W	M	25			
Rutherford, Elizabeth	W	F	75	housekeeper	100	
Frith, John	W	M	37	retail liquor	500	100
Frith, William	W	M	10			
Frith, Elizabeth	W	F	4			
Frith, Mary	W	F	1			
Pench, Annie	W	F	45	housekeeper		
Johnson, Milly	B	F	30	domestic servant		
Washington, George	B	M	58	farm laborer	350	
Washington, Sarah	B	F	40			
Washington, Georgelle	B	F	25			
Washington, John W. H.	B	M	25			
Washington, Edward L.	B	M	21			
Washington, LaFayette	B	M	18			
Washington, Daniel	B	M	12			
Washington, Louisa	W	F	24	domestic		

Name	Race/Sex		Age	Occupation	Real Estate	Personal Property
Washington, Walter	B	M	7			
Washington, Osinna	W	F	6/12			
Jackson, Lewis	W	M	48	farm laborer	300	
Jackson, Hannah	B	F	37	house keeper		
Jackson, Benjamin	B	M	18	farm laborer		
Jackson, John L.	B	M	13			
Jackson, Lucy	B	F	4			
Fitzgerald, Garret	W	M	78			
Fitzgerald, Thomas	W	M	40	railroad worker	100	
Fitzgerald, Mary	W	F	30	housekeeper		
Fitzgerald, James	W	M	6			
Fitzgerald, Thomas	W	M	4			
Fitzgerald, Michael	W	M	2			
Burnett, Sarah	W	F	48	housekeeper		
Burnett, Ellen	W	F	19			
Burnett, Robert	W	M	14			
Thompson, John A.	W	M	61	retired lawyer	6,000	400
Thompson, Mary G.	W	F	25	housekeeper		
Thompson, Augustus	W	M	20	physician		
Thompson, Clara H.	W	M	21			
Thompson, John T.	W	M	16			
Lemen, William L.	W	M	35	farmer	1,200	
Lemen, Susan M.	W	F	34	housekeeper		
Lemen, Elizabeth	W	F	9			
Lemen, Hester H.	W	F	7			
Lemen, Robert W.	W	M	5			
Lemen, Susan M.	W	F	5 or 3			
Homsher, Theo	W	M	41	store keeper	6,000	
Homsher, Letitia	W	F	38			
Homsher, Mary	W	F	14			
Homsher, Arabella	W	F	12			
Homsher, Franklin	W	M	9			
Drawbaugh, Alex C.	W	M	36			

Name	Race/Sex		Age	Occupation	Real Estate	Personal Property
Camanra, Eliza	W	F	20	domestic servant		
Hart, Macena W.	M	M	31	stone mason		
Hart, Sallie	M	F	28	housekeeper		
Hart, Lula A.	M	F	8			
Hart, Emma	M	F	6			
Hart, William O.	M	M	5			
Hart, Cora O.	M	F	3			
Hart, Mary E.	M	F	5/12			
Goens, William	M	M	9			
Washington, David	M	M	52	farm laborer		
Washington, Nelly	B	F	51	housekeeper		
Washington, Milly	B	F	21	domestic servant		
Washington, Margaret	B	F	18			
Washington, Lucy	B	F	17			
Washington, Charles	B	M	15			
Washington, David	B	M	13			
Washington, Robert	B	M	11			
Washington, Evaline	B	F	9			
Washington, Harriet	B	F	5			
Turner, Thomas	W	M	48	farmer	4,000	1,500
Turner, Sarah	W	F	38	housekeeper		
Turner, Robert G.	W	M	20	farm laborer		
Turner, Winfield S.	W	M	18			
Turner, May S.	W	F	15			
Turner, Jemima E.	W	F	13			
Turner, Martha	W	F	11			
Turner, Rhoda	W	F	9			
Turner, Sarah A.	W	F	7			
Turner, David	W	M	3			
Turner, Joseph	W	M	8/12			
Philips, Aaron	B	M	40	farm laborer	200	
Philips, Belle	B	F	39	housekeeper		

Name	Race/Sex		Age	Occupation	Real Estate	Personal Property
Philips, George	B	M	20	farm laborer		
Johnson, Albin	B	M	36	farm laborer		
Johnson, Fanny	B	F	37	domestic servant		
Johnson, Peter	B	M	11			
Johnson, Shellborn	B	M	10			
Johnson, Mahala	B	F	9			
Johnson, Armistos	B	M	7			
Johnson, Albin	B	M	6			
Johnson, Peggy	B	F	5			
Johnson, Jupiter	B	M	2			
Johnson, David	B	M	16			
Whittington, George	W	M	38	Blacksmith		
Whittington, Pansia	W	F	22			
Whittington, John T.	W	M	5			
Whittington, Charles C.	W	M			3	
Whittington, George W.	W	M			1	

Selected from Federal Census of Jefferson County 1880

Name	Race/Sex		Age	Occupation	Relationship
Burns, Charles	B	M	50	laborer	
Burns, Fanny	B	F	42		
Burns, Nancy	B	F	22	at work	
Burns, Lucinda	B	F	20	at work	
Burns, Kitty	B	F	18	at work	
Burns, Charles	B	M	17	at work	
Burns, Bettie	B	F	16	at work	
Burns, Julia	B	F	14	at work	
Burns, William	B	M	11		
Burns, Irene	B	F	9	at home	
Burns, Kelly	B	M	7		
Burns, Queen	B	F	5		
Burns, Porter	B	M	3		
Burns, Luckman	B	M	8/12		
Carter, Benjamin	B	M	43	laborer	
Carter, Mary Ellen	B	F	34		

Name	Race/Sex		Age	Occupation	Relationship
Carter, Lucinda	B	F	15		
Carter, Alice	B	F	10		
Carter, Moses	B	M	5		
Carter, Lizzie	B	F	3		
Carter, Ellen	B	F	6/12		
Ford, Daniel	B	M	35		laborer
Ford, Milly	B	F	30		wife
Ford, Emily	B	F	12		daughter
Ford, Margaret	B	F	8		daughter
Ford, David	B	M	6		son
Ford, Hannah	B	M	5		daughter
Ford, Sarah	B	F	2		daughter
Ford, Lavinia	B	F	1/12		daughter
Washington, David	B	M	60	laborer	
Washington, Nelly	B	F	53		wife
Washington, Charles	B	M	29		son
Washington, Harriet	B	F	13		daughter
Washington, David Jr.	B	M	23		son
Thomas, Wilber	W	M	39	B&O gang boss	
Thomas, Amelia	W	F	36		wife
Thomas, Mary D.	W	F	13		daughter
Thomas, Carrie	W	F	10		daughter
Thomas, Walter	W	M	8		son
Thomas, Elizabeth	W	F	6		daughter
Thomas, Estella	W	F	9/12		daughter
Burnett, William H.	W	M	31	farm laborer	
Burnett, Arra J.	W	F	29		wife
Burnett, Lottie C.	W	F	10		daughter
Burnett, Robert	W	M	8		son
Burnett, Leenora B.	W	F	5		daughter
Burnett, May C.	W	F	4		daughter
Burnett, (unnamed)	W	M&F	2/12		son & daughter
Henkle, Grove	W	M	64	farmer	
Henkle, Eliza	W	F	65		wife
Henkle, Jessie	W	F	27		daughter
Smith, Ann	B	F	29		servant
Smith, Lewis	B	M	8		servant
Smith, Vinson	B	M	2		servant
Smith, Erby	B	M	62		servant
Trussell, James T.	W	M	50	farmer	
Trussell, Virginia	W	F	35		wife
Trussell, Sarah T.	W	F	5		daughter

Name	Race/Sex		Age	Occupation	Relationship
Trussell, James	W	M	2		son
Trussell, Mary D.	W	F	8/12		daughter
Trussell, Gervis G.	W	M	20		nephew
Hess, John	W	M	71	farmer	
Hess, Elizabeth	W	F	59		wife
Hess, Joseph A.	W	M	38		son
Hess, Mary C.	W	F	19		wife
Logie, James	W	M	57	doctor	
Logie, Mary C.	W	F	48		wife
Logie, John H.	W	M	27	educator	
Logie, William	W	M	17		son
Logie, Benjamin	W	M	13		son
Logie, Frank	W	M	11		son
Logie, Jessie	W	F	7		daughter
Strider, Isaac H.	W	M	39	farmer	
Strider, Sarah E.	W	F	39		wife
Strider, Georgia	W	F	13		daughter
Strider, James W.	W	M	11		daughter
Strider, Rebecca	W	F	9		daughter
Strider, Harry	W	M	7		son
Strider, Edgar	W	M	1		son
Trump, Augustus	W	M	42	merchant	
Trump, Julie	W	F	39		wife
Trump, Harry	W	M	12		son
Trump, Sevilla	W	F	11		daughter
Trump, Frank	W	M	6		son
Miller, A. S.	W	M	32	farmer	
Miller, Susan	W	F	26		wife
Miller, Alice	W	F	5		daughter
Miller, Gilbert	W	M	2		son
Fulk, William	W	M	50	farmer	
Fulk, Katherine	W	F	41		wife
Fulk, Daniel S.	W	M	21		son
Fulk, William A.	W	M	15		son
Fulk, Susan C. V.	W	F	14		daughter
Fulk, Charles H. R.	W	M	8		son
Fulk, Emma E. G.	W	F	5		daughter
McCoy, Sallie	W	F	40	servant	
McCoy, Mary E.	W	F	15	servant	
Getzendanner, Daniel	W	M	52	farmer	
Getzendanner, Margaret	W	F	43		wife
Getzendanner, Phoebe	W	F	12		daughter
Getzendanner, Frank	W	M	12		son
Getzendanner, May	W	F	7		daughter

Name	Race/Sex		Age	Occupation	Relationship
Hart, Macina	M	M	40	stone mason	
Hart, Sallie	M	F	39		wife
Hart, Emma	M	F	16		daughter
Hart, Osbourn	M	M	14		son
Hart, Howard	M	M	9		son
Hart, Nellie	M	F	6		daughter
Hart, Elizabeth	M	F	2		daughter
Hart, Kate	M	F	2/12		daughter
Stephens, Charles	W	M	64	farmer	
Stephens, Virginia	W	F	61		wife
Stephenson, Philip	W	M	67	physician	
Stephenson, Elizabeth	W	F	55		wife
Stephenson, Ella	W	F	20		daughter
Stephenson, Harry W.	W	M	4		grand son
Stephenson, Ethel	W	F	2		grand daughter
Stump, Casper	W	M	39	saddle maker	
Sites, William A.	W	M	40	farmer	
Sites, Fannie M.	W	F	42		wife
Sites, Bessie H.	W	F	5		daughter
Sites, Mary	W	F	1		daughter
Fox, John H.	M	M	33	farmer	
Fox, Lucy E.	M	F	25		wife
Fox, Lucinda	M	F	12		daughter
Fox, Robert E.	M	M	2		son
Fox, Bertha E.	M	F	9/12		daughter
Denis, Howard	B	M	21	farm laborer	
Denis, Oliver	B	M	17	farm laborer	
Border, Daniel	W	M		physician	
Border, Clara	W	F			wife
Bowmen, Alexander	W	M		servant	
Moore, James W.	W	M	64	B&O detective	
Moore, Phebe	W	F	60		wife
Moore, Vincent G.	W	M	36		son
Wyatt, Bettie	W	F	38		daughter
Wyatt, Annie V.	W	F	10		grand daughter
Blew, Sallie	W	F	6		grand niece
Mason, Alice	B	F	20	servant	
Mason, Daisy	B	F	2/12		daughter
Clower, John	W	M	43	track hand	
Clower, Ellen	W	F	28		wife
Clower, Bertha	W	F	9		daughter
Clower, Robert	W	M	4		son

Name	Race/Sex		Age	Occupation	Relationship
Clower, Wade	W	M	1		son
Collins, Motrin	W	M	50	farmer	
Collins, Georgetta	W	F	47		wife
Collins, Carter	W	M	21		son
Collins, Frederick	W	M	19		son
Collins, Caroline	W	F	17		daughter
Collins, Lizzie	W	F	13		daughter
Collins, Horace	W	M	7		son
Collins, Samuel	W	M	78		father
Homsher, Theodore	W	M	52	merchant	
Homsher, Letitia	W	F	48		wife
Homsher, Mary T.	W	F	24		daughter
Homsher, Arabella	W	F	22		daughter
Homsher, Franklin C.	W	M	18		son
Homsher, Virginia	W	F	9/12		daughter
Ford, Margaret	B	F	9	servant	
Goens, John H.	B	M	41	farmer	
Goens, Mary	B	F	43		sister
Goens, Trice	B	F	80		mother
Goens, William F.	B	M	10		adopted
McDaniel, George	B	M	17	farm hand	
Bitner, John C.	W	M	34	retired farmer	
Bitner, Bettie H.	W	F	31		wife
Bitner, Sarah	W	F	7		daughter
Bitner, Blanche	W	F	6		daughter
Bitner, Eliza	W	F	1		daughter
Mason, John	B	M	40	laborer	
Mason, Rebecca	B	F	30		wife
Mason, Albert	B	M	8		son
Mason, Gertrude	B	F	2		daughter
Brady, Randolf	M	M	38	laborer	
Brady, Emma Hart	M	F	22		wife
Brady, Benjamin	M	M	6		son
Brady, Maybel	M	F	2		daughter
Brady, Mary	M	F	2/12		daughter
Brown, William	M	M	70	laborer	
Brown, Virginia	M	F	48		wife
Brown, Benjamin	M	M	21		son
Brown, Mary	M	F	16		daughter
Brown, Sarah	M	F	14		daughter
Brown, Salina	M	F	10		daughter
Brown, George	M	M	7		son
Roper, Douglas	M	M	43	blacksmith	
Roper, Fanny	M	F	42		wife

Name	Race/Sex		Age	Occupation	Relationship
Roper, Mary V.	M	F	20		daughter
Roper, George W.	M	M	16		son
Roper, Charles E.	M	M	12		son
Roper, James G.	M	M	7		son
Roper, Sarah	M	F	10		daughter
Roper, Lavinia	M	F	5		daughter
Roper, Martha	M	F	5		daughter

Selected from Federal Census of Middleway Magisterial District 1900

Name	Relationship	Race/Sex		Date of Birth	Children	Occupation
Price, Sam	head	W	M	April 1872		
Price, Mary	wife	W	F	Jan. 1882	1	
Price, Effie	daughter	W	F	May 1898		
Frith, Charles	head	W	M	July 1874		
Frith, Lucy E	wife	W	F	Aug. 1875	2	
Frith, Flossie Lee	daughter	W	F	Sept. 1897		
Frith, Charles G.	son	W	M	Dec. 1899		
Frith, Lee	sister	W	F	Mar. 1877		
Frith, Eugene G.	brother	W	M	Mar. 1883		
McDowell, James	head	B	M	Sept. 1862		
McDowell, Ella	wife	B	F	Dec. 1860	12	
McDowell, Robert	son	B	M	Oct. 1883		
McDowell, Mary	daughter	B	F	Apr. 1885		
McDowell, James W.	son	B	M	Aug. 1886		
McDowell, Harley	son	B	M	Feb. 1888		
McDowell, Benjamin	son	B	M	Aug. 1889		
McDowell, Amelia	daughter	B	F	July 1891		
McDowell, Maggie	daughter	B	F	Feb. 1893		
McDowell, Lucy	daughter	B	F	Oct. 1895		
McDowell, Charles	son	B	M	Mar. 1898		
McDowell, Jacob	son	B	M	Feb. 1900		
McDowell, ------	son	B	M	Feb. 1900		
Woodfork, George	head	B	M	Aug. 1855		farmer
Woodfork, Alice	wife	B	F	May 1867	3	
Woodfork, William	son	B	M	Apr. 1883		
Woodfork, George D.	son	B	M	Apr. 1885		
Woodfork, Amanda	daughter	B	F	Apr. 1888		
Roper, Edward	head	B	M	Aug. 1866		farmer

Name	Relationship	Race/Sex		Date of Birth	Children	Occupation
Roper, Lucinda	wife	B	F	May 1868	8	
Roper, Mary	daughter	B	F	July 1886		
Roper, Emma	daughter	B	F	Feb. 1888		
Roper, Charles	son	B	M	Dec. 1890		
Roper, John	son	B	M	Feb. 1893		
Roper, Estella	daughter	B	F	May 1895		
Roper, George	son	B	M	May 1897		
Roper, Racheal	daughter	B	F	May 1900		
Roper, Ruth	daughter	B	F	May 1900		
Briscoe, Baccus	head	B	M	Mar. 1821		
Briscoe, Betty	wife	B	F	Apr. 1840	5	
Granigan, -------	head	W	M	----- 1867		
Granigan, -------	wife	W	F	----- 1868		
Granigan, Robert	son	W	M	Mar. 1890		
Granigan, Isaac	son	W	M	June 1892		
Granigan, Randolf	son	W	M	Nov. 189-		
Granigan, Laura	daughter	W	F	Apr. 1897		
Granigan, Daisy	daughter	W	F	Mar. 1900		
Allen, David	head	B	M	Apr. 1850		quarry
Allen, Mary	wife	B	F	May 1855	12	
Allen, William	son	B	M	----- 1870		quarry
Allen, Harry	son	B	M	Apr. 1886		
Allen, Emma	daughter	B	F	Mar. 1887		
Allen, Bertha	daughter	B	F	July 1894		
Allen, Mary	daughter	B	F	July 1895		
Nicely, Leo	head	W	M	May 1872		day laborer
Nicely, Alice	sister	W	F	Sept. 1867		
Brown, Lucy	niece	W	F	Dec. 1881		
Brown, Henry	nephew	W	M	Mar. 1883		
Johnson, G. D.	head	W	M	June 1845		farmer
Johnson, Annie E.	wife	W	F	Feb. 1846		
Johnson, Emma E.	daughter	W	F	Feb. 1869		
Johnson, Rosie	daughter	W	F	Dec. 1879		
Johnson, Cora F.	daughter	W	F	Feb. 1876		
Johnson, Phillip M.	son	W	M	Aug. 1882		
Locke, Nathaniel	head	W	M	June 1850		
Locke, Mollie	wife	W	F	June 1852	4	
Locke, Fannie	daughter	W	F	Apr. 1882		
Locke, Curtis	son	W	M	Apr. 1883		
Locke, Effie	daughter	W	F	Nov. 1887		
Locke, Maggie	daughter	W	F	Feb. 1893		
Miller, M. F.	head	W	M	Dec. 1844		

Name	Relationship	Race/Sex		Date of Birth	Children	Occupation
Miller, Hattie B.	wife	W	F	Apr. 1855	7	
Miller, Mabel E.	daughter	W	F	Dec. 1878		
Miller, Florence	daughter	W	F	Mar. 1880		
Miller, Mary Baker	daughter	W	F	Mar. 1882		
Miller, Charles J.	son	W	M	May 1884		
Miller, Anna R.	daughter	W	F	Dec. 1886		
Miller, William F.	son	W	M	Aug. 1890		
Miller, James J.	son	W	M	Feb. 1897		
Jackson, J	head	W	M	Oct. 1860		
Jackson, Mary	wife	W	F	Apr. 1867	2	
Jackson, Lilly M.	daughter	W	F	July 1893		
Jackson, Lute Miller	daughter	W	F	Oct. 1897		
Dorsey, J. I.	head	W	M	Feb. 1857		
Dorsey, Ida	wife	W	F	Nov. 1862	5	
Dorsey, Strother M.	son	W	M	Sept. 1884		
Dorsey, Charles E.	son	W	M	July 1886		
Dorsey, Edith M.	daughter	W	F	Aug. 1887		
Dorsey, Lena A.	daughter	W	F	Oct. 1889		
Dorsey, Earl K. E.	son	W	M	Apr. 1891		
McDonald, -------	head	W	M	Apr. 1854		
McDonald, Annie	wife	W	F	Feb. 1868		
McDonald, Blanch	daughter	W	F	Apr. 1883		
McDonald, Robert W.	son	W	M	Apr. 1884		
McDonald, Frank D.	son	W	M	Sept. 1886		
McDonald, James W.	son	W	M	Jan. 1887		
McDonald, Annie W.	daughter	W	F	Feb. 1889		
McDonald, Ardell	daughter	W	F	Nov. 1890		
McDonald, Leonard	son	W	M	Aug. 1893		
McDonald, Charles H.	son	W	M	Jan. 1896		
Heinz, John	head	W	M	Mar. 1873		plasterer
Heinz, Emma C.	wife	W	F	Dec. 1867	2	
Heinz, Samuel	son	W	M	Nov. 1894		
Heinz, Laura L.	daughter	W	F	Dec. 1896		
Rutherford, C. E.	head	W	M	May 1870		well driller
Rutherford, Samuel D.	brother	W	M	May 1852		carpenter
Rutherford, Elizabeth	mother	W	F	Sept. 1812		
Willis, James	head	B	M	Mar. 1871		engineer
Willis, Ellen	wife	B	F	Oct. 1869	6	
Willis, Charles Brown	son	B	M	Mar. 1886		laborer
Willis, Lettie Brown	daughter	B	F	July 1885		servant

Name	Relationship	Race/Sex		Date of Birth	Children	Occupation
Willis, Albert Brown	son	B	M	May 1888		
Willis, Emert	son	B	M	May 1892		
Willis, Susan	daughter	B	F	Apr. 1895		
Willis, Silas	son	B	M	Apr. 1898		
Churchmen, Huff	head	B	M	Oct. 1858		stone quarry
Churchmen, Cornelia	wife	B	F	Mar. 1871	4	
Churchmen, Hattie	daughter	B	F	July 1886		
Carter, George	head	B	M	Apr. 1850		stone quarry
Carter, Annie M.	wife	B	F	May 1853	8	
Carter, Herbert	son	B	M	July 1883		
Carter, Boyd	son	B	M	Sept. 1887		
Carter, Frank	son	B	M	Nov. 1889		
Mason, Grapp	head	B	F	Mar. 1875		
Mason, Rebecca	mother	B	F	Nov. 1837		
Nott, Caroline	head	B	F	Apr. 1855	12	
Nott, Robert Hill	son	B	M	Dec. 1882		stone quarry
Hill, Clemendie	daughter	B	F	Feb. 1885		
Ford, Tucker	head	B	M	Dec. 1852		stone quarry
Ford, David	son	B	M	Mar. 1876		stone quarry
Ford, Anna	sister	B	F	Nov. 1842		
Lashorn, Fannie	head	W	F	Nov. 1866	2	
Lashorn, Myrtle	daughter	W	F	------ 1887		
Lashorn, Charles	son	W	M	------ 1889		
Carter, Benjamin	head	B	M	May 1837		farmer
Carter, Marria	wife	B	F	Mar. 1845	3	
Carter, Isaac	son	B	M	Aug. 1883		
Carter, Benjamin F.	son	B	M	Nov. 1886		
Carter, Thomas H.	son	B	M	Apr. 1889		
Carter, Angus		B	M	Mar. 1895		
Carter, Alice		B	F	Sept. 1898		
Goens, William	head	B	M	Sept. 1862		stone quarry
Goens, Harriet	wife	B	F	Dec. 1865		
Goens, Geneva E.	daughter	B	F	Feb. 1888		
Goens, Catherine K.	daughter	B	F	May 1893		
Goens, Paul B.	son	B	M	Mar. 1890		
Goens, Fannie E.	mother	B	F	Nov. 1838		

Name	Relationship	Race/Sex		Date of Birth	Children	Occupation
Thomas, Samuel W.	head	W	M	Jan. 1872		stone quarry
Thomas, Mary	wife	W	F	Aug. 1877	3	
Thomas, Wilber	son	W	M	Apr. 1894		
Thomas, Roy	son	W	M	Mar. 1896		
Thomas, Reba	daughter	W	F	Nov. 1897		
Thomas, Wilber	head	W	M	Sept. 1840		stone quarry
Thomas, Ann W.	wife	W	F	Nov. 18443	7	
Thomas, Bertha E.	daughter	W	F	Aug. 1879		
Thomas, May C.	daughter	W	F	Nov. 1881		
Thomas, Edith M.	daughter	W	F	May 1884		
Allen, William	head	B	M	July 1873		stone quarry
Allen, Nannie	wife	B	F	Sept. 1874	2	
Allen, Lillian	daughter	B	F	Jan. 1895		
Weaver, Charles	head	B	M	Apr. 1854	7	stone quarry
Weaver, Clarence	son	B	M	Sept. 1974		stone quarry
Weaver, Mary	daughter	B	F	Dec. 1879		house maid
Weaver, Isabella	daughter	B	F	May 1884		servant
Weaver, Hester	daughter	B	F	July 1887		
Weaver, Josie	daughter	B	F	Sept. 1889		
Weaver, Rosie	daughter	B	F	Jan. 1894		
Weaver, George	son	B	M	Apr. 1896		
Henderson, Edgar	head	B	M	May 1866		stone quarry
Henderson, Maggie	wife	B	F	May 1878	1	
Hill, Fannie	mother	B	M	Aug. 1847	9	
Williams, Blair	nephew	B	M	Jan. 1888		
Henderson, James	nephew	B	M	Aug. 1897		
Washington, James	head	B	M	May 1859		stone quarry
Washington, Lucinda	wife	B	F	July 1865	9	
Washington, Daniel	son	B	M	July 1884		farm laborer
Washington, Virginia	daughter	B	F	Sept. 1888		
Washington, Robert	son	B	M	July 1891		
Washington, Allen	son	B	M	June 1894		
Washington, Nellie	daughter	B	F	Feb. 1896		
Washington, Leona	daughter	B	F	July 1897		

Name	Relationship	Race/Sex		Date of Birth	Children	Occupation
Allen, Charles	head	B	M	July 1878		stone quarry
Allen, Gussie	wife	B	F	Aug. 1880	0	
Mason, Albert	head	B	M	----------------		brick yard
Mason, Fannie	wife	B	F	----------------	2	
Mason, Christian	son	B	M	----------------		
Mason, Rene	daughter	B	F			
Bradford, George	head	B	M	Sept. 1850		farm laborer
Bradford, Alice	wife	B	F	Dec. 1853	6	
Bradford, Hellen	daughter	B	F	Mar. 1893		
Mason, George	brother	B	M	May 1879		
Mason, Mary	wife	B	F	----------------	3	
Tucker, Thomas	head	W	M	Jan. 1850		B.O. foreman
Tucker, Jane	wife	W	F	Dec. 1850	9	
Tucker, Minnie	daughter	W	F	Apr. 1877		
Tucker, Melvin	son	W	M	Oct. 1881		stone quarry
Tucker, John D.	son	W	M	Apr. 1883		engineer
Tucker, William S.	son	W	M	July 1885		mail carrier
Tucker, Sadie	daughter	W	F	Oct. 1887		
Clower, Ellen	head	W	F	Apr. 1855	4	
Clower, Bertha	daughter	W	F	Apr. 1874		
Clower, Robert Wade	son	W	M	Feb. 1880		line man
Clower, Lidia	daughter	W	F	Dec. 1884		
Howard, Samuel	head	W	M	July 1856		engineer
Howard, Margaret	wife	W	F	Mar. 1868	7	
Howard, William	son	W	M	July 1880		brass finisher
Howard, Charles	son	W	M	June 1884		B.O. fireman
Howard, Sallie	daughter	W	F	Apr. 1886		
Howard, Elfie	daughter	W	F	Dec. 1895		
Hart, Mascena	head	M	M	June 1839		stone mason
Howard, Harry	son	W	F	May 1892		

Name	Relationship	Race/Sex		Date of Birth	Children	Occupation
Owens, S. M.	head	B	M	Jan. 1848	2	stone quarry
William, M. E.	daughter	B	F	Feb. 1872		quarry store
Whittington, J. T.	head	W	M	Jan. 1857		Chief engineer
Whittington, Annie E.	wife	W	F	Oct. 1856	8	
Whittington, Clarence	son	W	M	Apr. 1879		
Whittington, Ohamer	son	W	M	Feb. 1881		station engineer
Whittington, Fema W.	daughter	W	F	Sept. 1883		
Whittington, Boy C.	son	W	M	Jan. 1888		
Whittington, Daisy W.	daughter	W	F	Mar. 1890		
Whittington, Gracie	daughter	W	F	Jan. 1892		
Whittington, Florence	daughter	W	F	May 1895		
Wilt, Lewis	head	W	M	Feb. 1847		grocer
Wilt, Georgina	wife	W	F	May 1853	4	
Wilt, Walter F.	son	W	M	July 1874		grocer
Wilt, Irene M.	daughter	W	F	Mar. 1879		
Wilt, Margie L.	daughter	W	F	Apr. 1880		
Wilt, Mabel C.	daughter	W	F	Apr. 1880		
Homsher, T. H.	head	W	M	Feb. 1828		grocer
Homsher, Lucretia	wife	W	F	Feb. 1832	2	
Homsher, Arabella	daughter	W	F	Sept. 1860		
Homsher, Virginia	daughter	W	F	Aug. 1879		
Lucas, C. C.	head	W	M	Mar. 1861		doctor
Lucas, F. C.	wife	W	F	Mar. 1861		
Lucas, John	son	W	M	June 1890		
Lucas, Mary	daughter	W	F	Dec. 1892		
Lucas, Charles	son	W	M	Sept. 1894		
Lucas, S. E.	aunt	W	F	Feb. 1826		
Wyndlam, J. E.	head	W	M	July 1864		carpenter
Wyndlam, Anna B.	wife	W	F	June 1875	4	
Wyndlam, John W.	son	W	M	June 1893		
Wyndlam, Della V.	daughter	W	F	Aug. 1895		
Wyndlam, Sarah M.	daughter	W	F	Mar. 1897		
Wyndlam, James E.	son	W	M	Apr. 1899		
Licklider, S. D.	head	W	M	Apr. 1855		merchant
Licklider, Martha	daughter	W	F	Aug. 18-		
Licklider, Samuel S.	son	W	M	Aug. 1899		
Sinclair, Virginia	head	W	F	Dec. 1854	2	
Licklider, Sallie D.	wife	W	F	Mar. 1869	2	
Sinclair, Harold	son	W	M	May 1892		

Name	Relationship	Race/Sex		Date of Birth	Children	Occupation
Ramsburg, Violet	daughter	W	F	Oct. 1862		
Ramsburg, Willie	daughter	W	F	Dec. 1894		
Ramsburg, Joseph	son	W	M	Mar. 1900		
Fletcher, Thomas	head	B	M	Dec. 1874		stone quarry
Fletcher, Adelio	wife	B	F	Mar. 1875	2	
Fletcher, Norman B.	son	B	M	Nov. 1897		
Fletcher, Bertie	daughter	B	F	Apr. 1900		
Whitelock, W. E.	head	W	M	Dec. 1873		setting tele. poles
Whitelock, Carrie F.	wife	W	F	Sept. 1870	2	
Whitelock, Clyde	son	W	M	Dec. 1896		
Whitelock, Herman	son	W	M	Aug. 1898		
Cox, William	head	W	M	Jan. 1835		cooper
Cox, Rebecca	wife	W	F	Apr. 1838	2	
Cox, George	son	W	M	Aug. 1879		stone quarry
Cox, Edward	son	W	M	Apr. 1881		stone quarry
Hunter, Isreal	head	B	M	July 1860		stone quarry
Hunter, Laura	wife	B	F	Apr. 1865	8	
Hunter, Henry E.	son	B	M	Dec. 1884		laborer
Hunter, Albert	son	B	M	May 1888		
Hunter, Levenia	daughter	B	F	Aug. 1890		
Hunter, Martha	daughter	B	F	July 1892		
Hunter, Georgia	daughter	B	F	July 1894		
Hunter, Elizabeth	daughter	B	F	Sept. 1896		
Briscoe, Fannie	head	B	F	Feb. 1883		
Sharff, J. E.	head	W	M	July 1873		station foreman
Sharff, M. N.	wife	W	F	Dec. 1878	4	
Sharff, Christopher	son	W	M	Aug. 1896		
Sharff, ----------	daughter	W	F	Dec. 1897		
Sharff, Dewey	son	W	M	June 1898		
Sharff, Ernest	son	W	M	Mar. 1900		
Hunter, John	head	B	M	Aug. 1863		farm laborer
Hunter, Hannah	wife	B	F	Jan. 1873	3	
Hunter, Robert	son	B	M	June 1893		
Hunter, Ernest	son	B	M	Oct. 1894		
Hunter, Rhoda	daughter	B	F	Apr. 1895		

Name	Relationship	Race/Sex		Date of Birth	Children	Occupation
Thompson, Bettie B.	daughter	W	F	Feb. 1883		
Thompson, John C.	son	W	M	Jan. 1888		
Thompson, Sarah E.	daughter	W	F	Jan. 1888		
Burnett, J. W.	head	W	M	July 1878		farmer
Burnett, Mary A.	sister	W	F	Dec. 1877		
Patterson, R. W.	head	W	M	Jan. 1872		doctor
Patterson, V. A. M.	wife	W	F	Aug. 1880		
Miller A.	head	W	M	Dec. 1847		farmer
Miller, Mary F.	wife	W	F	Oct. 1848	7	
Miller, Gilbert C.	son	W	M	Feb. 1878		farm laborerr
Miller, Herbert. A.	son	W	M	Apr. 1880		farm laborer
Miller, Elija W.	son	W	M	Aug. 1882		farm laborer
Miller, Laura	daughter	W	F	Mar. 1886		
Miller, A. S. Jr.	son	W	M	Aug. 1888		
Miller, Paul E.	son	W	M	Mar. 1895		
Amey, William	head	W	M	Aug. 1838		telegraph operator
Amey, Eliza	wife	W	F	July 1843	12	
Amey, Jacob	son	W	M	Oct. 1872		telegraph
Amey, Joseph	son	W	M	Mar. 1874		telegraph
Amey, Edgar	son	W	M	June 1881		telegraph
Amey, Bessie	daughter	W	F	Mar. 1885		
Border, D. W.	head	W	M	June 1850		doctor
Border, Clara C.	wife	W	F	Dec. 1857	2	
Border, Ralph W.	son	W	M	Feb. 1887		
Border, Margaret W.	daughter	W	F	Nov. 1894		
Kerfott, J. P.	head	W	M	Dec. 1844		farmer
Kerfott, May S.	wife	W	F	May 1844	6	
Kerfott, W. H.	son	W	M	Sept. 1868		
Kerfott, Nannie B.	daughter	W	F	June 1870		
Kerfott, Mary	daughter	W	F	Sept. 1889		
Kerfott, John P.	son	W	M	Sept. 1891		
Kerfott, W. H.	son	W	M	Sept. 1893		
Kerfott, Sidney	daughter	W	F	Dec. 1895		
Anderson, W. O.	servant	B	M	May 1860		
Kisner, Lydia	servant	B	F	Dec. 1876		
Ferguson, C.	head	B	M	July 1871		farm laborer
Ferguson, Katie	wife	B	F	Nov. 1876	3	

Name	Relationship	Race/Sex		Date of Birth	Children	Occupation
Campbell, Jane	daughter	W	F	Sept. 1896		
Campbell, Sarah	daughter	W	F	Dec. 1898		
Abrose, Taylor		W	M	Oct. 1861		farm laborer
Rice, William	head	W	M	Dec. 1852		farm laborer
Rice, M. E.	wife	W	F	Sept. 1867	11	
Rice, K. R.	daughter	W	F	Aug. 1879		
Rice, J. W.	son	W	M	Oct. 1881		
Rice, Grace H.	daughter	W	F	Aug. 1883		
Rice, William M.	son	W	M	Nov. 1884		
Rice, Edward C.	son	W	M	Feb. 1887		
Rice, Ida L.	daughter	W	F	Apr. 1889		
Rice, Samuel R.	son	W	M	Mar. 1891		
Rice, Rosie M.	daughter	W	F	Mar. 1893		
Rice, Carl B.	son	W	M	May 1895		
Sibert, G. W.	head	W	M	July 1836		land lord
Sibert, Sarah E.	wife	W	F	Jan. 1845	2	
Ellis, Sarah	niece	W	F	Mar. 1878		
Bitner, J. C.	head	W	M	Aug. 1845		farmer
Bitner, Betty H.	wife	W	F	Sept. 1849	4	
Bitner, Blanch	daughter	W	F	Apr. 1874		teacher
Bitner, Leila	daughter	W	F	Apr. 1879		
Bitner, Ernest H.	son	W	M	Sept. 1884		
Widmyer A. M.	head	W	M	Jan. 1845		farmer
Widmyer, Ellen	wife	W	F	Feb. 1840	3	
Widmyer, C. C.	son	W	M	Mar. 1875		
Widmyer, Sarah	daughter	W	F	Dec. 1870		
Widmyer, John	son	W	M	Mar. 1890		
Head, --------	head	B	M	May 1867		day laborer
------, Richard	pauper	B	M	Feb. 1873		day laborer
Jones, C. E.	head	W	M	June 1865		farmer
Jones, Mary P.	wife	W	F	May 1872	3	
Jones, D. P.	son	W	M	Aug. 1895		
Jones, P. M.	son	W	M	May 1899		
Jones, M. C.	mother	W	F	Sept. 1832		
Brown, Edyth	servant	B	F	Mar. 1866		servant
Washington, F.	servant	B	F	------ 1855		servant
Benner J. W.	head	W	M	Feb. 1846		farmer

Name	Relationship	Race/Sex		Age	Occupation
McDaniel, Robert A.	son	B	M	25	
McDaniel, May	daughter	B	F	23	
McDaniel, Benjamin	son	B	M	20	farm laborer
McDaniel, Amelia	daughter	B	F	19	
McDaniel, Alama	daughter	B	F	17	
McDaniel, Lucia	daughter	B	F	14	
McDaniel, Charlie	son	B	M	12	
McDaniel, Edward	son	B	M	10	
McDaniel, Jacob	son	B	M	10	
Serbert, J. C.	head	W	M	32	farm owner
Serbert, Sophia	wife	W	F	25	
Serbert, Harry	son	W	M	12	
Serbert, Alice	daughter	W	F	3	
Serbert, Sallie E.	mother	W	F	ill.	
Willis, J. W.	head	W	M	38	farmer
Willis, Ella	wife	W	F	27	
Williams, Hugh	hired hand	W	M	19	herds man/farm laborer
Milbourns, Milton	head	W	M	38	farmer
Milbourns, Rose Anna	wife	W	F	32	
Milbourns, James	son	W	M	7	
Milbourns, William	son	W	M	5	
Milbourns, Sara	mother	W	F	60	
Socks, Daniel	head	W	M	60	farm laborer
Socks, Eliza	wife	W	F	62	
Socks, John	son	W	M	26	railroad worker
Socks, Lara	wife	W	F	22	
Socks, Leona	daughter	W	F	3	
Socks, Ida	daughter	W	F	2	
Fleming, C. H.	head	W	M	22	farm laborer
Fleming, Stacia	wife	W	F	32	
Fleming, Thelma	daughter	W	F	7	
Fleming, Zack	son	W	M	2	
Walkins, Emma	servant	B	F	22	servant
Lloyd, J. W.	head	W	M	ill.	
Lloyd, Martha	wife	W	F	ill.	
Socks, Daniel	head	W	M	28	railroad worker
Socks, Bessie	wife	W	F	26	
Socks, Charles Edgar	son	W	M	8	
Socks, Hellen	daughter	W	F	ill.	
Tharpe, B. E.	head	W	M	40	farmer
Tharpe, Cora	wife	W	F	25	
Tharpe, Viola	daughter	W	F	18	
Tharpe, Wilbur	son	W	M	17	home farmer

Name	Relationship	Race/Sex		Date of Birth	Children	Occupation
Sinclair, Willie Sager	grandson	W	M	Aug. 1896		
Horner, Mary	mother	W	F	Dec. 1822		
Timbers, Thomas	head	B	M	July 1849		farm laborer
Timbers, Julia	wife	B	F	Sept. 1864	2	
Timbers, Fred D.	son	B	M	Dec. 1855		stone quarry
Faye, J. U.	head	W	M	Aug. 1849		farmer
Faye, Josephine	daughter	W	F	Feb. 1882		
Faye, Lizzie	daughter	W	F	Apr. 1886		
Faye, Fannie	daughter	W	F	Oct. 1888		
Campbell, Jerry	head	B	M	Oct. 1860		farm laborer
Campbell, Belle E.	wife	B	F	Dec. 1857		
Campbell, Carter	son	B	M	Jan. 1886		farm laborer
Campbell, Thomas	son	B	M	Feb. 1888		
Campbell, William	son	B	M	May 1891		
Stump, C. M.	head	W	M	Dec. 1837		runs grain elevator
Whittington, Edgar	head	W	M	Feb. 1861		watchman of the quarry
Whittington, Isabella	wife	W	F	Nov. 1864	6	
Whittington, Francis	son	W	M	July 1884		
Whittington, Liddia	daughter	W	F	July 1881		
Whittington, Raymond	son	W	M	July 1893		
Whittington, Mary,	daughter	W	F	Sept. 1895		
Whittington, Virginia	daughter	W	F	Jan. 1898		
Smallwood, Scott	head	W	M	Oct. 1875		R. R. worker
Smallwood, Cora	wife	W	F	May 1872	1	
Smallwood, Lelia	daughter	W	F	June 1899		
McIntire, B. S.	head	W	M	Oct. 1835		R. R. agent
McIntire, Effie	daughter	W	F	May 1874		
McIntire, Elmyra	daughter	W	F	Jan. 1881		
Ramsburg, C. J.	head	W	M	Apr. 1867		R. R. agent
Ramsburg, Carrie	wife	W	F	Mar. 1870	3	
McIntire, May C.	daughter	W	F	June 1877		
McIntire, L. G.	daughter	W	F	Sept. 1879		

Name	Relationship	Race/Sex		Age	Occupation
Tharpe, Pearl	daughter	W	F	13	
Tharpe, Nannie	daughter	W	F	11	
Tharpe, Virginia	daughter	W	F	1	
Lucas, Reilly	head	B	M	54	farm laborer
Lucas, Robert	son	B	M	23	farm laborer
Lucas, Luke	son	B	M	21	farm laborer
Lucas, Clarence	son	B	M	17	farm laborer
Lucas, Harry	son	B	M	17	
Lucas, Johnson	son	B	M	14	
Lucas, Sallie	daughter	B	F	12	
Hoffman, G. W.	head	W	M	36	orchard owner
Hoffman, Betty	wife	W	F	35	
Hoffman, Elizabeth	mother	W	F	60	
Frith, C. M.	head	W	M	35	farm laborer
Frith, Lucy	wife	W	F	34	
Frith, Flossie	daughter	W	F	11	
Frith, Charles	son	W	M	10	
Frith, Verona	daughter	W	F	5	
Frith, Gladys G.	daughter	W	F	2	
Everhart, Alberta	servant	W	F	15	
Brown, Edward	head	B	M	49	fruit laborer
Brown, Suetta	wife	B	F	37	
Brown, Lida M.	daughter	B	F	14	
Brown, Sara	daughter	B	F	11	
Brown, Eva	daughter	B	F	10	
Brown, Charles	son	B	M	6	
Brown, Gilbert	son	B	M	2	
Brown, Benjamin	son	B	M	6/12	
Allen, David	head	B	M	59	stone mason
Allen, Mary	wife	B	F	56	
Allen, ------	daughter	B	F	14	
Allen, Ella	daughter	B	F	12	
Moore, Vincent	head	W	M	54	farm owner
Moore, Mary	wife	W	F	58	
Davidson, Hugh	hired hand	W	M	12	laborer
-------, Giles	hired hand	W	M	11	laborer
Woodfork, George	head	B	M	60	fruit laborer
Woodfork, Alice	wife	B	F	58	
Woodfork, George	son	B	M	23	
Hackley, Edward	head	B	M	40	railroad worker
Hackley, Louise	wife	B	F	49	
Burden, Maybel	daughter	B	F	16	cook
---------, Elsie	daughter	B	F	7	

Name	Relationship	Race/Sex		Date of Birth	Children	Occupation
Benner, Sarah	wife	W	F	Feb. 1850	6	
Benner, Anna C.	daughter	W	F	June 1873		
Benner, Arthur B.	son	W	M	Jan. 1881		farm laborer
Benner, James	son	W	M	Apr. 1884		farm laborer
Benner, Franklin	son	W	M	May 1886		
Benner, Leila	daughter	W	F	Nov. 1890		
Benner, Stanley	son	W	M	July 1892		
Benner, Ada	daughter`	W	F	Apr. 1895		

Selected from Federal Census of Middleway District 1910

Name	Relationship	Race/Sex		Age	Occupation
Magruder, D. L.	head	W	M	48	farmer
Magruder, Jane L.	wife	W	F	43	
Magruder, Evard L.	son	W	M	23	
Magruder, Arnold B.	son	W	M	20	
Magruder, Norman	son	W	M	17	
Magruder, Ruth W.	daughter	W	F	11	
Gibbin, Rachel	orphan	W	F	12	
Miles, Ice	orphan	W	M	12	
Border, Dr. D. W.	head	W	M	59	orchardist, doctor
Border, Clara	wife	W	F	51	
Border, Marguerite	daughter	W	F	15	
Bitner, J. C.	head	W	M		
Bitner, Bettie	wife	W	F	61	
Bitner, Blanch	daughter	W	F		college
Bitner, Leila	daughter	W	F		college
Henkle, Jessie	sister in law	W	F	78	
Galloway, Henry	servant				servant
Morgan, Douglas	hired hand				herd man
Frith, E. G.	head	W	M	27	farm and orchard worker
Frith, Edith	wife	W	F	22	
Frith, Mary	daughter	W	F	8	
Frith, John	son	W	M	2	
McDaniel, James W.	head	B	M	49	farm owner

217

Name	Relationship	Race/Sex		Date of Birth	Children	Occupation
Ferguson, Sallie	daughter	B	F	Jan. 1892		
Ferguson, John	son	B	M	Jan. 1894		
Ferguson, Charles	son	B	M	Dec. 1896		
Ferguson, ------	brother	B	M	Nov. 1876		
Moore, J. V.	head	W	M	Apr. 1843		farmer
Moore, Mary H.	wife	W	F	Dec. 1856		
Moore, J. V.	father	W	M	Mar. 1816		
Trump, Henry A.	head	W	M	Nov. 1837		exp. lumber
Trump, Julia S.	wife	W	F	Nov. 1838	2	
Trump, F. O.	son	W	M	Apr. 1874		merchant
Trump, Rua	wife	W	F	Nov. 1875		
Trump, George H.	son	W	M	Mar. 1868		lumber
Rogers, R. H.	head	W	M	Feb. 1854		blacksmith
Rogers, Sallie	wife	W	F	Mar. 1868	5	
Rogers, Robert R.	son	W	M	Jan. 1889		
Rogers, Herbert Henry	son	W	M	Feb. 1891		
Rogers, Beatrice	daughter	W	F	May 1894		
Rogers, Angia	son	W	M	May 1897		
Hammill, S.	head	W	M	June 1854		day laborer
Hammill, Alivia	brother	W	M	June 1816		
Cook, Elgin		W	F	Aug. 1865		house keeper
Allen, -----	head	B	M	Dec. 1869		farm laborer
Allen, Mary	wife	B	F	1891	4	
Allen, Joseph	son	B	M	Dec. 1891		
Allen, Mary C.	daughter	B	F	June 1893		
Allen, Delphia	daughter	B	F	July 1895		
Allen, William	son	B	M	Mar. 1898		
Campbell, T.	head	W	M	Feb. 1860		farmer
Campbell, Rebecca	wife	W	F	June 1872	2	
Getzendanner, C.	head	W	M	Dec. 1855		landlord
Getzendanner, Margaret E.	mother	W	F	Jan. 1837	7	
Getzendanner, May	daughter	W	F	Jan. 1876		
Getzendanner, Phoebe	daughter	W	F	June 1870		
Braxton, Sally	servant	W	F	------ 1889	11	

Name	Relationship	Race/Sex		Date of Birth	Children	Occupation
Twyman, Frank	head	B	M	Apr. 1875		stone quarry
Twyman, Sallie	wife	B	F	May 1876	2	
Twyman, James	son	B	M	May 1895		
Twyman, Harriet B.	daughter	B	F	Dec. 1898		
Cox, Charles	head	W	M	May 1866		stone quarry
Cox, Leola	wife	W	F	Sept. 1874	4	
Cox, Arthur	son	W	M	Feb. 1895		
Cox, George W.	son	W	M	July 1896		
Cox, Charles M.	son	W	M	Mar. 1898		
Cox, Huston	son	W	M	May 1900		
Henrietta, Mary	head	W	F	Aug. 1878	1	
Henrietta, Edward	husband	W	M	July 1873		
Henrietta, Emma	sister	W	F	Apr. 1881		
Henrietta, Arby	son	W	M	June 1897		
Cox, David E.	head	W	M	July 1868		laborer
Cox, Annie	wife	W	F	Jan. 1872	5	
Cox, Pearl B.	daughter	W	F	June 1895		
Cox, Roy C.	son	W	M	July 1897		
Cox, Mildred W.	daughter	W	F	Aug. 1898		
Mc-, Charles	head	W	M	Aug. 1861		
Mc-, Mary C.	wife	W	F	May 1861	6	
Mc-, Isaact L.	daughter	W	F	Dec. 18-		
Mc-, John S.	son	W	M	Mar. 1894		
Mc-, Charles James	son	W	M	Dec. 1895		
Mc-, Ernest	son	W	M	Feb. 1898		
Hess, Joseph A.		W	M	Feb. 1842		
Whittington, John	head	W	M	Aug. 1871		farm laborer
Whittington, Sarah	wife	W	F	Oct. 1866	3	
Whittington, Elmer L.	son	W	M	Jan. 1895		
Whittington, Nellie M.	daughter	W	F	Sept. 1896		
Whittington, Millie	daughter	W	F	Aug. 1989		
Thompson, John	head	W	M	Dec. 1835		farm laborer
Thompson, Pamelipia	wife	W	F	Apr. 1857	6	
Thompson, George W.	son	W	M	Mar. 1870		farm laborer
Thompson, James H.	son	W	M	Apr. 1877		farm laborer
Thompson, Frank C.	son	W	M	Mar. 1879		farm laborer

219

Name	Relationship	Race/Sex		Age	Occupation
Whittington, C. O.	head	W	M	29	laborer
Whittington, Mary	wife	W	F	28	
Whittington, Kenneth	son	W	M	6	
Whittington, Ernie	son	W	M	3	
Whittington, Andrew	son	W	M	1	
Allen, Charlie	head	B	M	30	laborer
Allen, Bessie	wife	B	F		
Allen, Hugh	son	B	M	9	
Allen, Harry	son	B	M	7	
Allen, Andrew	son	B	M	5	
Allen, Viola	daughter	B	F	4	
Allen, Dazie	daughter	B	F	1	
Bradford, George	head	B	M	49	farm laborer
Bradford, Alice	wife	B	F	53	
Bradford, Helen	daughter	B	F	17	
Allen, William	head	B	M	39	laborer
Allen, Nannie	wife	B	F	35	
Allen, Lilian	daughter	B	F	15	
Allen, William	son	B	M	6	
Allen, David	son	B	M	4	
Allen, Daniel	son	B	M	3	
Carter, George	head	B	M	56	laborer
Carter, Annie	wife	B	F	50	
Carter, Boyd	son	B	M	21	laborer
Wise, Richard	head	W	M	65	laborer
Wise, Eliza	wife	W	F	45	
Wise, Charlie	son	W	M	27	laborer
Wise, Mollie	daughter	W	F	21	
Wise, William	son	W	M	19	laborer
Wise, Emillia	daughter	W	F	15	
Wise, Sharlott	daughter	W	F	12	
Wise, Robert	son	W	M	10	
Wise, Sara	daughter	W	F	8	
Wise, Marshall	son	W	M	6	
Wise, Nellie	daughter	W	F	4	
Lee, Robert	head	W	M	36	farm laborer
Lee, Mary	wife	W	F	32	
Lee, Mary	daughter	W	F	3	
Whittington, G. W.	head	W	M	41	
Whittington, Lottie	wife	W	F	40	
Whittington, Jennie	daughter	W	F	18	
Whittington, Burnett	son	W	M	12	
Whittington, Mary	daughter	W	F	5	
Winters, G. W.	head	W	M	40	

Name	Relationship	Race/Sex		Age	Occupation
Winters, Emma	wife	W	F	36	
Winters, Katerina	daughter	W	F	7	
Folk, Katherine	mother	W	F	69	
McCoy, Lizzie	servant	W	F	45	servant
Brandenberg, Elmer	servant	W	M	12	servant
Manuel, James C.	head	W	M	31	farm owner
Manuel, Virginia	mother	W	F	70	
Manuel, Sara	sister	W	F	32	
Jones, C. E.	head	W	M	44	manager of an orchard
Jones, Mary P.	wife	W	F	37	
Jones, David L.	son	W	M	15	
Jones, Paxton	son	W	M	10	
Jones, William B.	son	W	M	2/12	
Marshall, P. P.	father-in-law	W	M	75	
Marshall, Isabell	mother-in-law	W	F	72	
Jones, Mary C.	mother	W	M	77	
Paine, Leila	servant	B	F	25	servant
Paine, John	hired hand	B	M	30	laborer
Paine, Edna	daughter	B	F	3	
Paine, Florence	daughter	B	F	3	
Paine, Raymond	son	B	M	1/12	
Jones, Edith	servant	B	F	22	
Widmyer, C. E.	head	W	M	35	owns farm
Widmyer, Lenora	wife	W	F	28	
Widmyer, Irving	son	W	M	1	
Widmyer, Clara V.	mother	W	F	69	
Fulk, W. A.	head	W	M	45	farm owner
Fulk, Mary E. Enther	wife	W	F	45	
Fulk, Harry	son	W	M	18	
Fulk, Charlie	son	W	M	8	
Fulk, Nellie	daughter	W	F	6	
Enther, Sallie	sister	W	F	50	
McCoy, Sallie	servant	W	F	65	servant
Campbell, J. F.	head	W	M	48	
Campbell, Rebecca	wife	W	M	35	
Campbell, Sara	daughter	W	F	11	
Campbell, Philip	son	W	M	7	
Campbell, John	son	W	M	4	
Campbell, Rebecca	daughter	W	F	3	
Jordan, Becke	servant	B	F		
Roman, Helen	servant	B	F	40	
Campbell, Carter	head	B	M	24	farmer
Campbell, Lilliam	wife	B	F	21	

Name	Relationship	Race/Sex		Age	Occupation
Clipp, Martha	head	W	F	55	
Clipp, Dora	daughter	W	F	24	
Clipp, Edgar	son	W	M	22	laborer
Lingamow, John	head	B	M	39	dairy farmer
Lingamow, Emma	wife	B	F	29	
Lingamow, Hugh	son	B	M	14	
Lingamow, Viola	daughter	B	F	7	
Lingamow, Anguns	son	B	M	4	
Lingamow, Ardella	daughter	B	F	2/12	
Everhart, T. O.	head	W	M	39	dairy farmer
Everhart, Cora	wife	W	F	33	
Everhart, Herbert	son	W	M	3	
Miller, A. S.	head	W	M	62	orchard and a farm
Miller, Mary	wife	W	M	54	
Miller, Herbert	son	W	M	30	salesman
Miller, Laura	daughter	W	F	23	teacher
Miller, Abram S.	son	W	M	22	home farmer
Miller, Paul E.	son	W	M	16	home farmer
Brown, J. P.	head	W	M	43	home farmer
Brown, Irene	wife	W	F	32	
Brown, Max	son	W	M	7	
Brown, Tracie J.	son	W	M	4	
Brown, Lucilla	daughter	W	F	2	
Brown, Tyler	son	W	M	1/12	
Horn, W. B.	head	W	M	40	laborer
Horn, Bertha	wife	W	F	38	seamstress
Horn, Mark	son	W	M	21	
Horn, Dorothea	daughter	W	F	2	
Burhman, J. E.	head	W	M	40	foreman at the railroad
Burhman, Pearl	wife	W	F	36	
Burhman, Grace	daughter	W	F	16	
Burhman, Harold	son	W	M	6	
Mason, G. M.	head	B	M	32	odd jobs
Mason, Mary	wife	B	F	38	
Mason, Robert	son	B	M	22	odd jobs
Mason, Susan	daughter	B	F	19	servant
Mason, Sallie	daughter	B	B	15	servant
McIntyre, E. M	head	W	F	45	teacher
McIntyre, Leona	sister	W	F	37	
McIntyre, Ervie	sister	W	F	32	
Wilt, W. F.	head	W	M	35	merchant
Wilt, Virginia	wife	W	F	30	

Name	Relationship	Race/Sex		Age	Occupation
Homsher, Bell	sister	W	F	50	
Campbell, E. D.	head	W	M	48	farmer
Campbell, Fannie	wife	W	F	38	
Campbell, Edgar	son	W	M	9	
Campbell, Katherine	daughter	W	F	6	
Campbell, Elizabeth	daughter	W	F	5	
Campbell, Francis	daughter	W	F	3	
Ross, Virginia	servant	B	F	20	servant
Corbin, William	head	W	M	27	laborer
Corbin, Georgia	wife	W	F		
Corbin, Elsie	daughter	W	F		
Corbin, Frank	son	W	M		
Young, Ralph	head	W	M	27	
Young, Edith	wife	W	F	20	
Young, H. Mary	daughter	W	F	7	
Young, Chester	son	W	M	3	
Trump, Frank O.	head	W	M	36	postmaster
Trump, Rua M.	wife	W	F	34	
Trump, Fannie	daughter	W	F	7	
Trump, Elizabeth	daughter	W	F	6	
Trump, James	son	W	M	3	
Trump, Julia	mother	W	F	72	
Amey, W. F.	head	W	M	70	laborer
Amey, Eliza	wife	W	F	68	
Amey, Jacob	son	W	M	48	
Amey, Josephy	son	W	M	36	
Amey, C. L.	son	W	M	29	
Tryman, Frank	head	B	M	46	laborer
Tryman, Sallie	wife	B	F	40	
Tryman, James	son	B	M	14	
Tryman, Hattie	daughter	B	F	11	
Tryman, Cora	daughter	B	F	7	
Tryman, Harry	son	B	M	3	
Morgan, Harrison	head	B	M	78	laborer
Morgan, Elban	daughter	B	F	29	
Morgan, Mahia	daughter	B	F	8	
Morgan, Consula	daughter	B	F	3	
Morgan, Grace	daughter	B	F	2	
Preston, Liza	head	B	F	63	
Othenfarger, Luther	head	B	M	28	laborer
Othenfarger, Flora	wife	B	F	21	
Othenfarger, Effleter	daughter	B	F	4	
Goens, Dino	head	B	M	40	laborer
Goens, Mary	wife	B	F	38	

Name	Relationship	Race/Sex		Age	Occupation
Goens, Rodney	son	B	M	17	laborer
Goens, Lizzie	daughter	B	F	15	
Goens, Robert	son	B	M	13	
Goens, Mary Arter	daughter	B	F	11	
Goens, Emma	daughter	B	F	5	
Goens, John	son	B	M	2	
Goens, Rachel	mother	B	F	55	
Roderford, James	head	W	M	39	laborer
Roderford, Bell	wife	W	F	35	
Roderford, Andrew	son	W	M	12	
Roderford, Ema	daughter	W	F	10	
Roderford, Frances	daughter	W	F	7	
Roderford, Carl	son	W	M	4	
Roderford, May	daughter	W	F	1	
Tyston, William	head	W	M	60	laborer
Tyston, Anna	wife	W	F	50	
Rose, William	head	W	M	36	laborer
Rose, Minnie	wife	W	F	36	
Rose, Vernon	son	W	M	9	
Rose, Robert	son	W	M	8	
Rose, Mary	daughter	W	F	8/12	
Carpenter, Albert	head	W	M	52	laborer
Carpenter, Annie	wife	W	F	55	
Smallwood, J. L.	head	W	M	35	
Smallwood, Cora	wife	W	F	33	
Smallwood, Lelia	daughter	W	F	11	
Smallwood, Margie Lee	daughter	W	F	8	
Smallwood, Stewart	son	W	M	6	
Smallwood, Jacob	son	W	M	4	
Smallwood, Hattie	daughter	W	F	2	
Stanley, J. F.	head	W	M	32	carpenter
Stanley, Blanch	wife	W	F	29	
Stanley, David	son	W	M	3	
Stanley, Marguerite	daughter	W	F	1	
Myers, J. P.	head	W	M	40	barber
Myers, Jane	wife	W	F	37	
Myers, Tom	son	W	M	17	farm laborer
Tucker, J. D.	head	W	M	27	laborer
Tucker, Lillie	wife	W	F	27	
Tucker, Richard	son	W	M	6	
Tucker, Raymond	son	W	M	5	
Tucker, Minnie	daughter	W	F	3	
Tucker, Leonard	son	W	M	1	
Whittington, J. L.	head	W	M	53	merchant

Name	Relationship	Race/Sex		Age	Occupation
Whittington, Emma	wife	W	F	53	
Whittington, Clarence	son	W	M	30	book keeper for quarry
Whittington, Boyd	son	W	M	20	machinist
Whittington, Grace	daughter	W	F	18	
Whittington, Florence	daughter	W	F	14	
Whittington, Harry	head	W	M	32	engineer for the railroad
Whittington, Mable	wife	W	F	29	
Whittington, Charles	son	W	M	9	
Whittington, James	son	W	M	7	
Whittington, Lawrence	son	W	M	4	
Whittington, Elizabeth	daughter	W	F	1	
Allen, Harry	head	B	M	24	laborer, railroad
Allen, Ella	wife	B	F	22	
Allen, Myrtle	daughter	B	F	4	
Allen, Georgie	son	B	M	2	
Allen, Hattie	daughter	B	F	6/12	
Allen, Newton	head	B	M	27	laborer
Allen, Victoria	wife	B	F	26	
Allen, Raymond	son	B	M	3	
Allen, Mack	son	B	M	2/12	
Washington, Dave Jr.	head	B	M	50	laborer
Washington, Lucinda	wife	B	F	44	
Washington, Daniel	son	B	M	26	laborer
Washington, Robert	son	B	M	19	laborer
Washington, Allen	son	B	M	15	laborer
Washington, Nellie	daughter	B	F	14	
Washington, Leonard	son	B	M	12	
Washington, Phoebe	daughter	B	F	9	
Washington, William	son	B	M	7	
Washington, Alice	daughter	B	F	4	
Washington, John	son	B	M	2	
Washington, Grace	daughter	B	F	1	
Campbell, Bell	head	B	F	48	
Campbell, Tom	son	B	M	24	laborer
Head, James	head	B	M	40	stone quarry
Hart, Howard	head	B	M	38	stone quarry
Hart, Lucinda	wife	B	F	35	
Goens, James	boarder	B	M	14	laborer
Campbell, Abram	head	B	M	37	laborer
Campbell, Sadie	wife	B	F	31	
Campbell, George	son	B	M	13	
Campbell, Hugh	son	B	M	8	

Name	Relationship	Race/Sex		Age	Occupation
Campbell, Dora	daughter	B	F	7	
Campbell, Carol	daughter	B	F	4	
Campbell, Esther	daughter	B	F	2	
Campbell, Elmer	son	B	M	8/12	
Carter, Herbert	head	B	M	20	railroad
Carter, Lenia	wife	B	F	23	
Carter, Margarite	daughter	B	F	1	
Carter, George	son	B	M	4/12	
Carter, Becky	grandmother	B	F	75	
Roper, C. E.	head	B	M	44	
Roper, Lucinda	wife	B	F	42	
Roper, Emma	daughter	B	F	22	
Roper, Charles	son	B	M	19	laborer
Roper, Clifton	son	B	M	16	
Roper, Stella	daughter	B	F	15	
Roper, Ruth	daughter	B	F	11	
Roper, ---------	son	B	M	7	
Roper, Theresa	daughter	B	F	5	
Carter, Ben	head	B	M	74	
Carter, Alice	wife	B	F		
Carter, Isaac	son	B	M	26	laborer
Carter, Ben Jr.	son	B	M	24	laborer
Carter, -----------	son	B	M	21	laborer
Ford, Daniel	head	B	M	55	laborer
Ford, Ella	wife	B	F	26	
Ford, Effie	daughter	B	F	5	
Ford, ----------	son	B	M	3	
Ford, William	head	B	M	47	laborer
Ford, Harriet	wife	B	F	40	
Ford, Paul	son	B	F	20	laborer
Ford, Catherine	daughter	B	F	16	
Granigan, H. A.	head	W	M	43	railroad
Granigan, Robert	son	W	M	20	railroad
Granigan, D. R.	son	W	M	19	railroad
Granigan, Thomas R.	son	W	M	17	laborer
Granigan, Laura	daughter	W	F	13	
Granigan, Daisy	daughter	W	F	12	
Granigan, Minnie	daughter	W	F	6	
Granigan, Alice	daughter	W	F	2	
Granigan, Charles	son	W	M	5/12	
Thomas, S. Walter	head	W	M	38	railroad foreman
Thomas, Mary D.	wife	W	F	35	
Thomas, Wilber B.	son	W	M	16	

Name	Relationship	Race/Sex		Age	Occupation
Thomas, Roy C.	son	W	M	14	
Thomas, Reba A.	daughter	W	F	12	
Thomas, Mary A.	daughter	W	F	10	
Thomas, Alton B.	son	W	M	6	
Thomas, William Jr.	son	W	M	2	
Thomas, Annie A.	mother	W	F	65	
Sharff, J. E.	head	W	M	37	railroad fireman
Sharff, Annie	wife	W	F	33	
Sharff, Christopher	son	W	M	14	
Sharff, Maggie	daughter	W	F	13	
Sharff, Dewey	son	W	M	11	
Sharff, Joe	son	W	M	10	
Sharff, Rosie	daughter	W	F	4	
Ritcharson, John	head	B	M	30	stone quarry
Ritcharson, Eva	wife	B	F	31	
Boyd, Russell	boarder	B	M	21	stone quarry
Johnson, Harry	son	B	M	2	
Lockley, George	head	B	M	25	laborer
Lockley, Emma	wife	B	F	23	
Lockley, Georgie	son	B	M		
Comb, John	head	B	M	38	stone quarry
Comb, Sara	wife	B	F	22	
Comb, Mary	daughter	B	F	2	
Comb, Katie	daughter	B	F	1	
Mason, Eliza	boarder				
Winston, Fred	head	B	M	22	laborer
Winston, Sadie	wife	B	F	20	
Winston, Flora	daughter	B	F	2	
Arrington, Luther	head	B	M	35	blacksmith for railroad
Arrington, Marry	wife	B	F	33	
Arrington, Leonia	daughter	B	F	13	
Arrington, Thomas	son	B	M	10	
Arrington, Manda	daughter	B	F	8	
Arrington, Luther	son	B	M	7	
Arrington, Mittie	daughter	B	F	3	
Walker, Frank	head	B	M	38	stone quarry
Walker, Damey	wife	B	F	40	
Walker, Esther	daughter	B	F	16	
Walker, Myrtle	daughter	B	F	10	
Walker, Bertha	daughter	B	F	7	
Wyndham, J. E.	head	B	M	41	carpenter
Wyndham, Anna	wife	B	F	35	
Wyndham, John W.	son	B	M	16	

Name	Relationship	Race/Sex		Age	Occupation
Wyndham, Della V.	daughter	B	F	14	
Wyndham, Sara	daughter	B	F	12	
Wyndham, James E.	son	B	M	10	
Wyndham, Nellie	daughter	B	F	8	
Wyndham, Charles	son	B	M	4	
Wilt, G. R.	head	W	M	61	merchant
Wilt, Georgie	wife	W	F	58	
Wilt, Mabel	daughter	W	F		
Hunter, Isiah	head	B	M	48	merchant
Hunter, Laura	wife	B	F	47	
Hunter, Robert	son	B	M	22	railroad laborer
Hunter, Howard	son	B	M	24	railroad laborer
Hunter, George	son	B	M	16	railroad laborer
Hunter, Effie	daughter	B	F	13	
Footer, William	head	B	M	29	railroad laborer
Footer, Dora	wife	B	F	29	
Footer, Anna M.	daughter	B	F	5	
Footer, William	son	B	F	2/12	
Prather, James	head	W	M	22	stone quarry
Prather, Grace	wife	W	F	22	
Prather, Virginia	daughter	W	F	1	
Licklider, Rua	head	W	F	72	
Licklider, Bessie	daughter	W	F	25	
Briscoe, Rachel	head	B	F	33	
Briscoe, Ruth	daughter	B	F	12	
Whittington, C. G.	head	W	M	49	mail carrier
Whittington, Isabell	wife	W	F	48	
Whittington, Francis	son	W	M	21	
Whittington, Ruth	daughter	W	F	18	
Whittington, Raymond	son	W	M	17	
Whittington, Virginia	daughter	W	F	12	
Whittington, Charlie	son	W	M	9	
Whittington, Gertrude	daughter	W	F	7	
Whittington, Ruth	daughter	W	F	3	
Whittington, ------	daughter	W	F	1	
Taylor, James	head	B	M	25	coachman
Taylor, Lavinnia	wife	B	F	19	
Taylor, Lora	sister	B	F	17	
Powell, Ella	head	W	F	56	
Owens, Florence	daughter	W	F	31	
Owens, Frank	son	W	M	11	
Owens, Floyd	son	W	M	8	
Powell, Julia	daughter	W	F	21	
Powell, Frank	son	W	M	15	laborer

Name	Relationship	Race/Sex		Age	Occupation
Jackson, J. H.	head	W	M	49	laborer
Jackson, Martha	wife	W	F	46	
Jackson, Ruth	daughter	W	F	12	
Jackson, John W.	son	W	M	2	
Mc Alister, Henry	head	W	M	20	railroad laborer
Mc Alister, Lillian	wife	W	F	17	
Mc Alister, Oscar	son	W	M	1	
Licklider, W. B.	head	W	M	29	merchant
Licklider, Virginia	wife	W	F	25	
Licklider, William	son	W	M	3	
Petrie, R. H.	head	W	M	38	merchant
Petrie, Lillian	wife	W	F	38	
Petrie, Ruth	daughter	W	F	17	
Petrie, Arthur	son	W	M	15	clerk
Petrie, Milton	son	W	M	9	
Moore, C. H.	head	W	M	28	railroad laborer
Moore, Mary C.	wife	W	F	25	
Moore, Julia M.	daughter	W	F	5	
Moore, Harry M.	son	W	M	2	
Lucas, C. C.	head	W	M	49	physician
Lucas, Frances	wife	W	F	49	
Lucas, Mary E.	daughter	W	F	18	
Lucas, Charles	son	W	M	15	
Cave, G. W.	head	W	M	28	railroad laborer
Cave, Bessie	wife	W	F	35	
Cave, Margarita May	daughter	W	F	14	
Cave, Bertie	daughter	W	F	12	
Cave, Anna B.	daughter	W	F	9	
Cave, Robert L.	son	W	M	6	
Cave, Franklin	son	W	M	3	
Cave, Charles	son	W	M	1	
Kearfott, J. P.	head	W	M	65	farmer
Kearfott, May Sidney	wife	W	F	66	
Anderson, Nellie	servant	W	F	53	
Kearfott, W. L.	head	W	M	42	real estate
Kearfott, Nannie B.	wife	W	F	38	
Kearfott, Genevieve	daughter	W	F	20	
Kearfott, John P.	son	W	M	17	
Kearfott, William E.	son	W	M	15	
Kearfott, Sidney W.	son	W	M	13	
Mason, Albert	head	B	M	41	laborer
Mason, Fannie	wife	B	F	40	
Mason, Florence	daughter	B	F	18	
Mason, Christopher	son	B	M	15	

Name	Relationship	Race/Sex		Age	Occupation
Mason, Irene	daughter	B	F	12	
Mason, Edward	son	B	M	8	
Mason, Marshal	son	B	M	2	
Rogers, R. R.	head	W	M	46	buggy maker
Rogers, Sallie Creamer	wife	W	F	48	
Rogers, Lester	son	W	M	20	
Rogers, Harry	son	W	M	19	
Rogers Bettice	daughter	W	F	14	
Rogers, Kenneth	son	W	M	12	
Rogers, Randolph	son	W	M	8	
Rogers, Lionel	son	W	M	6	
Rogers, Irene	daughter	W	F	10	
Trussel, A. E.	head	W	M	31	mail carrier
Trussel, Edith	wife	W	F	29	
Trussel, Margarite	daughter	W	F	5	
Jackson, B. F.	head	B	M	56	laborer
Jackson, Emma	wife	B	F	53	
Jackson, Alexander	son	B	M	18	laborer
Jackson, Richard	son	B	M	14	laborer
Jackson, Emma	daughter	B	F	25	
Arnold, Margarite	niece	B	F	6	
Johnston, William	head	W	M	55	laborer
Johnston, Carolina	wife	W	F	54	
Johnston, Lissie	daughter	W	F	25	
Johnston, Laura	daughter	W	F	22	
Washington, G. W.	head	W	M	39	laborer
King, Henry	head	B	M	24	laborer
King, Vernia	wife	B	F	25	
King, Robert	son	B	M	8	
King, Katherine	daughter	B	F	6	
King, Ester	daughter	B	F	5	
King, Helan	daughter	B	F	3	
King, Gladis	daughter	B	F	5/12	
Fletcher, Marshal	brother	B	M	19	
Prater, Newton	head	W	M	72	stone quarry
Prater, Eliza	wife	W	F	57	
Prater, Annie	daughter	W	F	17	
Prater, Geo	son	W	M	12	
Prater, Florence	daughter	W	F	8	
Prater, Bell	daughter	W	F	5	
Getzendanner, Charles	head	W	M	55	farmer
Young, Mary	servant	W	F	45	
King, Ed	head	B	M	58	railroad laborer
King, Annie	wife	B	F	37	

Name	Relationship	Race/Sex		Age	Occupation
King, George	son	B	M	13	
King, Edward	son	B	M	13	
King, ----------	daughter	B	F	6	
King, Annie	daughter	B	F	5	
King, Paul	son	B	M	2	
Whittington, W. M.	head	W	M	31	farmer
Whittington, Nellie	wife	W	F	26	
Whittington, Taylor	son	W	M	6/12	
Whittington, Randolf	son	W	M	8	
Whittington, Angus	son	W	M	5	
Logie, J. V.	head	B	M	60	
Logie, Mary	wife	B	F	37	
Logie, Fannie	daughter	B	F	22	servant
Logie, John	son	B	M	4	
Logie, Edward	son	B	M	3	
Miller, M. S.	head	W	M	65	farmer
Miller, Hattie Bell	wife	W	F	52	
Miller, Ruth	daughter	W	F	23	teacher
Miller, Fred	son	W	M	19	
Miller, Joe	son	W	M	18	
Tucker, F. W.	head	W	M	62	railroad foreman
Tucker, Jane	wife	W	F	62	
Tucker, S. W.	son	W	M	24	railroad laborer
Clower, Ellen	head	W	F	56	
Clower, Wade Hampton	son	W	M	30	laborer
Cox, G. H.	head	W	M	32	foreman
Cox, Fannie	wife	W	F	43	
Cox, Ruth	daughter	W	F	7	
Cox, Edward	son	W	M	6	
Cox, George	son	W	M	2	
Lashorn, Myrtle	daughter	W	F	24	
Lashorn, Charles	son	W	M	18	
Heinz, J. C.	head	W	M	37	concrete
Heinz, E. K	wife	W	F	39	
Heinz, Samuel	son	W	M	15	
Heinz, Robert	son	W	M	6	
Rutherford, C. E.		W	M	45	well digger
Turner, Charles	head	W	M	29	railroad laborer
Turner, Dora	wife	W	F	28	
Turner, Elsie M.	daughter	W	F	5	
Turner, Harry	son	W	M	3	

SELECTED FROM FEDERAL CENSUS OF MIDDLEWAY DISTRICT 1920

Name	Relationship	Race/Sex		Age	Student	Occupation
Ross, William	head	B	M	54		farmer
Ross, Lula T.	wife	B	F	31		laundress
Walker, --------	sister-in-law	B	F	16	yes	laundress
Ross, James	son	B	M	15		farm laborer
Ross, John	son	B	M	11	yes	
Ross, Alice	daughter	B	F	9	yes	
McDowell, Jerry	head	B	M	41		preacher
McDowell, Fanny	wife	B	F	38		laundress
McDowell, John	son	B	M	14		farm laborer
McDowell, Jerry	son	B	M	12		farm laborer
McDowell, Norman	son	B	M	11		farm laborer
McDowell, Robert	son	B	M	9	yes	
McDowell, William	son	B	M	7	yes	
McDowell, Dudley	son	B	M	6	yes	
McDowell, George	son	B	M	5		
McDowell, Sam	son	B	M	3		
McDowell, Kate	daughter	B	F	1		
Twyman, Frank	head	B	M	42		orchard worker
Twyman, Sallie	wife	B	F	38		
Twyman, Cora	daughter	B	F	17	yes	
Twyman, Harry	son	B	M	14		
Twyman, James	son	B	M	23		
Burnett, Clarence	head	W	M	42		carpenter
Burnett, ---------	wife	W	F	38		
Burnett, Ora	daughter	W	F	10	yes	
Burnett, Cora Belle	daughter	W	F	8	yes	
Burnett, Henry	son	W	M	5		
Miller, Paul	head	W	M	25		mail carrier
Miller, Kathleen	wife	W	F	23		
Miller, Paul Jr.	son	W	M	1		
Omps, A. L.	head	W	M	44		grain and dairy
Omps, Sarah E.	wife	W	F	39		
Triggs, Jerry	head	W	M	26		farm laborer
Triggs, Malinda R.	wife	W	F	26		
Triggs, Geraldine	daughter	W	F	2		
Woods, Bernice		W	F	14		
Brady, J. M.	head	W	M	55		grain & dairy farm

Name	Relationship	Race/Sex		Age	Student	Occupation
Brady, Virginia	wife	W	F	51		
Brady, Lee	son	W	M	17		laborer
Brady, Eugene	son	W	M	11	yes	
Brady, R. L.	son	W	M	25		farm laborer
Brady, Leila	wife	W	F	25		
Brady, Dorothea	daughter	W	F	2		
Bitner, J. C.	head	W	M	74		fruit & dairy farm
Bitner, Bettie	wife	W	F	71		
Bitner, Leila	daughter	W	F	39		teacher
Henkle, Jessie	sister-in-law	W	F	68		companion
Morgan, Douglas	head	W	M	45		farm laborer
Morgan, Stellie	wife	W	F	33		laundress
Morgan, Eliza	daughter	W	F	13	yes	
Miller, Herbert	head	W	M	38		
Miller, Nannie	wife	W	F	36		
Miller, Mary	daughter	W	F	6	yes	
Miller, Elijah White	son	W	M	2		
Williams, F. K.	mother-in-law	W	F	60		
McKee, Howard	head	W	M	49		fruit & dairy farm
McKee, Blanch	wife	W	F	45		
McKee, Bettie K.	daughter	W	F	11	yes	
McKee, Howard Jr.	son	W	M	2		
Blue, C. W.	Head	W	M	37		farmer
Blue, Mrs. C. W.	wife	W	F	39		
Blue, Judith	daughter	W	F	11	yes	
Magruder, D. L.	head	W	M	58		farm & live stock
Magruder Mrs. D. L	wife	W	F	52		
Miles, Ice	orphan	W	M	21		
Magruder, Ruth	daughter	W	F	21		
MaGoward, Frances	orphan	W	F	12	yes	
Cletus, Charles	orphan	W	M	9	yes	
Clemmon, Albert	head	W	M	46		farm laborer
Clemmon, Bessie	wife	W	F	36		
Clemmon, Mary	daughter	W	F	16		
Clemmon, Clarence	son	W	M	12	yes	
Clemmon, George	son	W	M	7	yes	
Clemmon, Stanley	son	W	M	6		
Clemmon, Hattie	daughter	W	F	3		
Clemmon, Dorothia	daughter	W	F	3		
Clemmon, Charles	son	W	M	2/12		

Name	Relationship	Race/Sex		Age	Student	Occupation
Johnson, William	head	W	W	64		farmer, dairy
Johnson, Jessie	daughter	W	F	34		
Johnson, Laura	daughter	W	F	32		
Jackson, Richard	head	B	M	66		farm laborer
Jackson, --------	wife	B	F	62		
Jackson, Richard	son	B	M	23		farm laborer
Jackson, Alexander	son	B	M	27		stone quarry
Jackson, Alinor	wife	B	F	26		laundress
Jackson, Mary	daughter	B	F	5	yes	
Jackson, Charles	son	B	M	4/12		
Trussell, A. E.	head	W	M	42		elevator operator
Trussell, Edith	wife	W	F	39		
Trussell, Margarite	daughter	W	F	14	yes	
Benner, Arthur	head	W	M	38		dairy farmer
Benner, Nannie	wife	W	F	38		
Benner, Hunter	son	W	M	15		
Benner, Bernard	son	W	M	10	yes	
Benner, Lena	daughter	W	F	11	yes	
Benner, Norman	son	W	F		yes	
Benner, Clarence	son	W	M	4		
Kearfott, John P.	head	W	M	75		fruit farmer
Kearfott, Nannie	wife	W	F	49		
Kearfott, Sidney	daughter	W	F	24		
Stubbs, Andrew	head	B	M	37		farm laborer
Stubbs, Belle	wife	B	F	38		laundress
Stubbs, Newton	son	B	M	12	yes	
Stubbs, Sarah	daughter	B	F	10	yes	
Stubbs, Andrew	son	B	M	8	yes	
Stubbs, James	son	B	M	7	yes	
Stubbs, Zenia	daughter	B	F	5		
Stubbs, John	son	B	M	3		
Stubbs, Isabella	daughter	B	F	1		
Miller, Charles	head	W	M	36		farmer
Miller, ---------	wife	W	F	34		
Miller, Locker	son	W	M	11	yes	
Miller, Dorothea	daughter	W	F	10	yes	
Miller, Helen E.	daughter	W	F	11/12		
Miller, Baker	son	W	M	5		
Miller, Ruth	sister	W	F	33		teacher
Jackson, Harry	head	W	M	59		fruit & grain labor
Jackson, Molly	wife	W	F	59		

Name	Relationship	Race/Sex		Age	Student	Occupation
Jackson, John	son	W	M	11	yes	
Mc Alister, Oscar	grandson	W	M	10	yes	
Mason, George	head	B	M	23		farm laborer
Mason, Mary	wife	B	F	25		laundress
Mason, Josephine	daughter	B	F	4		
Mason, Charles	son	B	M	2		
Mason, Zenia	daughter	B	F	1		
Dorsey, John	head	W	M	62		farm laborer
Dorsey, Mrs. John	wife	W	F	57		
Dorsey, Strother	son	W	M	36		stone quarry
Dorsey, Charles	son	W	M	32		shoe maker
Dorsey, Earl	son	W	M	29		B & O worker
Ramsburg, Miss E.	sister-in-law	W	F	43		factory worker
McIntire, E. F.	head	W	F	41		farm manager
McIntire, Lonia	sister	W	F	47		
McIntire, Effie	sister	W	F	54		teacher
Wilt, Walter	head	W	M	45		merchant
Wilt, Virginia	wife	W	F	40		
Homsher, Belle	sister-in-law	W	F	62		
Lucas, Charles	head	W	M	58		
Lucas, Francis	wife	W	F	58		
Lucas, Mary	daughter	W	M	28		nurse, social ser.
McDowell, William	head	B	M	39		laborer
McDowell, Carrie	wife	B	F	35		laundress
McDowell, Ellen	daughter	B	F	17	yes	
McDowell, Evalina	daughter	B	F	15	yes	
McDowell, William	son	B	M	13	yes	
McDowell, Frank	son	B	M	12	yes	
McDowell, Thomas	son	B	M	9	yes	
McDowell, Elizabeth	daughter	B	F	7	yes	
McDowell, Virginia	daughter	B	F	6	yes	
McDowell, Catherine	daughter	B	F	5		
McDowell, Clarence	son	B	M	3		
McDowell, Laura	daughter	B	M	1		
Horn, M. B.	head	W	M	43		carpenter
Horn, Bertha	wife	W	F	43		seamstress
Horn, Mark	son	W	M	14	yes	
Horn, Dorothy	daughter	W	F	11	yes	
Miller, A. S.	head	W	M	72		dairy farm
Miller, Susan	wife	W	M	56		

Name	Relationship	Race/Sex		Age	Student	Occupation
Everhart, Thomas O.	head	W	M	49		dairy farm
Everhart, Cora	wife	W	F	39		
Everhart, Herbert	son	W	M	13	yes	
Lucas, Philip	head	B	M	67		laborer
Lucas, Luke	son	B	M	32		
Lucas, Harry	son	B	M	29		
Lucas, James	son	B	M	24		
Lucas, Sallie	daughter	B	F	21		
Fleming, Carl	head	W	M	41		farmer
Fleming, Stacia	wife	W	F	40		
Fleming, Thelma	daughter	W	F	17		
Fleming, Zack	son	W	M	11	yes	
-------------------	father-in-law	W	M	73		
-------------------	mother-in-law	W	F	84		
Collis, -------	head	W	M	28		laborer
Collis, Lucy	wife	W	F	27		
Collis, William	son	W	M	8	yes	
Collis, Lula	daughter	W	F	5		
Collis, Martha	daughter	W	F	2		
Collis, Herbert	son	W	M	4/12		
Clipp, Martha	head	W	F	64		
Clipp, Dora	daughter	W	F	33		
Campbell, T.	head	W	M	60		farmer
Campbell, Rebecca	wife	W	F	47		
Campbell, Sarah	daughter	W	F	22		teacher
Campbell, John	son	W	M	14	yes	
Campbell, Amy	daughter	W	F	13	yes	
Campbell, Nancy	daughter	W	F	5	yes	
Roman, Helen	servant	B	F	39		servant
Widmyer, C.	head	W	M	45		farmer
Widmyer, Lenora	wife	W	F	39		
Widmyer, Eva	mother	W	F	79		
Widmyer, Irving	son	W	M	11	yes	
Widmyer, John M.	son	W	M	4		
Widmyer, Boyd	son	W	M	2		
Hammond, Roland	head	W	M	41		farmer
Hammond, Mabel	wife	W	F	41		
Hammond, Mary	daughter	W	F	17	yes	
Hammond, Thomas	son	W	F	16		
Hammond, Armstrong	son	W	M	14		
Hammond, Harry	son	W	M	11	yes	
Hammond, Emma	daughter	W	M	10	yes	
Hammond, Hester	daughter	W	F	8	yes	
Hammond, Mabel Lee	daughter	W	F	7	yes	

Name	Relationship	Race/Sex		Age	Student	Occupation
Hammond, Anna Ruth	daughter	W	F	5		
Hammond, Edith	daughter	W	F	4		
Hammond, Edgar	daughter	W	F	2		
-----------------	orphan					servant
Fleming, Harry	head	W	M	40		manager
Fleming, Daisy	wife	W	F	38		
Fleming, Virginia	daughter	W	F	3		
Fleming, Helen	daughter	W	F	1/12		
Trussell, James	head	W	F	41		farmer
----------, James		W	M	64		laborer
----------, Mrs. Annie		W	F	66		housekeeper
----------, Fred	son	W	M	8		
Bower, Mason K.	head	W	M	49		grain and dairy
Bower, Olivia	wife	W	F	47		
Bower, Mildred	daughter	W	F	18		
Whittington, George	head	W	M	60		Blacksmith
Whittington, Lottie	wife	W	F	48		
Whittington, Jennie	daughter	W	F	27		
Whittington, Burnette	son	W	M	22		mechanic
Whittington, May	daughter	W	F	14	yes	
Hart, Howard	head	B	M	49		farmer
Hart, Lucinda	wife	B	F	44		
Goens, James	nephew	B	M	24		laborer
Goens, Charles	brother-in-law	B	M	25		mechanic
Fulk, William	head	W	M	55		farmer
Fulk, Mary E.	wife	W	F	55		
Fulk, Charles	son	W	M	21		
Fulk, Nellie	daughter	W	F	15		
Entler, Sallie	sister-in-law	W	F	60		
McDaniel, James	head	B	M	57		farmer
McDaniel, Alice	wife	B	F	49		
Thornton, Susan	mother-in-law	B	F	83		
Thornton, Rachel	sister-in-law	B	F	39		servant
McDaniel, Charles	son	B	M	28		laborer
McDaniel, Esau	son	B	M	19		laborer
McDaniel, Jacob	son	B	M	19		laborer
McDaniel, Lucy	daughter	B	F	24		
McDaniel, Roy	cousin	B	M	16		laborer
Cooper, Rebecca	niece	B	F	19		
Cooper, Warner	nephew	B	M	17		laborer
Cooper, Nancy	niece	B	F	13	yes	
Cooper, Charles	nephew	B	M	13		

Name	Relationship	Race/Sex		Age	Student	Occupation
Woodfork, Willie	head	B	M	37		
Woodfork, Clara	wife	B	F	31		
Woodfork, Willie G.	son	B	M	9/12		
Allen, Louise	niece	B	F	3		
Edward, Charles	head	W	M	66		laborer
Edward, Rosae	wife	W	F	60		
Edward, Wesley	grandson	W	M	13		
Hardin, James	head	W	M	30		laborer
Hardin, Dora	wife	W	F	39		
Hardin, Hester	daughter	W	F	6		
Hardin, Charles	son	W	M	3		
Border, Ralph	head	W	M	37		farmer
Border, Annie	wife	W	F	36		
Border, Clara	daughter	W	F	5		
Border, Mary V.	daughter	W	F	3		
Border, Clara G.	mother	W	F	61		
Border, Margarite	sister	W	F	24		
Campbell, Abe	head	B	M	42		laborer
Campbell, Sadie	wife	B	F	40		
Campbell, Donald	son	B	M	17		
Campbell, Carl	son	B	M	14	yes	
Campbell, Hazel	daughter	B	F	19		servant
Campbell, Esther	daughter	B	F	12	yes	
Campbell, Elmer	son	B	M	10	yes	
Campbell, Minerva	daughter	B	F	8		
Campbell, Clinton	son	B	M	5		
Campbell, Mildred	daughter	B	F	3		
Campbell, Edna	daughter	B	F	3/12		
Fox, Robert E.	head	B	M	42		laborer
Fox, Idella	wife	B	F	33		
Fox, Robert	son	B	M	4		
McDaniel, Stephen	cousin	B	M	17		laborer
Sharpe, Wilbur	head	W	M	26		laborer
Sharpe, Flossie	wife	W	F	27		
Sharpe, Delphia	daughter	W	F	5		
Stanley, John F.	head	W	M	42		mechanic
Stanley, Blanch	wife	W	F	40		
Stanley, Henry	son	W	M	12		
Stanley, Margie	daughter	W	F	10		
Hogue, R. R.	boarder	W	M	45		manager creamery
Myers, Jane	head	B	F	44		
Brisco, Thomas	son	B	M	24		laborer
Arlington, Lou	boarder	B	M	21		blacksmith

Name	Relationship	Race/Sex		Age	Student	Occupation
Arlington, Keaty	boarder	B	M	26		
Fowler, R. F.	head	W	M	46		laborer
Fowler, Ella	wife	W	F	42		
Fowler, Mary	daughter	W	F	14		
Hill,---------	boarder	W	M	21		
Hill, Mrs. Florence		W	F	22		
Page, George	head	W	M	26		mechanic
Page, Florence	wife	W	F	24		
Page, Francis	daughter	W	F	3		
Page, Ernest	son	W	M	2		
Whittington, James	head	W	M	63		mechanic
Whittington, Ms. James	wife	W	F63			
Young, Laura	head	W	F	68		
Thomas, Walter	head	W	M	48		farm laborer
Thomas, Mary	wife	W	F	44		
Thomas, Wilbur	son	W	M	25		yard master
Thomas, Roy	son	W	M	24		laborer
Thomas, Reba	daughter	W	F	22		
Thomas, Mary	daughter	W	F	18		
Thomas, Alton	son	W	M	14		
Thomas, Parry	son	W	M	11		
Thomas, Woodrow	son	W	M	9	yes	
Thomas, Alma	daughter	W	F	7		
Thomas, Mildred	daughter	W	F	6/12		
Powell, Frank	head					truck driver
Powell, Frances	wife					
Powell, Eleanor	daughter					
Bradford, George	head	B	M	69		laborer
Bradford, Alice	wife	B	F	66		
Splon, Mrs. Helen	daughter	B	F	26		
Bradford, Rebecca	grand dau.	B	F	9		
Splon, Pauline	grand dau.	B	F	3		
Splon, Clarence	grand son	B	M	1/12		
Allen, Bessie	head	B	F	39		laundress
Allen, Andrew	son	B	M	15		laborer
Allen, Hugh	son	B	M	19		laborer
Allen, Mary	daughter	B	F	17		
Allen, Viola	daughter	B	F	13	yes	
Allen, Daisy	daughter	B	F	12	yes	
Allen, Anna Belle	daughter	B	F	5		
Kackley, Edgar	head	B	M	61		laborer
Kackley, Louise	wife	B	F	55		
Kackley, H. F.	brother	B	M	71		laborer
Allen, William	head	B	M	51		

Name	Relationship	Race/Sex		Age	Student	Occupation
Allen, Nannie	wife	B	F	41		laundress
Allen, David	son	B	M	15		
Allen, Daniel	son	B	M	12	yes	
Allen, ----------	son	B	M	9	yes	
Allen, Isaiah	son	B	M	6	yes	
Allen, Inez	grand dau.	B	F	4		
Carter, George	head	B	M	65		laborer
Carter, --------	wife	B	F	64		
Carter, Boyd	son	B	M	31		
Carter, Amelia	wife	B	F	38		
Tucker, John	head	W	M	37		
Tucker, Lillie	wife	W	F	38		
Tucker, Richard	son	W	M	16		railroad laborer
Tucker, Raymind	son	W	M	14		laborer
Tucker, Minnie	daughter	W	F	13	yes	
Tucker, Leonard	son	W	M	10	yes	
Tucker, Harry	son	W	M	9	yes	
Tucker, Edna	daughter	W	F	2		
Clower, Ella	head	W	F	66		
Clower, Wade	son	W	M	36		electrician
Allen, Harry	head	B	M	32		laborer
Allen, Helen	wife	B	F			
Allen, George	son	B	M	12		
Allen, Hattie	daughter	B	F	9		
Allen, Arthur	son	B	M	8		
Washington, David	head	B	M	60		laborer
Washington, Sylvia	wife	B	M	54		
Washington, Allen	son	B	M	25		laborer
Washington, William	son	B	M	16		laborer
Washington, Mary A.	daughter	B	F	14		
Washington, Grace	daughter	B	F	10		
Campbell, Belle	head	B	F	60		servant
Campbell, Thomas	son	B	M	32		laborer
Mason, Rebecca	mother	B	F	89		preacher
Law, Rev. L. A.	head	B	M	48		preacher
Law, Mrs. Georgia	wife	B	F	41		
Law, Benjamin	son	B	M	15	yes	
Law, Willis	son	B	M	13	yes	
Law, Leonidas	son	B	M	12	yes	
Law, Eva	daughter	B	F	8	yes	
Law, Nathaniel	son	B	M	7	yes	
Law, Robert	son	B	M	6		
Law, Irene	daughter	B	F	4		

Name	Relationship	Race/Sex		Age	Student	Occupation
Heinz, John	head	W	M	45		masonry
Heinz, Mrs. Kate	wife	W	F	49		
Heinz, Robert	son	W	M	15		laborer
Heinz, John	son	W	M	9	yes	
Rutherford, C. E.	brother	W	M	56		mechanic & well digger
Head, James	head	B	M	49		laborer
Head, Mrs. Mary	wife	B	F	33		
Winston, Fred	head	B	M	26		laborer
Winston, Sadie	wife	B	F	30		
Winston, Floyd	son	B	M	12		
Winston, James	son	B	M	2		
Carter, Herbert	head	B	M	25		laborer
Carter, Lucy	wife	B	F	30		
Carter, Margarita	daughter	B	F	1		
Roper, Edgar	head	B	M	53		store keeper, laborer
Roper, Lucinda	wife	B	F	51		
Roper, John C.	son	B	M	25		
Roper, Ruth	daughter	B	F	18		
Roper, Douglas	son	B	M	16		laborer
Roper, Theresa	daughter	B	F	14		
Roper, Hilda	daughter	B	F	10		
Roper, LeRoy	son	B	M	7		
Ford, Tucker	head	B	M			laborer
Ford, Eulia	daughter	B	M	15		housekeeper
Ford, Daniel	son	B	M			
Goens, Harriet	mother	B	F	59		
Goens, Paul	son	B	M	29		laborer
Goens, Delsia	daughter	B	F	24		
Goens, Edgar	grandson	B	M	5		
Turner, Charles C.	head	W	M	40		mechanic
Turner, Dora	wife	W	F	35		
Turner, Marie	daughter	W	F	16		
Turner, Harry	son	W	M	13	yes	
Turner, Charles	son	W	M	3		
Turner, Eula	daughter	W	F	7		
Frith, Charles	head	W	M	41		laborer
Frith, Lucy	wife	W	F	44		
Frith, Charles G.	son	W	M	20		laborer
Frith, Verona	daughter	W	F	14	yes	
Frith, Gladys	daughter	W	F	11	yes	
Welsh, Thomas	head	W	M	56		laborer

Name	Relationship	Race/Sex		Age	Student	Occupation
Welsh, Mary	wife	W	F	40		
Welsh, Luther	son	W	M	22		laborer
Welsh, Earl	son	W	M	18		laborer
Welsh, Thomas Jr.	son	W	M	3		
Painter, Pauline	grand dau.	W	F	5		
Welsh, Martin	head	W	M	48		laborer
Welsh, Mary	wife	W	F	22		
Welsh, Hugh	son	W	M	5		
Welsh, Elizabeth	daughter	W	F	2		
----------, Basie	head	W	M	24		labor quarry
----------, Martha	wife	W	F	19		
----------, Easie	daughter	W	F	3/12		
King, Edward	head	B	M	45		laborer
King, Mary		B	F	27		
King, Theodore	son	B	M	17		
King, Anna	daughter	B	F	15	yes	
King, Paul	son	B	M	12	yes	
King, Henry	head	B	M	38		laborer
King, Vernie	wife	B	F	37		
King, Esther	daughter	B	F	14	yes	
King, Helan	daughter	B	F	12	yes	
King, Garfield	son	B	M	8	yes	
King, ----------	daughter	B	F	6	yes	
King, ----------	daughter	B	F	4		
King, Herbert	son	B	M	2		
Fletcher, Herbert	head	B	M	32		laborer
Fletcher, Lillie	wife	B	F	25		servant
King, ----------	niece	B	F	4		
Washington, George	head	B	M	56		laborer
Washington, Mrs. E	wife	B	F	45		
Mason, Mary	sister-in-law	B	F	51		
Mason, Calvin		B	M	11	yes	
Brown, -------	head	B	F	45		
Brown, Charles	son	B	M	16		laborer
Brown, Gilbert	son	B	M	12		
Brown, Benjamin	son	B	M	10	yes	
Carter, Benjamin	head	B	M	33		laborer
Carter, Ellen	wife	B	F	21		
Carter, Harry Lee	son	B	M	4		
Carter, Benjamin	son	B	M	2		
Carter, Boyd	son	B	M	2/12		
Frye, John	head	B	M	70		laborer
Frye, Mary E.	wife	B	F	43		
Frye, John	son	B	M	14	yes	

Name	Relationship	Race/Sex		Age	Student	Occupation
Frye, Ernestine	daughter	B	F	12	yes	
Wilt, Lewis	head	W	M	71		merchant
Wilt, Georgiana	wife	W	F	69		
Brown, Irene	daughter	W	F	40		
Brown, Max	son	W	M	17		
Brown, Tracey	son	W	M	14	yes	
Brown, Lucilla	daughter	W	F	12	yes	
Brown, Tyler	son	W	M	10	yes	
Trout, Joe	head	W	M	37		cooper
Trout, Emma	wife	W	F	38		
Hopper, John	head	W	M	33		cooper
Hopper, Ida	wife	W	F	29		
Hopper, Preston	son	W	M	10	yes	
Hopper, Charlotte	daughter	W	F	7	yes	
Hopper, James	head	W	M	35		
Hopper, Lillian	wife	W	F	36		
Hopper, Alice	daughter	W	F	15	yes	
Miller, M. F.	head	W	M	29		R. F. D. carrier
Miller, Mabel	wife	W	F	26		
Miller, Florence	daughter	W	F	3/12		
Wyndham, Anna	head	W	F	45		
Wyndham, James	son	W	M	21		laborer
Wyndham, Nellie	daughter	W	F	17		
Wyndham, Fred	son	W	M	2		
Smallwood, Scott	head	W	M	45		laborer
Smallwood, Cora	wife	W	F	43		
Smallwood, Lelia	daughter	W	F	20		
Smallwood, Marjorie	daughter	W	F	17		
Smallwood, Steward	son	W	M	15		
Smallwood, Rector	son	W	M	13	yes	
Smallwood, Jacob	son	W	M	11	yes	
Smallwood, Hattie	daughter	W	F	7	yes	
Frith, Eugene	head	W	M	35		laborer
Frith, Edith	wife	W	F	32		
Frith, Juanita	daughter	W	F	13		
Frith, Garland	son	W	M	10	yes	
Arrington, Luther	head	B	M	48		blacksmith
Arrington, Mary	wife	B	F	39		
Arrington, Jessie	daughter	B	F	22		
Arrington, Amanda	daughter	B	F	18	yes	
Arrington, Luther Jr.	son	B	M	16		
Arrington, Mittie	daughter	B	F	13	yes	
Arrington, Fannie	daughter	B	F	9	yes	

Name	Relationship	Race/Sex		Age	Student	Occupation
Arrington, Robert	son	B	M	6	yes	
Arrington, Samuel	son	B	M	7	yes	
Coleman, William	head	B	M	48		blacksmith
Coleman, Lucy	wife	B	F	38		
Coleman, Ella May	daughter	B	F	12	yes	
Coleman, Dorothea	daughter	B	F	9	yes	
Coleman, Katherine	daughter	B	F	8/12		
Burhman, J. E.	head	W	M	49		state road foreman
Burhman, Mrs. J. E.	wife	W	F	45		
Burhman, Grace	daughter	W	F	25		teacher
Burhman, Harold	son	W	M	15		
Burhman, Phyllis	daughter	W	F	6		
Ferguson, Charles	head	B	M	48		laborer
Ferguson, Katie	wife	B	F	47		
Ferguson, John	son	B	M	24		laborer
Ferguson, Jerry	son	B	M	18		carpenter
Ferguson, Robert	son	B	M	17		laborer
Ferguson, Isabel	daughter	B	F	15	yes	
Ferguson, Richard	son	B	M	12	yes	laborer
Ferguson, Rose	daughter	B	F	11	yes	
Ferguson, Beulah	daughter	B	F	7	yes	
Ferguson, William	son	B	M	7		
Owens, Florence	head	W	M	40		
Owens, Frank	son	W	M	20		laborer
Owens, Floyd	son	W	M	28		laborer
Powell, Ella	mother	W	F	66		
Thompson, George	boarder	W	M	55		
----------------------	boarder	W	M	25		agent
Lockley, George	head	B	M	38		laborer
Lockley, Emma	wife	B	F	32		
Lockley, Georgina	daughter	B	F	11		
Lockley, ------------	son	B	M	9		
Lockley, Audrie	daughter	B	F	5		
Lockley, Billie	son	B	M	4		
Lockley, Boyd	son	B	M	3/12		
Madden, George	head	B	M	43		laborer
Madden, Mary Anna	wife	B	F	43		
Madden, James	son	B	M	19		laborer
Madden, Calvin	son	B	M	15		
Madden, Homer	son	B	M	13		
Madden, Charles	son	B	M	6		
Madden, Floyd	son	B	M	5		
Madden, John	head	B	M	39		laborer

Name	Relationship	Race/Sex		Age	Student	Occupation
Madden, Georgia	wife	B	F	29		
Timbers, Fred	head	B	M	37		laborer
Timbers, Georgia	wife	B	F	23		
Timbers, Mary	daughter	B	F	6		
Timbers, Israel	son	B	M	6		
Timbers, Julia	mother	B	F	68		
Amey, Eliza	head	W	F	78		
Amey, Jacob	son	W	M	53		electrician
Amey, Joseph	son	W	M	45		laborer
Amey, Edward	son	W	M	38		laborer
Trump, F. O.	head	W	M	45		ticket agent
Trump, Mrs. F. O. (Rua)	wife	W	F	44		
Trump, Fannie	daughter	W	F	18		teacher
Trump, Elizabeth	daughter	W	F	15	yes	
Trump, James	son	W	M	11	yes	
Trump, Franklin	son	W	M	8	yes	
Trump, Mrs. H. A.	mother	W	F	80		
Carpenter A.	head	W	M	65		laborer
Powell, Harry	head	B	M	28		
Powell, Phoebe	wife	B	F	19		
Powell, Elizabeth	daughter	B	F	2/12		
Rose, William	head	W	M	46		crippled
Rose, Minnie	wife	W	F	45		laundress
Rose, Lawrence	son	W	M	11	yes	
Rose, Eula	daughter	W	F	9	yes	
Rose, Bedford	son	W	M	5		
Burden, Nimrod	head	B	M	53		laborer
Burden, Henrietta	wife	B	F	50		laundress
Burden, Robert	son	B	M	12	yes	
Grantham, Lynn	head	W	M	40		farmer
Grantham, Mary	wife	W	F	38		
Grantham, Virginia	daughter	W	F	10	yes	
Grantham, Lynn	son	W	M	8	yes	
Hammond, William B.	head	W	M	31		farmer
Hammond, Laura	wife	W	F	29		nurse
Hammond, William W.	son	W	M	4		
Williamson, Mary Ann	boarder	W	F	27		teacher
Fox, Charles W.	head	B	M	34		farmer
Fox, Sarah R.	wife	B	F	32		
Fox, Anginia	daughter	B	F	8	yes	
Fox, Charles W. Jr.	son	B	M	6		
Fox, Lucinda	daughter	B	F	4		
Fox, Sarah Katherine	daughter	B	F	1		
Johnson, Ariana	sister-in-law	B	F	28		teacher

Name	Relationship	Race/Sex		Age	Student	Occupation
Tharp, Branson	head	W	M	52		farmer
Tharp, Dora	wife	W	F	36		
Tharp, Della	daughter	W	F	8	yes	
Tharp, Nannie	daughter	W	F	20		
Fox, Viola	daughter	W	F	28		
Fox, Gladys	daughter	W	F	10	yes	
Fox, Isabel	daughter	W	F	5	yes	
Fox, Edna	daughter	W	F	2		
Cox, George	head	W	M	40		stone quarry, carpenter
Cox, Fanny	wife	W	F	45		
Cox, Edgar	son	W	M	15		
Cox, George Jr.	son	W	M	12		
Whittington, --------	head	W	M	28		laborer
Whittington, Rose	wife	W	F	42		
Whittington, Anna V.	daughter	W	F	11	yes	
Whittington, Mary E.	daughter	W	F	9	yes	
Angelo, Henry	head	W	M	40		quarry foreman
Angelo, Lucia	wife	W	F	37		
Angelo, Olga	daughter	W	F	10	yes	
Angelo, Louis	son	W	M	7	yes	
Angelo, Cebenna	daughter	W	F	6		
Angelo, Christa	daughter	W	F	4		
Rossi, John	head	W	M	30		quarry
Rossi, Carena	wife	W	F	30		
Rossi, Mary	daughter	W	F	9	yes	
Rossi, Angelina	daughter	W	F	6	yes	
Rossi, Fronga	son	W	M	5/12		
Milbourne, Milton	head	W	M	51		farrier
Milbourne, Roseanna	wife	W	F	45		
Milbourne, James	son	W	M	16		laborer
Milbourne, Herbert	son	W	M	15		laborer
Milbourne, Cecil	son	W	M	10		laborer
Milbourne, Edith	daughter	W	F	8	yes	
Milbourne, Pearl	daughter	W	F	7	yes	
Milbourne, Robert	son	W	M	4		
Milbourne, Paul	son	W	M	3		

About the Author

Mrs. Hamstead, who traces her family through five generations in Kearneysville, has strong roots in her native village. She is a graduate of Shepherd College and taught Social Studies at Jefferson High School.

WA

www.ingramcontent.com/pod-product-compliance
Lightning Source LLC
Chambersburg PA
CBHW070132080526
44586CB00015B/1660